*H*idden for *G*lory

Destined for Adoption

by SuDawn Peters

Hidden for Glory – Destined for Adoption
ISBN 1-930285-10-8

Copyright©2002 by SuDawn Peters
Published by The Master Design
      PO Box 17865
      Memphis, TN 38187-0865
      Info@masterdesign.org
      www.masterdesign.org

Unless otherwise noted, Scripture quotations are from the HOLY BIBLE, Revised Standard Version © 1946, 1952, Thomas Nelson & Sons.

Scripture quotations marked NRSV are from the New Revised Standard Version Bible, Copyright © 1989 Division of Christian Education of the National Council of the Churches of Christ in the United States of America.

Scripture quotations marked NIV are from the HOLY BIBLE, NEW INTERNATIONAL VERSION © 1973, 1978, 1985 by the International Bible Society, used by permission of Zondervan Publishing House.

Scripture quotations marked KJV are from the KING JAMES VERSION of the Bible © 1973, Thomas Nelson, Inc., Publishers.

Printed by Bethany Press International in the USA.

JJ

Contents

Dedication

To those who chose to give life to our children:

I can only pray that on the chance any of our children's biological families find among these pages their stories, that they will read with open hearts and minds. Perhaps they will not remember the story as I have written it, but the story is, after all, from our adoptive parent perspective. Perhaps they will be reminded anew of the huge impact their decision to implement an adoption plan made in the lives of so many people. This story would not be possible without the unselfish decisions and commitment of the biological families to allow each child birthed to fly free as a butterfly to their destinies

To my father:

Who did not always understand our motivation or decisions, yet accepted our children unconditionally. Your encouragement and support ultimately made this project possible.

And to my husband:

Though we have disagreed on many decisions in our walk, we have truly been soul mates with regard to the addition of our children. May God bless your willingness and dedication to the family God has gifted us with. Thank you for your unconditional commitment to the Lord, the children and me.

Introduction

For John and me, adoption has always been and always will be a spiritual journey, a destiny, a calling from God. Even our first adoption over 28 years ago was a very spiritual event for us. It would forever change our lives and send us down a path we would never have chosen for ourselves.

The words within this text are taken from my journals: scribbled in the dark of night, the wee hours just before dawn, or during the children's nap times in the afternoon. As I reread my journals and prayed about what to include in this book, my soul experienced revival. My faith was restored as I rediscovered how God consistently had His hand on our lives.

There is no place I desire more to be than in the center of God's will and purpose. In the palm of His hand I feel immense protection, spiritual strength and joy unspeakable. But it was not always so. My writings also reveal how we have clearly faltered and often failed in our walk.

Like so many we have found ourselves caught up in the here and now: collecting possessions, catering to self-satisfying desires, dismissing the reality of eternity and losing sight of why we are here at this time in history.

In a perfect world all children would be conceived in love within a biblical marriage. All would live happily ever after. But alas, we live in a fallen world that increasingly devalues human life.

Lives are snuffed out by abortion at alarming rates in this nation, most usually for selfish reasons. Children are often trapped in a foster care system as complex as the fallen world we live in. Cultures are increasingly unable to care for their own and yet discourage or prevent the placement of children in stable families. Bureaucracies take authority as if they were God. Indeed, we have allowed these atrocities to creep into every realm of our lives.

We are not as isolated as we might believe. Every step we take, every decision we make, and every word we speak ripples throughout eternity.

Our free will choices have the potential to ensure or alter divine purposes in a way I am convinced we will never truly comprehend.

Apathy and agape love cannot occupy the same space; one must crowd out the other.

Love is what makes a society healthy, a people strong for God's kingdom.

As I grow older I am ever more fascinated with the realization that each life has a very specific purpose. I have begun to look at individuals; especially the children entrusted to us and wonder, will they opt to walk in faith, excited at the unknown? Will they reach out of comfort zones, motivated by love and touch another life? Or will they take the road more easily traveled, and in apathy seek no solutions? We each have a choice.

This book is a chronological presentation of the roads we have traveled in our marriage and more specifically in our adoption journey. To God be the glory for the way He not only orchestrated events, but also was able to work His plan in spite of our reluctance and controlling natures.

Many details will have to be left out to protect the privacy of those touched by our journey. As public as the life of an adoptive family is, there remains no other place where privacy is potentially more sacred.

Our children were always conceived in my spirit long before they arrived in our family. God has made it so.

At times John and I were truly puzzled by the child presented when we had a preconceived idea of who we 'thought' God was planning to bless us with next. Hopefully we have gotten better at walking briskly through doors held open by God and walking just as quickly away from doors divinely closed.

There could never be children who are more loved than those told about within these pages. Each has won our hearts and enriched our lives beyond our wildest imaginings. Our children are not angels; they make messes, mistakes, and require instruction just as other children do.

Nevertheless, as I will share with you, each child was divinely placed within our family and therein has or will experience exactly what God knows they need to experience in order to reach their full potentials. We are humbled in the knowledge and responsibility that comes with the task of parenting our unique family.

Throughout this book are sections of a poem that God inspired for presentation at Nicholas and Nathan's dedication to the Lord over 10 years ago. I have since written additions to the reading as we have added more children. It summarizes years of events and most importantly shows an overview of God's plan for each person in our family.

Finally, this is a work in progress. It shows God's continuous preparations, plans and provision when we choose to walk in faith toward our destinies. Herein are stories of God orchestrating events and guiding people down the pathways of life, frequently without human understanding or knowledge. Included are testimonies of God's faithfulness and love, even in hurtful situations and valleys of uncertainty. Hopefully, these realities will encourage others to realize conception is purposed and each life important in God's eyes. It is my prayer that you, the reader, will grasp anew how God can turn seemingly insignificant and often frightening events into stories of great spiritual significance.

SuDawn Peters
November 2002

From the Beginning

"My times are in Thy hands." Psalm 31:15

Christmas 1957

I unwrapped my presents with glee. Christmas was then and remains now, my favorite holiday of the year. Some of my fondest memories are of the holidays. I was not to be disappointed that year as I tore through the generous stack of brightly wrapped treasures. I am sure there were mounds of other gifts that year, but this is about one small baby doll.

The gift delighted me since doll babies and their accessories were my favorite toys. I don't recall noticing at the time that the doll had a different color of plastic skin from my other dolls. I was just excited at the new addition to my ever-growing collection. The doll came complete with new clothes and one of those cute little orange juice bottles.

I would be untruthful if I tried to quote the words that were spoken that day. I nevertheless have a vivid emotional memory of what I felt as I heard the adults around me discussing this newest toy. My aunt, whom I rarely saw, had mailed the doll to me, along with gifts for the rest of our family. I am certain she never knew the controversy her gift produced. I doubt she knew it was my first introduction to different skin tones. Nor, would she ever know that she prompted an event that God would bring to my attention a good many years later. While preparing to speak to prospective adoptive parents, God would use this odd event to show me how the little things in life often are seeds planted of dreams and visions that God has for all of us from the beginning of time.

My family was not particularly impressed with the gift. We lived in a rural area totally Caucasian in its population, at least to my limited recollection. If I had seen people of other skin colors, I don't remember it at that early age. It was a time when segregation was still reality. A time long before Martin Luther King, Jr. would 'have a dream' and boldly set out to change America and its history of racial prejudices.

As the adults conversed around me it was evident that they were surprised at my aunt's choice of a gift. They pondered what thoughts must have motivated her actions. In my memory the scene fades here and the next thing I recall is placing the doll proudly and with great care in a line of other dolls on my bed. As a child I would spend a good deal of my play time dressing and feeding and strolling around my baby dolls. I was in a dress rehearsal for adult life. Bedtime was a headache for my mother. She had to wait nightly while I dressed and tucked in each and every one of that large collection of "children." I can still vividly recall the names I gave them and where each one came from. It was all very serious play.

Perhaps it was the sheer number of dolls and the hopes of reducing the bedtime ritual that led to the disappearance of the black baby and likely others. Or, the well-intentioned actions of parents who wanted to stay away from the entire racial issue, even in a toy doll reminder. I'll never know for sure. I doubt anyone else would even remember such a seemingly insignificant event.

Regardless, as the years would go by I would be reminded of how "seemingly insignificant events" impact us and persuade us in our walk toward our destiny. It would be years before I would even be given recall of that event. I do not think for a moment that my parents were intentionally racially biased. I simply think that the doll served as a surprise and a reminder of how differently things are in various areas of our country and the world. The doll seemed a misfit in the line up of our lives.

Even as children we are in training for our life's work. This particular memory has served as a reminder to watch for my own children's natural bents and talents in the serious play of life, as they are practicing toward their destinies.

September 1962

The sun shines brightly. The blue sky is a canopy covering us. Pillows of white fluffy clouds meander across the horizon. Indian summer days sometimes prompt a bold recollection of that day long ago. I had no clue as to how that day, that moment in time, would one day be a determining factor in my destiny.

My uncle was standing in our front yard and proceeded to happily introduce us to his new wife and her three children. I recall the marriage as being a surprise to everyone. At age 10 I was most interested not in the news of the marriage, but in the new 'cousins' that were part of this package deal. A ready-made family, what a unique idea to me! Hovering near their mother was a boy near my age, and two girls nearly the same ages as my two younger brothers. We would all have new playmates near our own ages. What a bonus!

I had not thought much about that day for years…just another routine day in my childhood. A day buried in the recesses of my memory, until God chose to use the recollection a good many years later to confirm a purpose in my life. When in frustration I would begin to doubt my marriage and to lose sight of the plans God had for me, God would use the memory to remind me of the hand of divine providence in our lives. It was that day that I met my future husband. Once again I needed to be reminded that many years ago events were falling into place, which would shape and form the future. Now it is a memory I treasure, one with a special glow, a time of great significance in the purpose God had for many others and me.

1967

The sloped ceilings seemed closer than usual as I slowly opened my eyes and regained my sense of where exactly I was. Upstairs in my bedroom things were still quiet, the usual morning noises and the familiar smell of coffee not yet drifting up the stairwell.

I rubbed the last bits of sleep from my eyes and glanced at my Pekingese dog sleeping in a curled ball of blond fur at the foot of my bed as I floated back to reality. Slowly I realized I had just experienced a very unusual dream. It would once again be many years before I would comprehend or understand the significance of that moment in time, or how dramatically it affected the course of my life. I would be a mother of many children before I would accept the fact that God chose upon certain special occasions to reveal to me things through dreams and visions which He purposed to orchestrate at some unrevealed, future day.

The little girl in the dream was a mystery to me. I had never met anyone of Asian descent. I had seen pictures of these delicate ethnic dolls on brochures of needy children that frequented my grandparents' desk. They were continually sponsoring some child in a far off distant land. I assumed at the time of the dream that I was only putting into my dream life the pictures I had seen in real life. I did know somewhere deep within my being though, that this dream was different, but I could not have known nor understood how, as it was not yet time for God to reveal that mystery.

In fact, skip ahead a moment to 1995 where I have marked in my Bible the following passage:

"And the Lord answered me, and said, 'Write the vision, and make it plain upon tables, that he may run that readeth it. For the vision is yet for an appointed time, but at the end it shall speak, and not lie: though it tarry, wait for it; because it will surely come, it will not tarry. Behold his soul which is lifted up is not upright in him: but the just shall live by his faith'" (Habakkuk 2:2-4 KJV).

When the Lord spoke to me through that passage the first thought that popped into my mind was the above-mentioned dream once again, my first recollection of God giving me a vision for yet an appointed time.

The little girl in the dream was perhaps seven years old. She had nearly waist length hair, straight and dark. Her eyes were decidedly almond shaped and she was petite in her build. All I remembered of her was a flitting view as she moved with slow motion in front of my eyes, maybe in front of some sort of picture window. I do remember there was sunshine in the dream, and peace and joy in the scene. It was a mystery that would remain hidden for His glory and have everything to do with adoption, something I knew absolutely nothing about as teenager. I tucked away the memory in the recesses of my mind and went about my day and my life as usual. But in reality, I wasn't ever to be exactly the same again.

1968

I opened the box on my dresser to put away my watch. There amidst the various pieces of jewelry nestled an identification bracelet. As I picked it up my heart skipped a beat and at the same time a rather melancholy feeling encompassed me. John had apparently been visiting my brother that afternoon while I was gone. No doubt he had slipped into my room and placed the bracelet in my jewelry box. It was his quiet way of asking me to 'go steady'.

The past months had been rather awkward as we both quietly dealt with a new kind of attraction toward one another. It was an attraction I had fought hard to ignore, even deny. We were cousins by marriage. Our families were very close. We had shared family birthdays and holidays and fun evenings while adults played card games and we children played loudly all over the house and yard. Cousins certainly shouldn't get involved in this way with one another, and they surely don't go steady.

My mother seemed sympathetic to the confusion I expressed when I finally mustered enough courage to show her the secretly placed ID bracelet. I shall never know what she truly thought, but that day she was diplomatic and empathetic at least in my presence. I don't recall any specific instructions; I guess the decision was wisely left up to me. If I put the bracelet on, it bound me in a new way to this cousin of mine.

Going steady was a pretty serious event in those years, just a step away from marital engagement plans as far as I was concerned. I have never taken any relationship lightly; it is not my way. I prayed and thought about this new turn of events for hours on end, wondering about the right thing to do. There was no denying the subtle feelings we were beginning to have for one another. Still I had no previous experience to compare this to. Seemingly propelled to go down this dim pathway I began to wear the bracelet. Still there was an accompanying guilt that is still yet hard to define.

Spring 1969

Recent memories of working for hours on the floats, the decorations and the menu for prom were still floating around in my head. The crowded gymnasium, the laughter and nervous conversation surrounded us. It was time to enjoy the enchantment of an evening entitled "Gone with the Wind." My poetry was included in the scrolls by our plates. We were mystically transformed into a time in southern history that only Margaret Mitchell's book could inspire.

It was a magical, romantically memorable evening. How appropriate to end it with our first kiss! John's class ring and now his letter jacket would soon join my favorite things. This was becoming serious and somewhere deep inside we both knew it. We talked at length about the impact of a long-term relationship. We lamented over the problems it was causing between our families. We searched for a way to stifle the feelings that were increasing undeniably everyday. At the same time we couldn't spend enough time together.

Winter 1969

John and I were together at every possible opportunity. We were becoming helplessly dependent upon one another for companionship and support; we were the best of friends. We continued to test our relationship. At the same time we quit fighting what seemed to be the inevitable quite as hard. We struggled with the disappointment that we knew both sets of parents were experiencing.

Still, it all seemed destined in an indefinable sort of way. Eventually I couldn't imagine my life being spent with anyone else. I couldn't imagine being happy in my parents' home much longer. As strange as it all seemed then, we had fallen totally and unexpectedly in love. We were being made ready to commit to one another for a lifetime. We had not planned this at all.

Spring 1970

Graduation came upon us quickly. We shared a joint celebration with our families at his parents' house. Later we left the maddening crowd of younger brothers, sisters, aunts, uncles, grandparents and cousins and found ourselves on a quiet, dark country road. Reality slowly began to creep into our realm of thinking. No longer denying our love for one another we agreed our futures seemed hopelessly locked together. But, this was no simple thing. Just what were we to do about such a complicated situation? The Vietnam War raged in a distant land. Our time together more uncertain because of a war we didn't understand. Our options were limited with no savings account for either marriage or college. If he didn't quickly go to some sort of school the draft demanded immediate enlistment in the armed forces. We weren't ready for marriage in a practical way; we also had no specific career goals, at least that we could define. Suddenly, we faced adulthood with great trepidation. Was there even a future to plan?

Summer 1970

We spent as much time together as we could that summer. We were both working full time jobs so time together was difficult to manage. It was probably much more than our parents' hearts would have wished for us, but clearly not enough to us. There was so much to talk about, so much to plan, so many questions. We talked about a date for our wedding and tried to imagine what the future beyond a wedding ceremony would hold. We talked about the two children we would like to have, and surprisingly, about adoption. I don't have a clue why we would have even discussed adoption at this point in our young lives, except it be from God, but we surely did. Neither of us knew anyone who had adopted a child, except in a stepparent relationship, we certainly didn't have a clue about how to go about accomplishing such a thing. But, for sure, it was in our conversations, however briefly, even then.

In July John left for Denver, Colorado for computer technical school. I stayed behind to work and wait. We would save money and talk more about a wedding in January when the short school was completed. He could delay the draft while in school. Maybe the war would end and we could just go on with our lives after he completed technical school. We were buying time, and we were trying hard to be practical. We failed.

I was lonely and admittedly very hard to live with. Okay, probably horrible to live with! John was broke, hungry and scared living in a city ten times larger than any place he had ever even visited before. More than 20 hours away from home for the first time, he was completely alone, with no financial or emotional support from his family. He was a small town boy in one of the largest cities in America and he was homesick indeed.

He called me early one evening from a pay phone on a quaint street high in the Colorado Rockies. Totally unexpectedly he asked me if I would marry him, in two weeks! I fumbled and mumbled and lost all rational thinking. I said, yes!

September 1970

In a whirlwind wedding we managed to have all the traditional things that I deemed would be important for us to recall about our wedding day. John drove all night from Denver to our Missouri hometown. We managed a rehearsal the evening he arrived. We had a simple church ceremony the following evening. I had sewn my long white dress in the wee hours of the mornings in the days just before the wedding. Those two weeks from phone call to matrimony are a dim blur. A sweet reception followed at the home of my aunt and uncle and we were off for an overnight honeymoon to North-west Arkansas.

Early the next morning with a $100 and our station wagon packed full of wedding presents we were off to Colorado to begin our lives together. Suddenly reality set in. I cried all the way to Kansas City and at frequent intervals over the next 90 days. My young student husband must have doubted greatly just what he had gotten himself into. It was the beginning of a walk we could never have imagined.

In the Wilderness
— a Call

The ultimate escape had been accomplished! We rented a tin box trailer located atop an unsafe landfill in Denver, Colorado. Neither of us had ever been away from home more than a few nights, and then always with trusted family members. Living in rural Missouri and suddenly being thrust into a huge metropolitan area was indeed culture shock at its worst!

Suddenly I found myself amidst wedding gifts and the clutter of college textbooks, missing terribly the parents I thought had placed complicated and unreasonable rules upon my life.

I was homesick and oblivious to the fact that we were at the beginning of a journey that would take us through many wilderness experiences, and ultimately into the arms of God. These experiences would force us to get in touch with our own strengths and to be humbled by our inadequacies. Women's liberation and the Vietnam War were causing a constant conflict within me as I struggled to identify who I was and just what my goals were to be. As intensely as I had wanted to escape the rules and dependence upon my parents, I now wanted to return. It was a wilderness of confusion. I longed for the safeness that I had experienced in the womb of my family.

While we struggled along, military life was forcing itself upon us in full force. John graduated from technical school and we returned to Missouri only to find out he would not likely be hired because of his present draft status. He opted to enlist in the Air Force, thinking he might have more options with regard to career choices while enlisted. It was a close call; the next day he received his draft papers for the Army! How quickly and simply our life paths can be altered.

John was excited when the recruiter promised a job in computer operations. On-the-job training would be a wonderful asset, making mandatory time in military service beneficial after all! Ultimately he would never see a computer, let alone work on one, but would be trained as a security policeman, a field he had little interest in. During times of war young men have few choices.

We were separated while John went to basic training. I lived alone for the first time ever. At times all wilderness experiences become filled with loneliness, and this was to be no exception. The sins of apathy, pity, and dependence upon others instead of God were taking their toll on me. It was time for a wake-up call.

I had been taking some prescribed sulfa medication. Suddenly, during the predawn hours I had the sensation of being above my sleeping body. I felt an urgency to wake myself up but was unable to will myself to a conscious state of mind.

Somehow I realized I was totally unable to move any part of my body. It was as if I was encased in concrete. I tried to breathe, but no breath would come. I knew I needed to wake up, to breathe, but I was helpless to rouse myself and I knew too, that there was no one likely to come to my rescue. How I knew these things remains a mystery to me.

I recall feeling that I would like to just continue to float away. I would not have to be lonely or mixed up anymore; I would not have to endure separations from those I loved. There was a peace while I was floating in this silent world.

I am not sure what happened to bring me back, but eventually I felt the tingling of life returning to my legs and then my arms. I took a shallow breath. Then with great relief I realized that I could move my fingers, then my toes, and now take deep reviving breaths of wonderful air. I glanced at the clock, still not lifting my head from the pillow. It had only been about 15 minutes since I recalled looking at the clock, but it seemed much longer. Apparently I had an allergic reaction to the medication. The combination of my physical illness, my desire to escape reality, obvious depression, and the reaction to the medication had caused me to nearly die.

I was peaceful and glad that I was awake. I really felt fine now, healed. I knew though, that I had just experienced something very unique.

As I pondered what had just happened, I was suddenly bursting with thanks to God. I felt a completely new awareness of wanting to be nearer to the heart of God and more pleasing and dependent upon Him. It was all so supernatural, so life changing. I knew there was much yet to do.

Soon after this experience John returned from his basic training. He didn't understand this new urgency for religion in my life, but agreed to being baptized into the church I had attended all of my life. It was a step in the right direction, symbolic of our agreement to attempt to walk more closely with God than we had done in our past.

Within days we traveled together to Texas where he continued on with his training. For a season we enjoyed a reprieve from recent challenges, an oasis in the wilderness walk. We enjoyed some of the most precious times of our lives over the next 12 weeks. It was a time of rest and getting reacquainted. God was good, life was exciting, and we were immensely happy.

We had not been married quite two years when John received his orders to go to the Philippines. It was with many tears and a very humbled attitude that we read and reread the orders. He was now a security policeman, with special training in canine narcotic detection. Going to Vietnam was something he pretty much expected to do.

So, when the orders were handed out, and he was one of only two men who had orders for the Philippines, we knew that God had just set us on a special path. We didn't have a clue why we should be spared the fearsomeness of war. Most of his friends who received orders that day did not return from Vietnam alive. Though we were sad about the pending separation, the P.I. seemed like a paradise compared to the war zone of Vietnam. We openly thanked God for His mercy.

We had no clue just how important the coming months would be in the building of a foundation for the rest of our lives. God was positioning us for a most memorable year, possibly the most significant milestone of our lives. The coming year would change forever our plans and our pathway through life.

The months had gone by and I shut my eyes as the plane flew overhead carrying out of my sight the half of my life that meant the very most to me. I said a silent prayer into the hazy blue sky that John would return safely. The tightness in my throat nearly strangled me.

The orders were for an unaccompanied 15 month tour of duty. Words can't express how long that separation seemed to me as we looked into the future. I was terribly alone once again. Days crawled by as John and I settled into our lives in two separate worlds. Selfishly, I took small comfort in knowing full well that for some reason we were being protected from the ravages of the war. It did not ease the pain of separation or the thoughts of the empty holidays that loomed ahead. I felt robbed of anticipated happy Christmas memories. I imagine my attitude dampened the spirits of my poor family as well. I have recalled with great remorse some of the unkind remarks I made during that holiday season. Thank goodness for the unconditional love and the forgiveness of friends and family.

Days were eternally long. Finally I talked to John long distance on Christmas night. We talked about the possibility of my joining him in the Philippines. We weren't sure joining him would even be an option. I was doubtful and depressed after the conversation. Though the orders were for an unaccompanied tour, John decided to approach his superior officer about the possibility of my coming to the Philippines. I endured immunizations and filed piles of requested paperwork as we waited.

I realized many years later how much God had His hand on all of the legalities that were completed in record time. Sooner than we even hoped, I learned I would be in that mystical foreign country in just a few days! I was traveling so quickly that John barely had time to prepare a place off base for us to live.

While in high school I had prayed to be able to go to a foreign country. Somehow I felt if I left the safety of my family, and had an opportunity to experience another culture, I would be able to find my purpose in life. I didn't have a clue how precisely that prayer was about to be played out! Indeed, I had forgotten that prayer until a time when God chose to remind me of it years later.

In a rare mood I confided a secret wish to my mother-in-law: nothing could be more rewarding than to adopt a Filipino child. I assured her that the probability of adoption was unlikely. When considering it some months before, John and I had been told that we would not be allowed to adopt while on a tour of duty in any foreign country. Though it was never mentioned again, the spark of a dream glowed warm in my heart as I anticipated what the new adventure might have to offer.

I will never forget the sights and smells as I deplaned in Manila! A slight moment of fear shocked through me when I couldn't see John anywhere in that strange terminal. But, once through customs, I saw he was anxiously waiting at the end of the long lines. We were quickly in a taxi and I was in for the ride of my life!

God had orchestrated places and people once again. Our neighbors in the Philippines had in their custody a Filipino-American baby. The little girl was beautiful and especially enchanting to John and me as we spent day after day hoping I would become pregnant and at the same time considering adoption.

We spent long nights musing as far as possible into the future. We were trying to foresee the adjustments involved if we pursed the adoption of a Filipino child, an option that had unexpectedly presented itself as result of the location of the rental house John had chosen, and the neighbors we now counted as friends. We were trying to imagine what might be forthcoming if we were to adopt. Our hometown was a place where only white families lived.

How would the community reactions affect the overall development of a non-Caucasian child? Finally, we decided that with God's help, we were ready to meet the challenge, if indeed there was to be one.

We filed an application with the Department of Social Welfare, Republic of the Philippines. Thus began an experience John and I will never forget. For several months we searched for a child. We began to spend every possible hour riding in the back of hired jeepneys, maneuvered over rough and treacherous roads with expertise, by local drivers. We toured hospitals and clinics in search of abandoned children. We saw many children, and most remain etched in our hearts. None of the children or situations we encountered seemed exactly right.

We had been enduring fertility testing in hopes of conceiving. Without any warning, I miscarried and experienced quite an emotional blow. Our neighbors with the little girl had taken me to and from the base hospital. Back at home I waited on the couch for John to return from duty. He had been on a remote post when they had contacted him that I was in the outpatient clinic.

The tropical heat was intense; I was nauseated, in minor physical pain and major emotional distress. I was so angry that it scared me.

When would this wandering in the wilderness ever end? I truly could not understand why God would take my baby. I raised my fists in anger. I felt so alone. John would be expected to continue his work schedule, and I would have no family or friends to help me during my recovery. Oh how quickly self-pity can consume us, causing emotional and physical pain, as well as an open door to sin!

I wept until there were no more tears. I was totally exhausted when John finally returned from base. We went over all the things I could have done to prevent the miscarriage. I needed to find a reason. There was none. I felt like I had failed John. He assured me I had not. Sad as we were, we felt a closeness we'd never experienced before. Still, a dreadful feeling of doom dominated my life. We were a million miles from 'the world'. Not only had we just lost what we thought would bring true happiness; recently it had seemed there were no babies to consider for legal adoption.

> I was broken and sad,
> Hurting and mad.
> My pain others could not see.
> I longed for a child, a baby.
> Why God? Why not me?
> Others had children to snuggle and hold,
> You're young, there is time, it's okay I was told.
> I was longing, yes aching for God's very best,
> I felt robbed and angry,
> I tossed without rest.
> I conceived and lost, I wretched in my pain.
> I was puzzled and hurting, surely nothing to gain.
> But God is so good, when I falter and fall,
> Often then in my sorrow I hear my God call.

I have only come to realize in recent years the provision of comfort God made for me while in that wilderness. The neighbor that took me to the clinic had suffered numerous miscarriages herself. Her eyes showed me that she shared my grief and had compassion and understanding that I failed to comprehend at the time. Pity is a dangerous thing; we miss so many blessings when we allow its talons to get a grip on us.

John was to leave for a six week training school in Okinawa. If we didn't get a child soon, it would just be too late to even consider adoption. We had to allow time for the mandatory paperwork. If God wanted us to travel this road, He had to open a door quickly.

One day, John came home unexpectedly from the base. He had received a phone call while on duty. We were to meet one of our Filipino acquaintances. She was to accompany us to see a baby girl, just 10 days old. John and I, numb from so many disappointments, tried not to get excited. I hesitantly prepared for the trip. I had to wonder at the timing of this baby's birth and my recent miscarriage. Was it coincidence that they would have happened on or about the same day?

Often when we think there are no answers to our questions, God intervenes in a way we least expect. Interestingly it had been just over nine months since John had departed for the Philippines. The phone call John had received that day on base was about to initiate a divine appointment.

> *It was a dark humid room in an Asian tropic land,*
> *That God brought together through the miracle of His hand,*
> *A woman who gave birth to a treasurer oh, so dear!*
> *And a young wife and her husband on a tour of duty there.*
> *Empty our arms, our wounded hearts open wide.*
> *We held her, we touched her, we felt humbled inside*
> *This baby, this treasure from another's womb*
> *Was to be our daughter, God had made the room.*

As we walked into that small basement apartment I felt a divine presence like I had never experienced before. I knew that God had led us to this place. The baby's mother talked at length to our Filipino friends. John and I were completely humbled as we stood to the side, hands clasped, never taking our eyes off of that perfect bundle of divine creation. She was snuggled down sleeping peacefully in the center of a double bed. She was so innocent, so unaware that her entire future was being discussed.

She was the most beautiful baby we had ever seen! Years later I came to realize that if the match of a parent and child is God's divine plan, then it matters not whether the child is biological or adopted, or imperfect in any way physically or mentally, that child is still perfect in the eyes of the new parents. This is as it should be with a gift as great as the life of a child.

Using an interpreter, Leah's mother asked us many questions. Would she be taken to church? What was our denomination? Would she have shoes? Could we clothe her and feed her properly? Would she see snow? Would we love her? Those questions have echoed in my mind many times as the years have passed.

During adoptive pregnancy there is often little to do but discuss names. We had never found one that seemed exactly right for a girl. As I was tenderly holding the baby for the first time, her birth mother asked us what we would name her. That was the moment in time when John and I realized that this time something was really happening, we were finally holding our very own gift from God!

We asked her name. Without hesitation, the mother said, "Leah." In an instant John and I agreed, it was exactly the right name, one we had not even considered. As our eyes locked for a brief moment, I instantly knew that Leah's mother was blessed by our acceptance of not only her child, but the name she had chosen for her as well. It seemed to seal the covenant we were about to enter.

As with any divinely arranged appointment, there was never really any question about the validity of this meeting, or of the outcome. We knew that this meeting was different from all of the others we had experienced in our searching for a child. Somehow, we just knew that this time things were going to work out.

From the moment I held Leah in my arms the months of searching, the pain and the emptiness of previous months became a misty memory. The labor was over and I now cradled in my arms the most delicate amazing creature I had ever beheld.

Her birth mother dressed Leah and prepared to give her to us. Carefully she mixed a bottle, the last maternal ritual she would probably ever do for Leah. It was silent in the room. There can be no courage on earth like that of a mother who must make sacrificial plans for her child. And then, it was time to go.

I have never been able to completely put into words the emotional magnitude of receiving a child through adoption; of turning and walking out of the door with a parcel as valuable as that of another human life. As we left the apartment that day, I could feel the eyes of Leah's birth mother clinging to the memory of our departure like only one who has released a child can understand. I knew I could not look back; to do so would perhaps change our destinies forever. I could not have borne the pain I am sure was in her eyes. I could barely carry the weight of our new responsibility; the burden of a birth mother's heart would have made the load too great that day.

I can remember the smell of the car and the intense heat as we prepared to leave. It seemed there should be more we could do. Leah was in my arms, she felt like a perfect fit, yet we were leaving her roots behind. With prayers, intense silent prayers, I begged that all of us would be protected in a mighty and awesome way.

The house was empty upon our arrival home. Where was the welcoming committee? The great numbers of family that I had always envisioned would greet us upon our arrival home with the first grandchild on either side of the family? Oh yes, we were in a foreign country; we were a 'world' away from any familiar faces. I wanted to shout: "Do you see what is going on here? We have a child, do you hear me? A beautiful baby girl"! But, there was no one. People walked by on the streets outside our house, and they didn't even look our way. It was the middle of the night back in the state of Missouri, and besides, there were only designated times we could call from the base. Our parents were grandparents, and they didn't even know we were expecting! We couldn't call and tell anyone. We were alone, and I cried.

As I sat silently holding that precious bundle I could feel God smiling, hands clasped, watching, as this scene of love unfolded, just as He had known it would. He had watched our grief and experienced our pain at not bearing a biological child. At the same time, across the city, another woman was experiencing grief and pain for having conceived a child she could not parent. Neither of us could have known that we were going through our wilderness of pain so that we might be a part of a plan much bigger than any of us could ever have understood.

I suspect in that little dark apartment Leah's birth mother was suffering too. Maybe she was thinking, "Don't you see? They just drove off with my baby! She is gone; I will likely never see her again!" The pain, yes, the grief, possibly was not unlike the ache we experience when someone close to us dies. The people walked on down her street, never looking her way. Her friends went back to work; hopefully the one who had helped deliver Leah stayed awhile offering emotional support. But, then she too, would have to go on with routine.

It must have been hard to be alone, folding up the baby clothes, putting away the powdered milk that we left on the counter. Perhaps she touched the warm spot on the bed, where just a short time before her precious bundle had been innocently sleeping. She was alone, and she cried.

I am sure through the years when she would hear of a snowfall she would wonder if Leah was there, touching the cold ice crystals, walking through the powdery wonderland. She might have wondered when she walked by local vendors peddling shoes if Leah had shoes to fit her feet. On her birthday did her birth mother wonder what Leah looked like now? Could she have known that she surely did make the right decision that day so long ago?

When I would clean out Leah's closet and discard pairs and pairs of shoes, tears would well into my eyes and I would remember those loving questions. When her closet would overflow with more clothing than she would ever need, or when she could eat no more food, I would remember. Perhaps because her birth mother will likely never see snow, I am especially touched when I see Leah and her siblings, or now her own little daughter, laughing and playing in fresh fallen snow. At an early age when Leah learned to recite the Lord's Prayer, and now as she takes her own daughter diligently to church I want to tell her mother: your prayers have been greatly answered. Somehow I hope that she knows what a precious gift she has given us and that we do love Leah so.

In our broken hearts and in the purpose of our days
God is greater and mightier, a mystery are His ways.
The years tumbled by and our hearts opened wide,
Her dad and I welcomed Leah, our hearts swelled with pride.
Words can't express the emotions of that day,
Nor, could we have known of our future, or the way
That God was answering our prayers that we knew!
It began our journey down a path that is traveled by few.

I brought Leah to the states for her first Christmas. It was so very special bringing home such a treasure to share with our families that year. It would be the last holiday my paternal grandmother would be physically able to be with our family and I am so grateful for the memory of her holding Leah for the first and only time that Christmas Eve.

I know my grandparents would be full of joy if they were to know how many children have since joined our family! They had a special love for children and were mostly responsible for planting the seeds of compassion and caring that have been the focus of my life. Their example and unconditional caring for those less fortunate than themselves has indeed rippled through many people's lives in just a few short years.

Leah's adoption helped John and me learn that even when we do not realize it, God is orchestrating our lives, urging us to go down certain paths. From the unlikely orders to the Philippines, the quickly obtained international papers and traveling permission, to our neighbors in the Philippines with an adopted little girl, through the wilderness we plunged. Onward through the loss of a child and ultimate meeting with people who would become a part of this adoption story, God was nudging us ever toward the desires He had planted in our hearts. Since we were sometimes so blind, it was a good thing God continued to drive!

When I could get no relief from flu-like symptoms, I gave in and went to the doctor. I was shocked and full of disbelief when the doctor told me that I was pregnant! When I questioned him for a second time, he laughingly assured me that antibiotics would not take care of my horrible, awful nausea, and relentless headache.

During the drive home fear stepped in where disbelief was gradually giving way to reality. I had miscarried more times than I cared to recall. It was very likely that I would do so again, I couldn't count on this pregnancy being any different than the devastating times in the past. I consoled myself with the reminder that we had already initiated paperwork hoping to adopt from Korea. If this pregnancy ended in grief I would at least have something to look forward to. I wanted to have a baby so desperately, but at the same time, I was so very afraid to get my hopes up and then face the extreme pain of loss once again.

John was no less surprised than I had been when I found him at work, and told him the news. He was cautiously optimistic, and tried to be empathetic and supportive in my fears. There was nothing to do now but proceed through the months and depend upon God for the outcome.

As the weeks went by I realized I had a doctor who was serious about helping me through this pregnancy and I became just a bit more excited. There would be biweekly injections, numerous medications, and almost complete bed rest, but I was determined to carry this baby full-term. In the end, it also took every ounce of energy I had, and I had to make the tough decision to close the business that we had opened upon our discharge from the military. It was a small price to pay for the life of my long-awaited birth child.

I was so desperately ill. I couldn't drink a sip of water without throwing it back up. I had to wonder how there were so many people on this earth if every pregnancy was as difficult as this one! I knew they weren't, but then, I did question why I was having such a hard time birthing something I had desired for so long to do. I really never found any answers to those questions, and as the years would go by, my thorn in the flesh continued to be female attributed difficulties. I wondered how anyone who desired children so badly could have that very birthing ability become impossible. Many years later when our house was bursting at the seams with children of all ages and races, those empty arms seemed like a fleeting illusion, somewhere in my misty past.

John was gone a good deal of the pregnancy. With our business closed and his burnout on college classes, he searched for new employment. It was a recessionary time in this country and jobs were very difficult to find. Things were more complicated because of the previous years of military police work and college training in a completely different field of computer science. Like so many other things in our lives, even his career direction was a collage of experience without purpose or direction. So, he took a job that required much travel and tried in his own way to provide for his now growing family.

It was another lonely time. All of the hopes and dreams we had for our future seemed to get dashed at every turn in the road. Returning to our hometown was not turning out in the least as we had expected. Even a much desired pregnancy was presently more like a nightmare. It was a time as dark as midnight.

Finally, there was nothing left in me to fight the battles or try and figure out plans for the future. Alone in my bed, in the final weeks of my pregnancy I totally relinquished my life and my situation into God's hands. I had always loved the Lord. I could not recall a time when Jesus and the love of God were not an intricate part of my thoughts and feelings. Still, I was trying so hard to do things under my own strength and I was beginning to understand that was an impossible feat, if my greatest desire was to truly please God and serve Him. Hands down, I had to give it all to God. The burdens and the pain were too much to carry. I am sure my Lord wondered why I had taken so long to hand over the reins to my life.

> *God plants His desires in our hearts with love,*
> *So that we might know when He sends from above,*
> *An answer to prayer for the things we seek*
> *At a moment in time when we are humbled and weak.*

I felt so ignorant; there had been so many obvious events that had been divinely orchestrated over the years. Why were we so blind? Why was I so unaware of my need for total sanctification? I wept, and in those tears came a great release of all of the anger, the questions, and fears. I knew that I would soon be required to handle things in a different fashion.

Just shy of four years after Leah arrived in our family, I gave birth to a perfectly healthy, full-term baby boy. Nine months of nausea, doubts, and fears melted away in an instant when I saw our precious newborn son. A daughter and now a son, we had the perfect family!

God answered my prayers, I conceived and bore,
A child we had longed for, we sorrowed no more.
The pain of labor, the peace of God's love
When a child, God's gift, comes on the wings of His dove.
Now I knew how it felt to grieve
And also knew the joy of giving birth, when in love we conceive.
Destined to share parents that were uniquely his own,
Designed to share a family where all nations are represented in the home.
From the smile on his face, to the compassion in his heart,
Genetically our own, and yet God's from the start.
The years had tumbled by and our hearts opened wide,
There were three of us to welcome Jared, our hearts swelled with pride.

Having Jared was certainly one of the most memorable and gratifying events in my life. I now understood pregnancy better, how intense the love and emotions can be between a mother and her child. I think giving birth created in me a greater compassion for life and a respect for birth mothers that I might not have gained in any other way. As a young man, Jared is without a doubt a unique combination of his father and me, genetically our own and specifically designed to be a part of this divine call. If anyone has made a sacrifice for this walk, it would be Jared. I am convinced that God will richly reward him, and completely use his experiences as the years of maturity bring realization and submission to God's plan for our son's life.

Submission, both to God and to my husband, would be the first and most important and ongoing lesson I would have to learn. For a take-charge personality, the submission part of the Christian walk has got to be the greatest challenge! My sincerity would soon be put to the test.

If our marriage was to survive, John was going to have to come home. He finally found a computer operator position in another part of the state. Without consulting me, John made the decision to relocate us once again. I was not happy about the decision, and reluctantly sold our home and made the move. This would be the first of many lessons in submission, and I confess it was not with a joyful spirit that I followed my husband's lead.

It was both our faults when things began to get tough in our relationship. However, it was me that God had dealt with, and I now began to understand the spiritual importance of submission. Now, for me to not submit with a willing and compliant spirit was a sin. That sin of discontentment and resentment was building a wall that would have to come tumbling down if we were to keep our relationship intact for the long haul.

We would go through an incredible valley of despair and pain, and seriously consider divorce. But in the end, our commitment to each other and our children gave us a sincere determination to find what God had for us and would help us climb out of that valley. It would take years for the wounds to heal. In fact, there would always be scars of those troubling times, but God is good, and gently helped us work through the stages of reconstruction one building block at a time. With time, the foundation was more solid and our purpose more clearly united.

Out of the wilderness of life had come a call. Now the foundation was laid and the four of us would travel a path destined to be touched in an intricate way by both physical and spiritual adoption.

On the Job Training

We had a nice new home, healthy, happy children and John was finally working in his chosen career field. Still, I felt like something was missing. I couldn't quite define what I was looking for.

The word "adoption" kept jumping out at me from unlikely places. I just knew there were more children for us. What I hadn't learned was the lesson of being content in whatever circumstances I found myself in, and my impatience grew. We agreed we weren't ready to take on permanent responsibility for more children. So, foster care seemed a good option.

After taking state training we became licensed foster parents. Our first child was a little boy that had been kept in a chicken coop and fed bread and water. We all had challenges adjusting to this deprived little guy. I was reminded repeatedly while this baby was in our home of how cruel the world can be to children, even in this land of plenty. Though this child was extremely hard for us to understand, we did find a measure of satisfaction in taking care of a child in need. Eventually he went to a childless couple who planned to adopt him; they were thrilled to have a son. At least we were helping others, and enjoyed knowing we could.

Primarily because of my discontent, we eventually returned to Southwest Missouri. It was also a good career move for John and he was happy with his new position. At last things seemed to be moving on the right track. We bought a larger house, because we were already thinking of the children we desired to help. Not surprisingly they were quick to arrive in our home, once our foster care license was transferred to the new county.

God was giving us specific on-the-job training that would suit us well in the years to come. In this new-found walk with the Lord, there was much to learn.

One particular child would find a special place in our hearts and home. Hers was a foster-adopt placement from the very beginning. When I received the phone call about Tracy I decided almost without thinking that we should take her. In retrospect I know that I was so eager to help someone that I plunged ahead without seeking directions from God. It's not that Tracy was not to be with us, indeed I believe she was, just not for the reasons that I had envisioned.

Even when things were not going well, it never occurred to me that the placement might not be permanent. The purpose of foster-adopt programs is to allow the child and the family to have a trial time of living together before final adoption plans are made. I just assumed that we were going for the "adopt" part of the agreement.

We had been going through the adoption home studies and learning a lot about ourselves in the process. After each visit John and I would talk for a long time. We feared that something wasn't just right, but yet felt committed to this child who was obviously so needy. When Tracy came I sensed then and there that it was going to be a full time job. But, I was expecting more physical work, not so much emotional baggage. The latter required endless effort to try and understand.

What we had not anticipated was the damage that had already been done to this beautiful little girl by the very system that was designed to help her. Tracy had been in at least eight foster placements in her 10 short years of life. She had every symptom of Reactive Attachment Disorder, or RAD, a recent catchall term for children who are prevented from having a chance to bond and build relationships with significant people early in their lives. Eventually these children build such armor to protect themselves that it takes a great deal of professional help and unconditional parental love sprinkled with enormous amounts of understanding to just begin to repair the damage previously done. All we knew then was that she was an expert at deception.

When I would try to confide in close friends or even professionals, they would look at me as if I were the one with the problems! This sweet little girl could effortlessly control anyone, especially those who were attempting to build a relationship with her. Sometimes I felt like I was trapped in a cage. People were floating around me, jeering and laughing, muttering and shaking their heads, then floating off again, leaving me with a lonely, helpless feeling of inadequacy.

I felt like a total failure, as a mother and as a Christian. Eventually, the teachers that spent many hours with her each day would come to see the seriousness of my concerns, but few others did.

I spent a great deal of time in prayer for Tracy and our entire family. Her challenges were affecting not only our other foster child, but Leah and Jared as well. I wrote in my journal in May of that year: I have never been as exhausted as I've been working with Tracy. She is so complicated and yet appears so normal that no one believes me when I explain the physical and emotional strain of living with her. She isn't even aware of the way she manipulates people, it is second nature to her. It comes as easy as breathing. She is such a victim of the systems mistakes. Few people will likely ever be able to totally relate or completely understand Tracy. God will be her only strength and stability.

We wanted so very much to help Tracy. To offer her a foundation, a safe haven in which to heal and begin to build a stable and productive life. We planned to love her, accept her, and give her everything that she needed. We wanted to make up for past hurts and prepare her for the future God had destined her for. We wanted desperately to protect her from being victimized again.

After a long talk one night with Leah, I knew that we were going to have to seriously reconsider our original commitment to Tracy. We were going to have to make decisions that would protect the children that had already been entrusted to us for a lifetime. After a lengthy conversation John and I agreed to call the social worker and try to explain the situation. The worker was very gracious, not condemning, as I had feared she might be. We agreed that it might be best for our family if Tracy were to leave.

Being constantly moved was part of what had prevented her from being able to form appropriate long-term relationships in the first place. Moving had taught her that she did not have to be accountable to anyone. When the going got tough, the tough moved on. The very cycle we had been trying to stop we became participants in. There seemed no other answer.

Tracy had requested a family that lived on a farm and had a horse. Surprisingly the worker soon found a family with only an older son, and they were eager to have a daughter. Much to Tracy's delight, they did have a farm and a horse. By her second visit to that family I knew we could all let Tracy go, and in fact were ready to do so.

When she walked out the door for the last time, backpack on and dolls in her arms, I was so very sad. Such mixed emotions: failure, exasperation, frustration, anger, fatigue-the thoughts just raced through my mind. I slithered to the floor against the closed door. In a defeated heap, weeping from the depth of my heart I cried out to God. I told Him I would rather parent 10 children for a lifetime, than deal with the complexities of children affected by long-term foster care.

Thankfully, there are those families that find fostering a very fulfilling and wonderful ministry. There is a huge need for good foster families, and I was hopeful that we would be one of those that were a blessing to the little children. Sadly, fostering was something I personally found incredibly difficult to do.

In June I wrote in my journal: Tracy has been gone several days and it still feels odd. There is a strange emptiness about the room where she slept and in the closet where her clothes were. The emotions we are all feeling are very complex. Not the same as the leaving of those children whom we never expected to stay long term. Our plans have all changed. Still, there is a peace and relief from all of the stress of the past several months. Now I struggle with wondering if Tracy will ever understand that we had the best of intentions. Will she ever know our love was sincere and straight from the heart of God, in spite of the difficult times?

Having Tracy taught us that we can NOT love unconditionally as I thought we could or should. It showed us that no matter how we tried, five individuals could not make another person happy. I do know that we could not have tried any harder to love her and help her without changing our very own personalities and that simply could not be.

Not long after Tracy moved there was a prose reading one night at church.

Tears welled in my eyes. That night when I returned home I wrote: I do love Tracy in a special way and I will always wonder if she is saying her prayers, if she'll know how to love others in an appropriate and accepting way. I wonder if she thinks of us and if she knows we tried our very best.

Unfortunately we never really found out if her new placement was truly successful or not. We lost all contact after Tracy's high school years. She still frequently comes to mind. I pray it is well with the soul of this special young lady.

After Tracy we decided to try and adopt from Korea again, perhaps that would fill the void in our lives that still existed. We had our children, a beautiful home, our own business, and we were living near our families. Why could I not find a peace? Always searching, always looking.

As a Christian there is value in searching and considering that which God would have us to do. With complacency comes lack of growth. We are among the movers and shakers of the world. God has continually used those often frustrating personality traits as assets over the years.

But, for now we were about to learn more about following God's will, and both John and I were going to have to learn yet another step in submission to God's plan. First individually, and then when we were together, God began to bring circumstances to our attention guiding us to consider a move. This would be a big difference compared to other moves. This time it was His request, and most of our previous moves had been as a result of our own impatience and searching.

This was our first conscious attempt at seeking God's will in the matter of moving. Prior to that time it seems we just stumbled around and eventually found a comfort zone. Sometimes, I am sure, our impatience was God's prompting, but many times we just moved on and paid the consequences in the long run. Relocating would mean leaving both of our families and letting go of the dream of raising our children near grandparents and family in a community that we loved. It was one of the harder decisions we have ever had to make.

We had no idea what God had for us, in the good of our days or the challenges that would certainly come. It was energizing though to be in agreement and know that God was leading.

Everything about living in Southwest Missouri had been conducive to maturing us as individuals within our marriage and certainly in our faith. We were growing to love and respect our God more each day. We were slowly comprehending how necessary He was to our happiness and well-being, and how intensely He wanted to be included in our day- to-day life. This was a very different concept for us to learn…. much different from the "Sunday morning God" we had experienced in our youth.

About this time I dated Proverbs 20:24 in my Bible: "All our steps are ordered by the Lord; how then can we understand our own ways?"

Indeed, we cannot understand. Our new direction meant that we had to stop adoption paperwork for a second time. I journaled the following prayer: To our little girl in Korea, may God be with you and your birth mother this day. May you both be strengthened and understand that there is a bright future ahead for you in this family. I do not understand the delay, but I know the Lord will send you to us when it is just right. I pray that the Lord will nudge us when we are to move forward and slow us when we walk too quickly. Even when our prayers are few we pray the Lord will be with you. I know you will be just the perfect girl for our family.

I reasoned our little girl wasn't ready to travel yet; otherwise we would not have felt such an urgency to move. I couldn't understand why I had felt driven to be doing something about our next adoption if we were moving and everything submitted would be invalid. I decided it was that immaturity and impatience once again. In that time of searching and trying to figure out what was the right thing to do we had no idea that all our wanderings were meandering down the right highway at last.

When the door opened effortlessly for a job in Oklahoma, John seized the opportunity and, borrowing his parents' small camping trailer, moved there ahead of us. We didn't have a clue why we were going. But we agreed it was the right thing to do. When our house didn't sell and impatience got the best of us once again, we decided to find a rental house in Oklahoma.

We moved to Tulsa during an employment boom, which caused rental houses to be in great demand and short supply. A friend and I had covered many miles and spent countless hours looking for a house for our family to rent. My faith had been wavering when after several days of searching I couldn't find anything that seemed right. At the end of a very long day we pulled up to one of the last houses on our list.

I don't think words can adequately explain how I felt when we pulled next to the curb. It was like the power of God came over me and I was inexplicably aware that this was the house I would finally rent. I announced without even getting out of the car that this was the house I wanted, and I was strangely confident in my statement. My friend suggested I might want to get out and at least look through the windows. I obliged, but I remember thinking that it wasn't going to make any difference, this was where we were going to live.

I came back to the car after peeking through the front door. I went immediately to the nearest pay phone and proceeded to call the rental agent. We were able to lease that house against all odds. We lived there peaceably, knowing we were right where we were supposed to be for several years.

It was the first time in a very long time that I had felt I was in the right place at the right time. That is a most wonderful and satisfying place to be.

When things are right with God, they are right with the world!

Soon a lady came by to welcome us to the neighborhood and to invite our children to Vacation Bible School. Ultimately we would join that small church and spend a good many years as part of a closely-knit church family.

In that congregation God used experience after experience to help us mature spiritually. John was a board member, a trustee, adult Sunday school teacher and youth leader, and served in a number of other positions over the years we attended that church. I would work in the nursery, teach ladies Bible studies and do various other jobs, including working with the youth. Those families became an extension of our family and supported us through a multitude of life experiences.

Our steps were becoming a bit more assured and though we still had no idea where it would lead, we were learning to trust God to get us safely to each rest stop. Along the way He was providing well for us in spite of the fact that our finances were in terrible shape. We tried to keep up a house payment on our home in Missouri and rental payments in Tulsa. Stress was high and it seemed the harder we worked the further behind we got on everything. We tried desperately to stay in control and to be good stewards of the money God was providing. Our cars were old and in constant need of repairs. I was as frugal as I knew how to be in all areas of our budget; still we were continually behind on our obligations.

It was in that house that I did home day care. Learning to deal with people and the numerous demands of several small children at the same time would prove to be great on- the-job training for the years to follow.

I was impressed and proud of the children as they adapted to the new surroundings and to life in a large city. Teachers were giving rave reports about Leah and Jared. Still, I had huge reservations about the time and energy I spent on the children in my home day care. I so wanted to be more available to my own children. But, the income was necessary and being home to work seemed much better than the alternative of working outside our home and having my own children go to someone else's home before and after school each day. It was slim consolation.

All the while Jared was a preschooler; there had been a constant coming and going of many babies and young children, first through foster care, and now with our home day care. I regretted horribly not being able to spend as much time with Jared as I had the four years with Leah prior to Jared being born. I always felt I cheated him somehow. Yet, I know that I was doing the best I could, one day at a time. I reminded myself constantly that God had His hand on all of the circumstances and He was more than able to fill the gaps of my inadequacies within the lives of those persons I held most dear.

I wrote in my journal during Jared's kindergarten year: He tries so hard to please. His smile is delightful and impish. He literally worships John. In spite of John's drive to work so much, I am thankful that Jared has a strong father for a role model. That is something so many young boys never have the privilege of experiencing.

Those months demanded patience as we dealt with repeated job disappointments and confusion over why the house in Missouri would not sell. This was especially hard to understand since it was certainly a marketable house. When we had felt that God was directing us to move to Tulsa, we assumed He had a buyer for the house we would leave behind. It was an albatross around our necks. We did not understand what we were to do. So, we held on and tried to work harder to meet our ever-growing obligations.

In the midst of the most unlikely circumstances God was obviously guiding us to our much-desired Asian daughter. As much as we did not understand what we were to do about finances we were very clearly being directed to a specific agency in order to pursue adoption once again. The agency name came at us from endless angles. Advertisements in the phone book jumped boldly from the pages. Acquaintances mentioned the name and total strangers confirmed the reputation and validity of this newly discovered agency.

When we made an appointment for our initial home study we didn't have the money to pay the social worker when she came calling. Nevertheless, I made the appointment.

It was a bright sunny day as I walked to the mailbox wondering what God was going to do about these latest instructions of proceeding with adoption plans. Adding a child had seemed more logical when we were living in our large house in Southwest Missouri. Were we really on the right path? How could we go toward this adoption without enough money to make our budget work, let alone pay the thousands of dollars that would be required to get a child via international adoption? I wondered if God truly understood how utterly stupid we were going to look when those given privy to the information found out how terribly messed up our financial situation was. Surely we were not understanding, surely I should cancel the appointment!

Amidst the expected past due bills, I found a check for the exact amount needed for this initial step in the adoption process! The check was a refund from a utility deposit made over six years before in another state. We had moved at least three times since that deposit had been made, in fact, we had forgotten even making it. We have no clue to this day why we would receive a refund.

But, when God writes the checks, the origin is irrelevant. Had the amount not been so obvious I think I would have proceeded to question the appropriate destination for the much-needed funds, there were so many bills that should have been paid. But, God made it abundantly clear that He had sent a specific amount for a specific purpose.

We learned over the coming months that in God's eyes the only poverty is a lack of faith. It was this knowledge that would sustain us through many a financial trial, knowledge that many never grasp.

There were so many things we learned during this time, so much training that would be applicable over the coming years. God helped us to grow by building on each of our life experiences.

While we lived in this house I bred canary birds and finches. The money I made from selling the young birds paid for the hobby, and occasionally gave me some extra spending money as well. I sewed for other ladies, as well as continuing on with day care. All of those many things working at the same time demanded people skills and physical energy. I would utilize the life skills I acquired during this point in time and again over the years. I also spent a lot of time reading organizational books and storage tips since we were living in a small house. This was also information that would be a great asset as I added children and possessions to our ever-increasing household.

Yes, God was teaching us every step of the way. But like high school students who see no reason for some of the required classes, neither John nor I could understand the reason for some of the circumstances God was allowing us to experience.

Thankfully, over time, even the worst of circumstances are not wasted! All things are working together, giving us on the job training for the next stage of our walk with God.

Past Missed Conceptions

In looking through some mementos, I found some journal notes written soon after our marriage in 1970. In those writings are signs of confusion and a longing for the morals and purposes of the past. Even then, I was not buying into the implications that the so-called freedoms afforded those involved in the women's movement were as decidedly liberating as influential women insisted. Indeed, time has proven those freedoms were certainly not as liberating as my generation hoped they would be. I wonder how many of us have struggled more in our women's lib bondage than our grandmothers and great-grandmothers did in their accepted material limitations and lifestyle of assumed submission to God and husband?

During the years I was a home day care provider, I saw women all around me trying to justify working outside the home. Most never really understood the cost of their choices-financially and emotionally-on themselves, their husbands, and their young children. I was never able to satisfactorily explain to a child in tears why mother or daddy had to leave them for another long day. Usually the child had been taken from a warm cozy bed, handed a toaster pastry, wrapped in a coat, and dropped at my door. I saw time and again parents walk dejectedly down my sidewalk, unable to look back into the eyes of their sad children. They were not "liberated." They were in bondage to creditors and a society that has persisted in devaluing the family unit and the Biblical foundations upon which this country was founded. It is no wonder then, that limiting the size of our family seemed so logical. The burden of paying daycare providers, purchasing name brand clothing and electronic games was too much to bear.

The days of caring for others' children were days of reflection and revelation for me. It was very stylish to have two incomes, establish credit histories, and accumulate the gadgets that it had taken a lifetime for our parents to acquire. Regretfully, many of us bought into this 'culturally correct' thinking and sought the materialism of our generations. We were so wrong. Still, like others, we continued to seek the happiness, security and peace for which people throughout history have searched. That happiness, we were told, would surely come with planned pregnancies, a wallet full of credit cards and a successful career. Many of us unexpectedly felt guilt, instead of liberating happiness when we began desiring a child instead of those "other things." It was a very confusing time.

Early in our marriage, a time of infertility confused me, and then miscarriage and conception complications exhausted our emotions. Finally, a difficult pregnancy and later reoccurring complications with birth control made a tubal legation a logical choice. Though it is very odd to us now, we never prayed about our decision to have my "tubes tied." As I recall, it received acceptance with friends and family and, with their approval, we just had the procedure done. I was glad to be rid of the medical concerns of conception and miscarriage and the alteration of my moods that the birth control drugs were obviously causing. Eventually, we realized that the "successful" outcome of all of these methods of birth control had left a very empty space in our lives.

We humans are such puzzling creatures. The further from our reach children seemed, the more precious to us they became. Like children stretching for a coveted toy that has been placed just out of reach, we found ourselves lifting our hands to God. If we had such a desire for more children, we finally realized, God must have a plan. After all, it is God who puts those desires there in the first place. John and I could never have imagined what God would have for us once we became willing to listen to His leading!

Life moved on, painfully at times, as I unexpectedly went through a season of frustration and anger, questioning God about what was wrong in our lives. We seemed to be searching for someone or something that would fill the void that was undeniably in our lives. When I realized that foster parenting and home day care weren't going to replace the children that I knew should fill our home, I began in earnest to find out what God would have us specifically to do. I felt victimized by the times I found myself living in. I found few people who could understand my anxiety. Rare was the person who could even begin to understand why we would feel that children were the answer to our longings. We had a beautiful adopted daughter, a wonderful biological son, and the additional blessings from time to time of foster children.

I pray that those reading these words will find encouragement in how God has blessed and increased our family in spite of the decisions we had already made. For us, and perhaps for some of you, the solution is as old as the stories of Moses, Esther and others throughout the Bible. We are still learning to let God weave together decisions of our past with the plans He has for us in the future. God not only knew, but He allowed us to make the decisions we made. He knew all along what we would do. Hopefully we are becoming a positive part of a plan to "work all things together for good" (Romans 8:28).

Uniqueness and differences are part of the wonder of the God who creates all things. Naturally, then, no two couples will have families that are alike. Not everyone will share the same convictions with regard to family planning, and also, even our convictions are subject to change over periods of time.

It is not my intent to press our example of a family upon anyone. It is my prayer that you will simply pray and seek what God would have you to do at the place in your walk that you currently find yourselves in. Each couple must prayerfully come to an agreement in the decision of birthing, fostering or adopting more children.

I can sense that the "success" of birth control has left an empty space in the lives of many people in this country. At a time when it is often assumed that less children in our families will allow us "more," we are realizing that the "more" we are seeking could quite possibly be found in the blessings of children. I believe, as I talk to couples all over the country, that there are at least three mistakes, maybe four, in our thinking. One of the mistakes is accepting that our past decisions are final. The second is in assuming that if we had the finances (there goes that material wealth thing again) we could make the wrongs right by having reversals of surgeries performed in the past, or could 'afford' more children. The third is in our struggle to discern whether we are having concerns because God desires to put more children into our homes. We cannot and should not become responsible for more lives without the express approval and motivation coming from the God of the universe. The task is simply too much. We must guard ourselves continually against a fourth battle opponent-deception. Deception encompasses all of the original three concerns. For, if we can be convinced that it is too late, or we do not have the finances, or that God does not want us to have more children, then many children that might find security, and eternity via fundamental Christian homes, will remain lost orphans.

I wonder as I reflect on the recent years of infertility in America, and a trend toward sterilization, if our merciful God doesn't have a redemptive plan. There are many children in need of Christian families. The orphans of the world are more numerous than my heart can bear to comprehend. Those children will be born, they will grow up, and they will be many in number in our world of immorality and promiscuous sex. We hold in our hands the capability to lift them out of their current situations and give them the gift of a destiny of love, security and family that they might possibly never know. We are told to go and make disciples of men (Matthew 28:19). Though I am not a missionary, nor even a bold witness in approaching strangers, I can make the difference in the lives of many by touching and investing in the life of just one child. Perhaps, our past decisions can be redeemed to become a part of God's solution to a failing welfare system and the plight of millions of children worldwide.

Thankfully the same God that is working within our hearts to bring us home, to reconsider how our children are taught, to reevaluate our goals and motivations, will enable us to adopt-if that is His plan for our family. But, I dare say, that in a nation where deception allows abortion to be used as birth control, the battle to frustrate those asking to adopt will be great.

In fact, it is one of many battlegrounds in this nation. Spots of heated battles have already received media attention, and will continue to do so as the devil begins to attack the lives of families and children from yet another angle. We must put on the full armor of God for this battle. As we know all too well, we do not fight against man, but against principalities and powers (Ephesians 6:10-12).

The change then, must come from within. With hindsight, we may need to adjust our way of thinking regarding the children we thought would fill or homes. We must release this area of our lives to God just as most of us are continually doing with regard to other lifestyle changes. Perhaps, an inability to bear children can be redeemed to become a part of a provision to move the children of the world into Christian homes. Homes that are, perhaps, the only safe haven soon to be found in a world gone astray. We have within our grasp the finances and the talents to completely change the destiny of this nation, and the world, one child at a time.

In the adoption of 12 children and the unexpected birth of our son, it is unlikely that one challenge you could mention has been spared our family.

We have been asked to adopt in nearly every kind of circumstance and against all odds. Though controversial, and not always accepted, God has specifically directed us to adopt across racial lines, or welcome special needs children into our family. We have adopted during times of unemployment, when exhaustion seemed inevitable, and more recently when our age should have been a negative factor. When those around us thought we had used no logic at all, we still chose to adopt. In working through the adoption process, God always supplied the needs and led us to the child He had created for our family.

Yes, we believe that just as the son born to us was supposed to be a part of our family, so were the other children, at the moment of their conception, destined for our arms. What God asks us to do, He always enables us to do.

We must remember that when we accept Christ as our Savior we, too, are *adopted* into the spiritual family of God (Ephesians 1:5-6). Within that family are people of every race, intellect and ability. Couldn't God then have plans for the nations of the world to be miraculously blended into the traditional families of this lifetime? We can each have an impact, changing the world not so much with large families, but in tiny proportions of one child at a time. The "unlovable", the older child, the handicapped, the challenging, the foreign-all are precious in His sight.

Silver Storks

The time involved from our first having a 'notion' about adopting a foreign child goes back many years. I can remember fleeting thoughts about how neat it would be to have an Asian daughter when I was just a girl myself. I remember how excited I would be over the tiny bits of information my grandparents would get in regard to the little girl they continually sponsored in a foreign country. But I wanted to have hands on contact with children. Sponsorship is necessary and good, but I wanted to directly affect the lives of children.

When John and I were dating I remember thinking about the children and life we might someday have. I assumed we would have our own birth children; still, a certain excitement flitted through my soul when I would think about adopting children that would otherwise not have a family.

Dreams are one of the ways that God shows us what to do. God has used that means several different times over the years, usually when I am least expecting it! It took a long time before I could accept that God spoke to me in this unusual way. I am sure as I write these words that the dream of a little Asian girl that I shared in the preface of this book was absolutely not only an instructional but a confirming way for God to direct our path.

I believe that God plants the desires He has for us in our hearts, and then proceeds to give us those desires as we seek His will and direction. It is in the search and discovery of these gifts that we discover our purpose in living. Few truly find that purpose in our present day materialistic world. Oh, the joy we as a people miss when we do not reach out and share the abundant blessings that God has so richly bestowed upon us and desires to gift us with.

The "reaching out" experience is divine and utterly breathtaking when we discover God's perfect will for our own lives. It is the longing of the spirit to find the desire of the Heavenly Father. When that desire is understood and sought after, life has purpose and meaning like at no other time in our walk on earth. One task of reaching out is not nobler than another. Oh, that more people would understand that they seek not their own gratification, but the hopes and dreams that God has purposed for each of us!

I believe that there is a "permissive will" and a "perfect will" in our walk down life's road. When I am in God's permissive will I often burn out and get so tired and frustrated, sometimes giving up on the entire project. In love, God gently watches and lets me struggle and fall again. There is no blatant sin in permissive will, just ignorance in not seeking, or perhaps failing to understand God's instructions. I will likely arrive at the same destination, but experience some delays and side trips. Like a stubborn child, I often have to learn things the hard way.

To find God's perfect will I am required to let go and let God direct. The destination may seem unreachable, but the trip day by day becomes similar to reading the pages of an exciting mystery. I never know what is going to happen, but I know all the pages will come together to climax in a very exciting and unpredictable ending. God knows what is written on the pages of our lives long before we try to muddle through. Though I often misunderstand the instructions or the purpose in our destination, it is nevertheless; His perfect will that I seek.

We had tried all of the normal ways to be "successful", even from a 'church' perspective. Both of us worked very hard at physically tiring jobs. We dedicated a good amount of time to church work and attendance. We tithed and did not otherwise waste our money, at least in our own understanding. Still, no matter what we tried it never worked out and we would struggle and suffer all the more for our human efforts. It appears we were not destined to be a middle class American family, living in the same house for a number of years and having an average of 2.5 children. We could not find rest in trying to fit the mold. It was logical, but it was not to be. Against all logic, through the past 30 years God almost continually moved us toward adoption and our next child.

Even after we had the pictures of TJ, our Asian baby, and the adoptive labor really began to become excitingly stressful, there would be obstacles to overcome and illogical provisions. The orphanage was considering keeping TJ in Korea for three more months while they did surgery to repair a hernia. Maternal instincts were flowing fast and furiously, and that was my baby, in spite of the miles that unfairly separated us. No one was going to be with MY baby through surgery except me. Still, no scheduled arrival date was to be had.

We couldn't find the reason for the delay in her travel arrangements. Finally after numerous phone calls we found that the Immigration and Naturalization Services (INS) office had 'misplaced' our entire packet of legal documents and it would be at least three months before they could process our baby's visa. This news came on the day after we received the picture showing the hernia demanding medical attention. It was a time of intense emotions and helplessness like I have rarely experienced.

John called a state representative when our request to expedite new papers to INS met with deaf ears. We didn't have a clue at the conclusion of that call whether it had been a move in the right direction or not. So, we were shocked when within 48 hours duplicates of legal papers from two states were gathered into an acceptable file at the INS office and approval granted for our baby to begin her journey home. God had divinely directed and intervened!

Throughout the process of waiting on this international miracle, God had repeatedly supplied the needs for the adoption. The church helped us pay for the visa we couldn't afford. If it had not been for the generous baby shower I don't know how we would have clothed her. She received more beautiful clothes than I can ever remember receiving at one time. We received rebate checks from a utility company, and letters from people we had never met encouraging us to pursue the adoption, all in spite of what our circumstances appeared to be. We received an income tax refund that year that just lacked a few cents of being what we needed to pay the Korean part of the adoption. We had never, nor have we since, received a refund remotely close to the amount it was that year. Of course none of these provisions came ahead of time, but arrived in the nick of time, just as we needed them. Typically, help came just as our faith would begin to waver.

The 'adoptive pregnancy' had involved mountains of paperwork and numerous disappointing postponements. At times the anticipation had made us sure we would burst! Now, the due date had arrived! It was to be a labor of love, warmly shared by many. The phone call came and the labor pains started in earnest.

I wrote: Thirteen days ago the phone call that TJ had a scheduled flight, finally came! We were all so excited! The kids jumped and shrieked for joy! I was so excited I almost forgot to call John at work. Then I did a totally crazy thing. I settled into doing dough art on the lids of discarded jars. (It seemed so very important!) When our pastor stopped by and heard the news he looked upon the project in disbelief, his expression confirming the fact that I was in shock!

Looking back, I must agree, he was absolutely correct. That day, I thought he simply did not understand the importance of getting all the little details done before the baby arrived home. I had planned to be so cool when the phone calls finally came, not giddy and restless like the other mothers I had seen just prior to the arrival of their new additions. But I failed! I didn't sleep at all that night. The next day we worked hard at organizing the house and cleaning. We were having so much fun in our excitement that the housework seemed like play. Every plane that flew overhead prompted Jared to ask if it was TJ coming home.

The arrival date did finally become reality and a large group of friends mingled in the "waiting room." The "hospital" was Tulsa International Airport.

Fondly called "Silver Storks", awesome jumbo jets arrive calmly and routinely into major airports across the world; among their cargo ride rosy cherubs with almond eyes. Akin to natural delivery, these "Silver Stork" deliveries are often delayed, taking much longer than we would like to wait.

We were totally deflated when we were told at the arrival gate the flight had been detained and was still on the ground in Denver. No one could tell us just how long or for what reason there was a delay. We were unprepared for an extended wait. I wondered how we would bear the predicted four or more hours of 'hard labor' in a room literally bursting with anticipation.

The news rippled through the crowd and welcome home signs and balloons came down to lap level as a dejected feeling floated over the room. Questions with no answers skirted across the crowd. Folks wondered if they should stay or go.

As we were considering what we should do, a rumor rumbled its way back across the vast crowd of people. Our family was pushed to the entrance gate. The computer had failed to keep track of our stork and it was rolling toward the 'delivery room' even as we spoke! There had been no airline announcement; the attendants claimed they had no clue that the plane had ever left the ground in Denver. No matter, there were now people coming down the ramp. Oh my, when would everyone finally get off of that plane? It seemed like the minutes were hours and the hours days as we strained to see for the first time our long awaited baby.

People around us were a blur and our attention centered on the last stages of labor before delivery. A hush fell over the crowd, then our applause spread as those oriental dolls, four in all, were delivered one by one to the waiting arms of their forever families. We endured one last agonizing moment as they teased us with a delay. Last, but certainly not least, she was here! The circle of love began months, even years before was now complete.

The labor of waiting was forgotten, the pains and fears erased. Months of prayers and preparation melted into a feeling of complete joy. We were sharing the miracle of a unique birth and a blessed beginning. Trista Jin-Joelle was home!

I have a journal entry from a few months after Trista's arrival. It says: When asked recently to write about the most special day in your life, Jared, (then about seven years old) wrote about the day TJ came home on an airplane from Korea. We would all have to agree! It would be just one of many very special days as our love and our family continued to grow.

A picture of an Asian girl in my mind years ago,
Is now before me a treasure to mold and let grow,
In the ways of the Lord, the way of a new land
With the strength of her God, and the love of her new parents' hands.

Sent to America to be all she can be,
For God has a purpose it's easy to see.
She's gifted and motivated like no other one
She knows Jesus and serves Him even so young.
Brought from Korea on a Silver Stork plane,
with God's hand as her guide, she has heaven to gain.
The years tumbled by us, our hearts opened wide,
There were four of us to welcome Trista, our hearts swelled with pride.

We know that at a time in our lives when adding a child seemed the least likely thing to do, the Lord provided for the adoption in numerous ways. He made miracles happen and brought beautiful people into our lives.

Some six months after Trista arrived in the States we would receive a much worn package from INS with the original legal documents. Who knows how many desks that folder had spent time on before finding its way back to us? I shudder still to think how long it would have taken our baby to get home to us if we had waited on the lost papers to be found and processed. We thank God we did not have to wait.

We were now more positive about the tasks ahead and looking forward with immense anticipation to what the Lord had planned. The lessons we had learned and the faith we had come to know were unexplainable, a vital and permanent part of our beings. We had a new desire to serve the Lord in a special way. We desired to serve Him with diligence and faith knowing that when we make the effort, God is sure to make a way for that which He desires us to do.

After her arrival in June, I wrote the following: TJ has been here about eight weeks. It has been a very difficult two months and I will never forget the fatigue and the confusion I have felt since her arrival.... We have spent an unbelievable amount of physical and emotional energy, both in getting the baby here and in caring for her since her arrival. She has been nearly impossible to make happy. We are considering sending to Korea for the formula she was on, in hopes that will somehow soothe her. As soon as I try to lay her down, she screams and carries on so. She only sleeps for short periods of time; I am running on empty and completely out of ideas.

As if that were not enough, the house in Southwest Missouri had not sold. It had been on the market for well over a year. John was not happy with his present employment, and we were still struggling financially. What were we doing wrong? I pondered my questions day in and day out. I could find no answers.

I noted this Scripture in my Bible about this time. First Corinthians 15:58 states: "Therefore my beloved brethren be steadfast, immovable, always abounding in the work of the Lord, knowing that in the Lord your labor is not in vain."

During those first few months after TJ arrived when I could not seem to comfort her, my heart cried out in fear. I was afraid I was not going to be able to meet the needs of this child. I even wondered if we had made a terrible mistake by adding a third child to our family. All the doubts and fears would tumble down on me in the night when I was at a low ebb of physical rest and mental energy. I thought about the fact that both Leah and Jared would be starting school in the fall. I could have started a career with no guilt trips and no toddlers demanding my attention. I knew I was rambling and deep in my heart I knew she was to be with us, but still, in weaker moments the sin of doubt would plague me.

Somehow I muddled through the days. There were never any answers, just an understanding that to get through this time I would have to take one day at a time. I could not look to the past, nor worry about the future; I just had to focus on today. Indeed, the same faith that had gotten us through the months of waiting on her to come home, continued to get us over the rocky path of the next few weeks after her arrival in the States. Ever so slowly Trista began to find her place in our family.

It would be three months after she came home before I could write in my journals that she was actually happy. One thing was for certain; in spite of her unhappiness at home she was still cordial and patient with people. Our church family was especially attached to her and she won the hearts of many people with that special smile the Lord gave her! It was like sunshine glowing on her face every time she smiled. I never did get use to the way people touched her, pinched her chubby little cheeks and kissed her in those early months, she was a true trooper and very tolerant.

In more recent years I have come to believe that Trista was experiencing a great deal of emotional trauma from leaving foster parents and familiar sights and sounds behind. As a young woman she still is cautious about making new acquaintances and once she has come to love someone, she takes her relationships very seriously. She is the sort of person that has pen pals from grade school and calls friends that she hasn't seen in years. It must have been very difficult to leave behind those you had dared to love, and yet be too young to effectively express your grief. I am sure also that she was experiencing great discomfort from the formula, but we were helpless to resolve the situation, try as we might. Still, she was our daughter by divine appointment and our God had made it so!

From Trista's arrival in our home I learned that there truly are things that God chooses to reveal to us long before the time designated for manifestation. We were boldly reminded that there are no country or racial boundaries in God's adoption plans. He has a specific family in mind for children, and if we are obedient to the leading of the Holy Spirit, He will divinely orchestrate details beyond our human comprehension to get that child to the family of His choice. There is no room for logic in most adoptive placements.

I was sitting at the dining room table one sunny day. *Trista, then about seven years old, flitted by the sunlit windows. Something about the way she smiled and the way her waist length hair flowed in seemingly slow motion around her face made me realize that she was for sure the little girl that God had shown me in that dream so many years before.* Because the child in my dream had been older, not an infant, John and I had assumed that one day we would adopt an older Asian girl. It was a wrong interpretation of God-given information. All the time we had been searching and looking for that specific little girl she had been living and breathing and laughing in our very home!

I cannot express how seeing her flow by the lacy curtains that day strengthened my faith and made me realize anew that God does have a hugely important plan for each of us if we are willing to totally submit to God and let Him be the director of our lives. Whatever God asks us to do, He will give us the strength to continue when in our own strength we cannot carry on. He is a God of great big promises obtained by taking little tiny steps of faith.

Strength and assurance for our walk come in so many different ways. As we struggled on through some of the worst financial times we had experienced, I became physically and emotionally exhausted, in spite of knowing that God could and would get us through. The flesh is so weak!

In early winter I put a note beside Proverbs 20:24: "A man's steps are directed by the Lord. How then can anyone understand his own way?" (NIV)

We knew that we were not done adopting, but our life was certainly not going in a way that was conducive to finalizing Trista's adoption, let alone searching for another addition so quickly. Still assurance that this was "the way, walk in it" (Isaiah 30:21), came to me indirectly through two different presentations in our small church. One was a visit by an evangelist who had a little girl adopted from Korea not many months before. Somehow, just meeting them strengthened me. Then a very large adoptive family came and presented a program of singing and testimony. God used that family to reassure John and me that He did indeed have unique plans for us. We knew we were headed for some sort of special missions, we just didn't know where or how!

Just by being accessible and open with their lives, strength was given and received in ways only the Spirit can understand. Through those church presentations I began to understand more clearly how our lives all too often speak much louder than the most carefully selected words. I am not a great evangelist giving alter calls to thousands, that is not the request God has for my life. But, perhaps somehow, when others see our family and hear out stories, they too will receive a lifeline to Jesus via the power of the Holy Spirit present in our lives. We can indeed attempt to be the only reflection of Jesus some will ever see.

In my journal I wrote: Today as Leah and Jared sang at church I couldn't hold back a tear of joy as the peace and assurance that seeps through us as Christians came over me. John and I are both so proud and excited to be the ones entrusted with raising these children as part of our family and in the church, allowing them opportunity to come to know Christ in a personal way.

Leah would have been about 10 years old at the time and Jared would have been about six years old. We were blessed to have a church that allowed everyone to participate in the services and testimonies as they felt led. Several times over the years that we were members there, each of us had opportunity to be on the podium. I hope we were a blessing!

Life Alternatives

God opened the door for us to move into a much larger and newer house. It was next door to friends of ours from church. We were all very excited and happy to have the opportunity to live there. I continued to baby-sit on a smaller scale. The house we were living in had a room off the kitchen just perfect for my small, part-time sewing business.

Meanwhile, even with all the head knowledge and Scripture reading I did, I wrote the following:

Lifelines do come on horrible days but our knees grow weary and our bodies tired with the pressures no matter how much we try to let the Lord carry us along. Submitting to an unseen force is so difficult, and yet so very necessary. Thankfully God carries us along until we are mature enough to stand on our own feet, steady in our commitment and firm in our faith. Oh, that we would become more steady!

Ever frustrated, I didn't feel like I had any long-term direction. Most everything I did seemed meaningless, with no eternal significance. I suppose it was one of those 'permissive will' times. There was nothing really wrong with what I was doing, but at the same time I couldn't accept the peace God is so willing to offer in those waiting rooms of life.

I'd read aimlessly throughout the Bible. Since I didn't have a clue what

I was searching for, it was hard to look for specific instructions or even specific passages. But as crazy as it seems, certain lines would jump out at me. I jotted them down in my journal and then each day went back over what I had read in the preceding days. As the list grew, the message began to make more sense. It seemed God was showing me that ever-bold lettered word: **adoption**. I thought it was a pretty unlikely idea. So did John.

He hoped my hints from God with regard to adoption might mean that I could somehow work in adoptions, bringing home an income instead of paying out those huge fees. We had not yet paid off the final bills attached to Trista's adoption, and that had to be done before we would or could pursue another placement.

If God had another child for us He was going to have to make it very clear because we did not see how we could ever justify more adoption expenses.

I prayed for understanding and a glimpse of what was to be came clearly to me one day, in a very unexpected manner. John was gone, the older children were at school and TJ must have been sleeping. I was washing dishes at the kitchen sink.

In the stillness of that afternoon, as clear as any thought can be, the Lord impressed upon me that there would be another child before Christmas. I was so sure of what God said that I began preparing a place for this child in our home. This clear word from God was to have enormous impact on my thoughts and actions from that time forward.

Just when that old sin of doubt would begin to creep in God would confirm my steps in a new and different way. For example, soon after that word from the Lord had been given to me, a friend stopped by for a visit. She told me about a crisis pregnancy center that she had heard about at her Bible study group. There was a need for volunteers. I knew as soon as she had spoken the words that I was to find out more information about this place called Life Alternative.

I did not know what I was to do, but I did know that I had my next set of instructions. She most likely doesn't remember, but when she left, my friend jokingly said, "You'll probably get a baby through Life Alternatives before Christmas." She walked on down the sidewalk, not having a clue the confirmation she had just given me. I said nothing to anyone.

I searched for a phone number and called this organization that was being so obviously brought to my attention. I felt compelled to do something in the pro-life movement. Adoption, in and of itself, is of course a very pro-life action. But I assumed this would be a diversion from my obsession with adoption. In fact, I probably would not have made an appointment and ultimately made plans to attend workshops in how to be an effective volunteer, if I had thought that my motive was to adopt a child. God knew that, so He proceeded to bring me through the back door of the plan and skillfully directed us over and around hurdles time and again.

I met with the director for the first time. We talked about my relationship with God and what I felt He was showing me to do. She and I concluded the meeting, agreeing to pray about exactly what it was the Lord desired for me to do within the organization. Even after the interview I was not sure why I had gone there. But I noted in my journal that I knew I was on the right path. For the time being, that knowledge was enough.

Meanwhile, God kept me seeking His directions with other confirmations. When I would listen to Christian music, I found it renewed my soul and often God used it to communicate to my spirit in ways I have yet to understand. There was Christian television. I am not an avid television fan, but at this point in my life I did feel drawn to certain shows. One day I actually felt God had set me down on the coffee table, dishtowel in hand so I would listen to a story. Tingling through my body verified my feeling that God was trying in a fatherly way to impress something upon me. I shed tears as I cried out for understanding regarding what God wanted me to specifically do. I fully expected to hear the answer in an audible voice. I never did, but God made His point through the show: It was about how faith had seen an adoptive family through some unusual circumstances. The details of the story are long gone from my memory, but the emotional impact upon my spirit I can remember to this day. In the days that followed God would use that television show in a number of ways, including two more programs that seemed designed for just my ears.

John and I prayed and considered what we were to do next. A show came on that proceeded to tell the story of a man who left his job as a computer operator and went into contract programming after he felt the Lord was directing him that way. As a result of his obedience this man's life was blessed in many ways and he was able to tithe more and contribute more to organizations and such things. As you will see, these were very timely stories.

When we take time to know more about God, and to communicate with Him, He begins to make apparent many of His desires. When we are willing to allow the Holy Spirit to move through us, many beautiful events can happen; things we never expect.

That summer I wrote: Everyone is still sleeping. I woke up early this morning with an urge to get up and begin the day with some quiet time in preparation for some serious heart to heart prayers with God. I don't feel a burden for the decisions for which I seek direction, just a need to be open this day to conversation with the Holy Spirit. It is a delightful summer morning; all is well in my world. Fresh hot coffee to enjoy on a patio that provides a setting to make me forget there is a busy, often cruel city just minutes away. The field behind the house is green and the grasses are waving as if praising the Lord with uplifted hands. The birds are fluttering everywhere catching their morning meal and calling exuberantly to one another, caught up in their morning bird activities. There is a warm, balmy breeze and a cheery sunshine peaking over the rooftops. Rejoice, this is truly a day that the Lord hath made!

Two days later John and I met for a sack lunch at a local park. We could just feel that things were going to change, and we wanted to talk about the possibilities. We considered adoption, job changes, even moving.

The questions hung in the trees as we wandered back to the car, still puzzled and yet somehow prepared, but for what?

I wrote in my journal: God seems to have so much more for me and I seem to be the only thing in the way of receiving my blessings and peace. Working in adoption is my first love and I want to continue to work toward that end, either adopting more children, helping to place children, or somehow working with underprivileged children or perhaps speaking to people encouraging others to adopt. I want to go wherever the doors open and the Lord leads. I just don't know where He is leading!

We decided to put out "feeler" letters, which introduce our family and our desire to adopt more children, to different adoption agencies Our thinking was if God had a child for us, then with just a simple letter of inquiry the Lord could then motivate the appropriate people to present our child to us. We have used this approach preceding other placements and feel, for us, this is a "faith under girded with works" approach.

We also filed a pre-application with the state that summer. We attended workshops that were required before we could adopt a child through the state. Again, this was simply because we felt God wanted us on the path of adoption and this was one of the few paths that appeared to be an option.

We did get a phone call from an agency in Kansas, asking us if we would consider a newborn with Down's syndrome. We were unsettled all that week as we considered what we should do. I remember the indecision and the huge step of faith we knew a special needs adoption would take. We finally called and told the caseworker that if the Lord so led we would take the baby. We were put on the list of families to be considered.

The Lord gave us a peace for the first time in several days and we felt the lesson in this particular case might have been about our own obedience and willingness to take a handicapped child. We never felt the need to pursue her, and we assume she was placed with another family. There would be others too numerous to mention that we called about or were contacted about. Nothing ever materialized, but we were open to anyone the Lord chose to place in our family.

This was in my journal: Our cars are running on a prayer and bills are rolling in like thunderclouds. It would be easy to let circumstances freeze us in a fearful state. We can choose to take hold of the situation and make positive decisions, all the while depending on God for the outcome, or we can mumble through life and never have the high that comes from living the mystery one page at a time.

Psalm 25:4, says "Make me to know your ways, O Lord; teach me your paths. Lead me in your truth, and teach me, for you are the God of my salvation; for you I wait all day long."

During that week I had a dream. *In the dream I was seated next to someone whose face I could not see. After considering the dream over and over I now believe the person was representative of the Holy Spirit (or Jesus). John was across the room, a bit of a distance from us. This 'person' handed me a blue check for a specific amount. Nothing was verbally said, but I remember knowing full well that John would not have to worry about the finances.*

I told John about the dream and we considered what it would mean and thought that amount of money would be so great to have! But, it was just a dream and we honestly didn't have a clue what it all meant. But for me, the peace was there again and the message was clear: don't worry about money.

Psalm 16:7, 8 says: "I bless the Lord who gives me counsel; in the night also my heart instructs me. I keep the Lord always before me; because he is at my right hand, I shall not be moved."

I had been selling some of the dresses I made as well as some other hand-crafted items at local craft shows, hoping to increase our income. John called while I was working at a craft show to tell me that he had abruptly been laid off. I came home immediately so we could figure out what we were going to do. We were finally sincerely seeking God's perfect will, even if we weren't sure at the time that we were going to like the answers and direction we would receive. We struggled hard to keep our faith and not panic with this new development. But we had to ask, now: what were we to do?

The Lord had provided John with a Scripture the very morning of the layoff. John would later say that helped him very much to get through that terrible day. He had been working an average of 90 hours per week, salaried. John was physically exhausted. Our conversations did meander back to the man who had left a salaried position to do contract programming because in that position not only is the hourly pay much better, but there is pay for hours worked. If John had only been getting paid straight time for the many overtime hours he had been working, we would not have been having the financial challenges we were having. Working so many hours with no extra pay had prohibited any of the occasional odd jobs he had become accustomed to doing in order to secure us the needed additional funds for our monthly obligations.

Just before John was laid off we had decided that we were going to let the house in Missouri go into foreclosure. Actually, holding on to it so long was what had caused us to get so terribly behind on other things. It had been a struggle for over three years. We had finally relinquished all thoughts of how to sell it, or how to hold on to it. We had reached peaceable terms within ourselves. To say we weren't hoping for a miracle in the situation would have been untrue, but we had both finally turned the entire situation over to God and it was refreshing to be in agreement about our decision to let go. We had tried virtually every way we knew to sell the property. So many people had prayed about the sale of that house. We had to accept that God's answer was no. As the days went by, God not only provided us spiritual strength but also made incredible financial provision for us as well.

We sat down several weeks after John's last day of work. It came as no big surprise that *the exact figure, $5,389.00, that God had shown me in the dream was the amount that had gone through the checking account.* That was nearly three times our normal income at that time. It was an amount we desperately needed to get our heads above water after a draining three years of hard work and unrealized dreams.

Trista's adoption had never been legally finalized in the United States because of a lack of funds. We had been paying on the debt as much as we were able every month. *The Lord kept impressing upon me to get the bill taken care of by the end of October.* We didn't have a clue how we were going to do that while we were out of work.

The money came on the 29th of October; the day the Lord had told me we needed to have the debt paid. This time my parents unexpectedly sent some money. I am sure they never intended it to be for an agency payment. I am just as certain they did expect it to help us pay some on our necessities. Again, it would have been so logical to spend that money in any number of other places, but God had shown me the amount and given me the date, I wasn't about to argue with the provision in the mail that day!

Without even knowing it, my family had been used by God to make an illogical provision for adoption. Oh, that we might all be willing to be the means through which others are blessed, even if it be unbeknownst to us!

Eventually I went to a Life Alternative meeting for volunteers. I can write with a totally clear conscience that adoption was not on my mind. In fact this was to be a pleasant diversion from John's employment situation and our waiting room regarding whatever God was going to show me to do.

I was politely interested in the meeting. I did enjoy the testimony about an overseas mission trip and equally enjoyed watching an especially beautiful black baby girl in our midst. I could hardly take my eyes off of her!

After the meeting we mingled and shared a time of fellowship and refreshments. The director motioned me aside and after some friendly chit-chat told me that my name had come to her during intercessory prayer a few days earlier. I fully expected her to tell me what God had shown her I was to do at the crisis pregnancy center. I was in a position to welcome any direction at all, and waited anxiously for her to tell me what God had revealed to her. Instead, she began asking how our adoption search was going. I told her about the workshops we were attending through the state and shared that in our present unemployment situation we were not actively pursing any specific adoptive situation.

My heart began pounding as she told me about a baby that was due in December. Would we be interested? This lady and others would soon learn to never ask me if I'm interested in adopting or if we would consider certain situations. I am ALWAYS intrigued! The rest of the evening is a blur as I did the silent argument routine with God. *Not wanting to get my hopes up, but I was unable to deny the witness of my spirit that had been so real while my friend talked.* I was a jumble of emotions when I finally excused myself from the meeting and headed home into the night.

The longer I drove on those back roads though the stillness of the evening the more sure I became that this little bit of information was from God. This was indeed a day of confirmations, but I was struggling greatly since there wasn't a bit of logic in any of the thoughts I was experiencing.

I had stopped at an intersection. With great power and strength the Holy Spirit seemed to fill the spaces of the car. In what seemed an audible voice I heard these words, "My ways are not your ways."

The glow and warmth of the Spirit were quickly gone, but the impact was real.

John was wiped out from all of the emotional craziness of no work and my obsession with finding what it was that God had for us. Unable to contain my enthusiasm, I replayed the evening to him in detail. I had found out in the conversation at the meeting that the baby would be biracial. Even that information somehow was a confirmation since we had been noticing biracial children when we were out and about as much as we had noticed Korean babies prior to Trista's arrival. Though he understood the events to be from God, John wasn't exactly able to share my excitement. I decided he would have had to experience the things I had just been through to know the intenseness of the revelations. He couldn't burst this bubble: I knew God was mightily at work!

The next morning I boldly highlighted Isaiah 55:8-9 in my Bible: "For My thoughts are not your thoughts, neither are your ways My ways, says the Lord. For as the heavens are higher than the earth, so are My ways higher than your ways and My thoughts than your thoughts." I added a hearty, Amen! I certainly did NOT understand what God was doing or thinking. He had a plan; of that I was sure.

God was not asking us to understand. He was just asking us to be obedient and to follow His leading, to walk in faith. Faith was just about all we had left. Our pride was gone. We weren't even providing in a way we would desire for our children, though they continued to lack for nothing. We had been humbled to our knees so many times by decisions we thought were right but turned out to be so apparently wrong. With no direction, no plans in sight, we called and said we would take the baby.

> At the kitchen sink I stood one day,
> "Before Christmas a child will come your way."
> I'd heard God in my heart, of that there was no doubt.
> How His plan was to work, I would have to patiently find out.
> As I drove down the road,
> God's will I would find
> The power of God entered my car and my mind.
> "Trust me," He said with a forceful voice,
> To follow or falter will soon be your choice.
> "My ways are not your ways" was the Scripture He gave
> How true that would be as our path God would pave
> Unemployed and scared through the course of our days,
> When God asked us to take her and question not His ways.

We found out that the baby was due December 15th, just another tiny confirmation that we were traveling down the right path. Now logic was settling in again. We thought insurance would be a problem since John was no longer employed full-time. We investigated and found out if we could come up with the premium our insurance could be extended throughout the end of December and would cover the baby as soon as we got legal custody. We no sooner found out that information than John received a call that the contract work that had been sustaining us through these crazy times was finished. Without that work we could not even pay the insurance premium.

Everywhere we turned we hit huge hurdles: they seemed endless. It was during this time that we were forced to accept a painful reality of life.

John considered the pastor of our church a very dear friend. Understanding our walk was not logical, John still sought the counsel of his pastor/friend. Instead of offers of prayers or even tough love answers, the pastor spoke some very cold words. He compared the adoption of children of color to the Save the Whales Program. The same pastor who had interceded on our behalf numerous times during the adoption of our Asian daughter now verbally compared a child of Black heritage to whales! John was visibly affected. We were further shocked when we realized that long term friendships became stressed when we discussed our recent motivations that we believed to be from God. There was undercurrent within our church and concerns in the ladies group about a mixed race child in the Sunday nursery.

Statements heard in the past about Sunday morning being the most segregated hour in America became painfully real. Soon after that discussion the pastor and his family left the area. I fear our convictions were factored into their decision. There was no biblical verse to support the opinions and reactions of the church, yet many held on to the prejudices learned over a lifetime and tolerated daily in the church. I have never grown used to that unjustified judgment. In later years we would learn yet another phase of that judgment...our children are wonderful blessings and add minority flavor to the local body of believers and for that they are readily accepted. However, when the children are older and dating or courtship becomes a possibility, true beliefs are readily seen, and they are not often positive and accepting of our children of color. It would seem they are all right to help meet quotas and grow youth groups, but not acceptable as potential marriage partners. We have at the same time, received many blessings and words of encouragement from the body of Christ, and certainly find many good and glorious people in any given congregation.

Knowing that we could not change our circumstances without divine intervention we waited a week for something to change and when nothing did we called and told the director at Life Alternative that though we truly felt the baby was ours they should find another family more able to financially provide. I don't know if she ever really searched for another family, knowing she was a true warrior and comfortable in her walk of faith, I suspect she opted to pray for us and leave the rest in God's hands.

We had no guarantee that we could pay the costs, even though at every turn many expenses were being miraculously taken care of. Meanwhile, although the attorney offered to do the termination of parental rights at no charge, we had to have some money for the anesthesiologist, and that had to come immediately. Since we had mailed the monthly installment for the medical insurance the day before, there was no cash for the newly presented need. But, God would use His resources once again. Several of our friends rallied around and gathered together a good portion of the money we needed to prepay the medical bill. We were still short some of the needed funds.

I wrote in my journal: Things are beginning to get testy around here and it is time I'm afraid for one of those low valley experiences that make the mountain peaks of life seem so awesome, and from a distance unconquerable. John is showing signs of faltering faith and weariness. If he loses his spirit, jobs will be difficult to secure. I feel we must come through this valley stretch with upside down palms, emptying all problems into God's hands.

Palms and hearts empty of burdens are necessary if we are to climb the mountain path and reach the peak of spiritual joy. Faith is essential and as the spiritual leader and provider of this family, it is critical that John keep his faith. I will pray diligently and without ceasing for my husband as he struggles to lead us through this valley.

Later I wrote: I thank the Lord that though I am weary I have not lost faith this time through the valley of life. Faith is not a gift I have been blessed with in other crazy times, but praise the Lord, this time He has been successful in carrying me through without a huge struggle on my part. Of course He has gone to some incredible lengths to keep me on track and show me His will. I still believe that we will get a child before Christmas. I believe John will get a good job and that when we look back to this valley we will find it was one of the most productive times we have yet endured. I write these thoughts with $60.00 in our bank account and no earthly way for things to work out. Still, I have seen so much of God at work in our lives recently, I must hold on.

It was a long dark weekend, but Monday came! John was able to work a few contract hours and would be paid the end of the following week. He finally received confirmation of a full-time position, but they had not given him a start date. The insurance lady had been out of the office the preceding Friday when we had taken the check by for the continuance of the medical insurance. When she found out that John would be starting a new job she returned the premium check to us, saying they would just continue our coverage until the end of the month, at which time we would be eligible for insurance with the new employer.

That returned check, combined with the amount that had been donated by friends, provided exactly the amount we needed to meet with the attorney and pay the anesthesiologist fees! When we left the attorney's office we felt totally peaceful. The commitment to this baby was now officially made and we knew we were doing the right thing. A decision and a commitment were delightful after weeks and weeks of living in a waiting room. We chose not to try and figure out what provision God had planned for the balance of the expenses.

When it was all said and done we had free medical insurance for the nine weeks that John was out of full-time work. I had minor surgery during this time and some other things happened. We filed more claims during that time than we had ever filed on insurance before, and his previous employer had carried us on the insurance program without charge!

Within hours of our making that firm commitment to the baby, John received a call to start work the next morning. Was God waiting on our obedience, or was the timing just ironic?

"For there is no distinction between Jew and Greek; the same Lord is Lord of all and bestows His riches upon all who call upon Him. For, 'everyone who calls upon the name of the Lord will be saved' " (Romans 10:12-13).

We went to Missouri over the holiday. Our family was not excited about the latest development regarding the addition of another child. We admitted, logically it made no sense. We didn't attempt to explain or make excuses. We just made our announcement, opened our gifts, enjoyed a distracted but memorable time, and then rushed back to Tulsa to await the arrival of our new baby.

Just before midnight the phone rang. The birth mother was in labor; we would be called first thing in the morning with an update!

Oh, the bliss of seeing those things which God has revealed begin to become reality. The excitement and anticipation of a new baby were no less the fourth time around than they had been the first, because this was God's plan and all was well. I slept peacefully. Our child was on its way just as God had promised so many long months ago. We didn't have our baby by Christmas, but we did have confirmation and that was enough.

Early the next morning we found out that we had a beautiful baby girl. We were ecstatic! We tossed around names, tried to figure out when and how her arrival would be orchestrated and generally flitted around. I wrote: We have our miracle, a perfectly beautiful, delicately painted and softly sculptured baby girl, and the desire of our hearts.

God made it so!

Then another call came that would burst our bubble and make me wonder if man's free will would be allowed to stop something that had been such a God plan all along. The hospital decided that they would not release the baby to us unless we paid the entire bill before we picked up the baby. The bill was several thousand dollars! This was a new twist; we had been assured that the delivery would be covered by insurance.

We were hurt and angry and had no time to try and figure things out. Our baby was being dismissed the following day, and if we were unable to pay the bill the hospital urged the attorney to find someone who could or the baby would go into state custody! We were frantic.

Phone calls flew to the director of the crisis pregnancy center who was on Christmas holiday out of state. She was helpless to do anything from such a distance. The attorney, who was already waiving his fees, was not too keen on spending a good deal of time on this already non-lucrative placement. The hospital refused to make a payment plan with us, and I honestly thought just as quickly as we had thought we were bringing our baby home, we were losing her to something totally crazy!

I was next door lamenting over the situation to a friend. The agony was literally physically painful, especially after the valley trip we had just been on over the past few weeks. John burst through the front door of our neighbor's house. The attorney had just called. The bill was taken care of. We had to meet the attorney in 30 minutes at the hospital and it was urgent; he didn't have anyone to take the baby and he had another appointment in just a couple of hours! My ears heard the words but my heart was still absorbing the news when we arrived at the hospital. We never did receive a bill for the medical charges and do not know to this day who or what took care of that mountain. Suddenly we were putting another precious gift from God safely into a car seat. She had already found a place in our hearts.

> *She was a treasure from God, a cherub to hold,*
> *A mystery, a promise, the way God had told.*
> *On Christmas she came just as God had said.*
> *Now she lay like an angel asleep in her bed.*
> *The space in our hearts God would continue to fill,*
> *We prayed and we searched as we sought God's will.*
> *The year tumbled by us, our hearts opened wide,*
> *There were five of us to welcome Andrea, our hearts swelled with pride.*

During Andrea's adoption I learned that my childlike acceptance had been absolutely correct. A person's skin color made no difference to the Jesus I loved.

God sees only the diversity and beauty in the skin color of the people He creates, not the differences we so often see. He had a plan for Andrea, and part of that plan was to be raised as our child.

God goes to great lengths to get all of us where He wants us to be. "For we are His workmanship, created in Christ Jesus for good works, which God prepared beforehand, that we should walk in them" (Ephesians 2:10).

There are alternatives to unplanned pregnancies, life-giving alternatives, and I am thankful when people choose life.

I wrote in my journal: I believe God gave us all of our children for special reasons we may not know for years or even until we join our heavenly family. But I know as I sit here and pray and write that God lent them to us for a season to love. I know all of our children have been divinely placed with John and me for a reason yet unrealized. Our children are a pure delight to me!

Pain
Prejudice &
Persecution

My coffee mug steams as I gaze out my dining room window, watching sunbeams playing chase with spring thunderclouds. The freshly mowed grass looks so tidy and crisp. Nature sings and God's love abounds! On this beautiful, calm morning in May the older children and John are gone for the day. The babies are still sleeping. I am tensed, lending one ear to insure I hear their first calls of the day.

Like clockwork, I climb those stairs every morning and open the door to their smiling happy faces. There is such a sense of God's presence in their warm, sunlit nursery!

Prayerfully I write: Help us all hold fast to Your promise of provision and to recall vividly and with new energy the uncountable times You have taken care of us in ways only You, God, could do. Oh, and God, please transcend the miles and reach out to each of the girl's birth mothers wherever they are Lord, and give them the gift of a smile this day and a blessing too, because of the love they have shown each of our daughters by making an adoption plan for them.

In spite of all the good things that were happening, I was still in a searching mode. I also had a great desire to be in a house that was my own, for there I could paint, or wallpaper or decorate to suit my own preferences. In a house that we owned I wouldn't worry about fingerprints and stained carpet, it would be ours and I would not be accountable to anyone else for the wear and tear that is inevitable in a household of children.

In my journal I wrote: We want more than nice houses and fancy cars. We want to have Your peace and direction in our lives. You are all knowing and can nudge us to find Your perfect plans and timing. Forgive us when we take matters into our own hands, and forgive us when we get sad and emotional, insisting on having our own way much like the toddlers in the nursery upstairs. Thank you Lord for answers to prayers, even when we don't always like the answers. Please continue to hold our hands and draw us closer to the throne of grace and a glorious peace on this earth. And, Lord, in Your time provide us with just the right property.

Sewing for other ladies had been going well, and was something that I really enjoyed. I was staying busy, and at times had more work than I could possibly do. John was also feeling productive in his programming position.

In addition, he had been working several weeks on specs for a possible contract job, negotiating the details on many occasions. It would add a good amount of income to our regular salary. John had many plans for this additional income and was really excited about the venture. The night he and a partner went to sign the final contract, the businessman whom they were to do the work for tore up the check in front of their faces. It was an awful thing. John always tries so very hard to provide well for us and works nearly without ceasing. I simply did not understand.

I prayed: Lord, please, heal the hurts and disappointments, give us an excitement and joy that can come only from You. Through our trials help us to emerge better prepared for service in building Your kingdom. Show us how to be good witnesses, even when people are misleading and deceitful. We praise You for open and closed doors and ask for a deeper love for You.

Leah and Jared sometimes talked about how things might be had we not gotten Trista and Andrea. Leah said we would be driving a neater car; specifically, in her preteen mind, a red sports car. My desire for a nicer van or newer station wagon simply showed the generational differences, not the lack of wanting material possessions. Jared chimed in and said we would have more money to spend on different things if we hadn't adopted the

girls. I had to wonder if he was thinking of the football we had been prom-
ising much too long.

I assured them that those things were wonderful to have, and there were
many things that Dad and I often desired as well. But I ask them if they
really thought those things would be important when they got to heaven
one day.

I shared that when I am tempted to want new things I don't necessarily
need, I test myself with this question:

"When I get to heaven someday and I stand face to face with Jesus, will
I be able to say I made the right choices?"

Could I justify saying no to a child, in this case Trista or Andrea, because I wanted a new van, or other things that I did not need?

With childlike frankness, Jared quickly reminded me that we were talking about now, and that going to be with Jesus would be much later! Oh,
how easy it is in our day-to-day walk to put those things of eternal significance on hold, choosing instead items that offer more immediate gratification. I suspect we are all very guilty of this sin from time to time.

I prayed: Lord, as John and I have a delay in acquiring more material
wealth, help us to remember that one of our main concerns for our children
is that they learn human life is far more valuable than anything money can
buy. Help us teach them by example that happiness cannot be purchased.
The wealthy may have their material wealth, the poor will likely have their
love and perhaps their basic needs, but to have both is a privilege beyond
measure.

"Remove far from me falsehood and lying; give me neither poverty nor
riches; feed me with the food that is needful for me, lest I be full, and deny
thee, and say, 'Who is the LORD?' or lest I be poor, and steal, and profane
the name of my God" (Proverbs 30:8-9).

I have come to understand that imagining things as they 'might have
been' is a normal healthy thought process, helping us to find purpose and
meaning in the situations we find ourselves in. Over the years, all of the
children have mused from time to time about what it would be like if there
were fewer children, or no babies, or no big sisters or brothers. Frank discussions usually follow a time of assumed unfairness, or stress.

Thankfully after conversation has flitted around the room, all conclude that everyone in our ever-growing family nucleus is needed. All are so intricately a part of our family that the thought of their not being in our lives is unimaginable.

Still, conversations such as the one Leah and Jared had seem to allow venting of frustrations unique to large families and to assist in getting a perspective regarding the obvious plans God has for each person. We are always stronger and more accepting of our purpose after these searching conversations.

Eventually we purchased a house in an older part of town on a "work for down payment" plan. It was fun to remodel and I loved the 1930's style. We now lived in a totally integrated area of the city, and we were hopeful that it would be of benefit to our racially mixed family.

We did a great deal of work in the area of child advocacy. The search seemed relentless to find God's way for us. Even writing this, years later, I do not completely understand why there was always such restlessness in all that we did. I am certain that a good deal of the time we were doing God's work, and we were sincerely trying to hear His voice and direction.

One day as I was praying I felt like the Lord said to me *"Build your house with expansion in mind."* I struggled with that, and sought Scriptures that might explain more clearly what God was trying to show me. I shared my puzzlement at this knowledge with some ladies at a local ministry. The next time I visited them, one of the ladies said that she had prayed about my questions and felt that God wanted me to read Isaiah 54. When I went home I looked up that chapter. I knew immediately that she was right.

It said "Sing, O barren one, who did not bear; break forth into singing and cry aloud, you who have not been in travail! For the children of the desolate one will be more than the children of her that is married, says the Lord. Enlarge the place of your tent, and let the curtains of your habitations be stretched out; hold not back, lengthen your cords, and strengthen your stakes" (Isaiah 54:1-2).

In this Scripture I found a promise from God that in the end we would not be put to shame. It was a profound time, and I now knew for sure that there were going to be more children, for we were to build our house with expansion in mind.

I had cried out loudly when I felt I could not have children. Now God was showing me that there is a purpose even in not being able to bear children, for there are those who will be asked to take the children of the many women who cannot parent. The time would come when there would be those who could not understand why we would adopt so many children. There would be those who would try to make the children in our home feel ashamed of their heritage or the circumstances under which they were born. But for then, I had no clue of how personally prophetic that specific Scripture would become in the years ahead.

It is so hard to wait upon the Lord, especially when we don't know the purpose of our days. An evangelist came to our church and his sermon was especially empathetic to us. He said that he had always had a knowing about God and God's love. I too cannot remember a time when I did not feel God's presence in my life. He also told of knowing in 1961 that God had called him to preach. He didn't answer the call until 1976. He changed jobs every few years and searched and looked but when he finally gave in to God's will he found happiness. I knew that was exactly what we were going through. I suppose some things in life just cannot be rushed.

For several months Leah had been having a very difficult time. It is hard to know when her trials began exactly. At first we just attributed it to the normal adolescence testing, as we knew that middle school years are typically turbulent years for anyone. I share this story in the hopes that perhaps our family's struggles will help some who find themselves in similar circumstances. For obvious reasons I will not share details of the many months of agony, both for Leah and for us, but I do believe as I write that God would want parts of this story told. Hopefully others might have a glimpse into the emotions and confusion that adopted children often feel, and approach the issues equipped with more understanding than we had at the time.

As she entered middle school, questions surrounding racial issues became more predominant in Leah's thoughts than ever before. Waiting for her to broach the subject, she finally came in from school one day and directly asked me with utter confusion in her dark brown eyes, "What color am I?" We talked at length that day about different races, the issues and the need to accept the color of skin that God has chosen to give us. It would be the first of many lessons where I would learn that often being of mixed heritage is more difficult to understand than assuming we are of one race. I eventually came to believe this is an unnecessary concern, put upon us by the society we live in. It is especially irrelevant in America, where few of us can prove that we are of a so-called "pure race."

Transracial adoption has always been a very controversial issue. We had struggled with the challenges it might create prior to bringing Leah into our family. Transracial placements may seem to complicate things, and perhaps for some it does. However, it is my opinion that children of mixed heritage struggle with identity, regardless of where they spend their childhood, in an adoptive home or with their biological family. Still that day I had no satisfactory answers for Leah. She was who she was because God had made it so, and to a young teen that is little consolation in facing the day-to-day remarks of immature and often-cruel peers.

As the months went on our confident, intelligent, talented daughter became progressively more depressed and defiant. All measures of discipline seemed to only fall on a hard shell that was not about to let anyone inside. Reminders of our unconditional love, her place in our family, and a thousand other reassurances all seemed to fall on deaf ears.

Leah insisted on being on the streets late at night and not being trustworthy when out of our sight. When she began doing things that would endanger her well-being, we were left no choice but to place her in a group therapeutic home for evaluation and safekeeping. The pain in my heart the day we drove her to the center is not something I can even put into words. Just as we had given our all to Tracy many years before, we had naturally invested even more love and dedication into Leah's life. Once again we were blatantly reminded that sometimes love is not enough.

Unless a person is willing to receive the love and acceptance that is offered, there is little that others can really do. We are all accountable for our own choices, including what we feel, how we react and what we do with our walk to or from the God who designed us.

Free will, oh how our heavenly Father must grieve day after day as we too act in rebellion to the love and instruction He so freely gives. If John and I were hurting so badly, how does our Father in Heaven ever bear the pain of so many rebellious people?

We entered a very dark and gloomy time. We could not explain to our other children why the older sister they adored was so distant and now living somewhere else. Sometimes, I explained to them, people make choices that we do not understand. Sometimes, parents can't make things better, as much as we always want to.

Sessions with clinical counselors seemed nonproductive as Leah learned to manipulate those trying so hard to help. The adults in her institutionalized world could see no reason for this acting out, and nothing seriously wrong in the way we parented. Being human, we have in the past, and continue to make our share of big mistakes, daily in fact. Still, most of the children living in the treatment center had totally dysfunctional families, often with abusive or unconcerned parents. These were not challenges Leah had to deal with.

After several weeks of this living arrangement and virtually no progress in her treatment, Leah requested to be placed in a state foster home. Righteously indignant, I was at my wit's end. I wondered if Jesus felt this way when He found the money-changers in the temple. It was so wrong! This horribly wrong scene had to be stopped! Wishing that I could toss tables and storm around, I chose instead to confront my dear daughter.

In front of the counselor I told Leah that placing her in any other living situation, besides our home, or the center she presently found herself in would never happen. With tearful eyes and my throat constricting so tightly I could barely say the words, I told her that no matter what she did, run away, chose to drop out of school, not see us again, even commit murder, she would still be our daughter. Wherever she ran on this planet the fact would remain that she was our daughter, and that we loved her. Just as you cannot truly run far enough to actually hide from God and His love, neither can you remove yourself from the love of committed parents or from a plan much bigger than most of us can even fathom.

I reminded her that we were not happy with the way things had been either. Running away is something many people think about from time to time, but in reality it is not an option for stable, caring individuals. God had made her our daughter and nothing that she did, or that we did would ever undo God's plan for our lives. Those plans were for us to be a part of a uniquely designed family. We all needed her, but she was upsetting the other kids, destroying her dad and me with the hurt, and worst of all, doing it all by choice. But, no matter the pain she tried to inflict on us, or for that matter on herself, nothing on earth would change the fact that she was our daughter. I looked deeply in her eyes for some sign of understanding, and saw only hardness in those glistening eyes.

I fled from that room literally gasping for breath as I hit the cool outside air. I had never experienced pain of that kind before. I have begged God to never ask us to endure such a trial again. John and I wept together when I returned to the car. We prayed for a miracle and drove slowly home to our other children. Death is the only comparison I can give, it was as if a part of us was dying "on the limb" and we had no clue how to save Leah's life.

Maybe someday Leah will tell her story, and feel comfortable with sharing her thoughts and feelings during that time. That is her choice, it is her story. I am certain her version of what transpired would be totally different than John's or mine. I think that in an odd and somewhat inappropriate way, Leah was searching for her roots, for something to identify with. She mentioned that she was not like us, but like her birth mother. Indeed we are all like those of our biological family, so there was nothing to do but agree.

However, we are all grafted into the family of God via adoption: "He destined us for adoption as his children through Jesus Christ, according to the good pleasure of his will, to the praise of his glorious grace that he freely bestowed on us in the Beloved" (Ephesians 1:5-6, NRSV), and it was no different in her adoption into our family.

She had a new future, a new hope. That did not make what might have been less, or bad, just different. We only met her birth mother for a brief time, and had no background information to share with Leah. We were helpless to find answers to her unspoken questions. We acknowledged the validity of the pain, but we could not, at that time offer a solution.

Leah seemed to assume that she would have been a street child, or a garbage dump survivor. So, thinking that her destiny had been altered, she attempted to set right what she thought in her adolescent mind had been made wrong. It was a dark and fearful time for Leah as well as those who loved her so much.

When I left the center that night, I was exceedingly worried that I had slammed shut a door. At the same time I hoped and prayed I had in reality, opened a window for Leah to go through. I agonized over every word that had spewed from my mouth and every tear that had hotly fallen down my cheeks. John and I wondered if we would ever have our daughter back. We were forced to release her to God. He alone could protect her. After all, we were only His appointed caretakers; God surely did not need us to keep our daughter safe. He knew the beginning and the end, and He knew this chapter in our lives as well. It is easier written than lived. The days were exhausting as we tried to go on in a normal fashion, yet with an important piece of the family missing.

A few days after my confrontation with Leah, we went out of town for the evening. The greatest words I have ever heard traveled from our answering machine when we returned home. "Mom, if you want, I would like to come home." She had called three times! What a day of rejoicing we had!

Since Leah had made the decision to come home, we felt confident that she was going to try and make it work. We did not force her to come; we allowed her the freedom to make that choice. Rules were still the same. Nothing on the surface had changed.

Spiritual surgery had gone on in the hearts of the entire family, and only time would tell if it had been a healing procedure. This we knew: all surgery leaves scars. In the end, most scars become painless.

Once again we began to fall into a more relaxed, although busy, routine. Leah was concentrating on trying to make correct choices, and obviously trying to stabilize herself. It was something that she had to do. In the years that followed her into adulthood there would be many times that her tenacity and endurance would be put to the test. She would run from God and His purpose for a good long season. No, she wasn't as openly rebellious as she had been as a preteen, but she still tested the rules, demanded some control and struggled for emotional stability, all the while expressing an incredible wisdom for her age. From the beginning, Leah was a survivor and our faith in her abilities had been renewed. One day, she too would find what God had for her to do. Until then, we would all do the best that we could do; it was all that could be expected.

Occasionally as the years have passed she has recalled and shared bits and pieces with us, and with each sharing comes more understanding. For the most part I believe that the very darkest times in the pits of life have a way of being buried in the recesses of our minds, and perhaps that is for the best. We did not dwell on, nor do we recall those times, it is irrelevant to our loving and moving on in a relationship of unconditional love. Some of life's experiences are not necessary to review and relive, it is enough that we have come through them, stronger for the lessons learned, more equipped in a silent sort of way for the remainder of our walk down the path of life. We must all persevere.

Then Came Jordan

In an exhilarating four days, John and I enjoyed the first opportunity for retreat and rest in the many years of our marriage. Ironically this trip without our children was totally about children. It was a national seminar on adoption. Among other volunteer jobs, John was on the state Foster Care Review Board and our state's Permanency Planning Committee. I served as president of an adoptive parent support group. Our many years of working within these local organizations prompted some people to help pay our expenses to the conference that year.

All too soon, the rush of the conference abruptly ended. Browsing through the airport gift shop, we were waiting on our return flight home when we saw Erin*, a friend from Oklahoma. We discovered we were on the same flight home. Later that day during a layover in the Knoxville, Tennessee airport the conversation was lively as several of us shared information we gained at the conference. Our over stimulated emotions and over loaded brains amidst the bustling racket in the airport caused the conversation to be somewhat disjointed. In the midst of a conversation about parenting, John and I were asked if we planned to adopt again. Although always open to that possibility we were, for the first time in a very long time, not in a particular hurry, **unless** God saw fit to open unexpected doors.

We prepared to board our next flight. While in the midst of seemingly unrelated conversation, Erin paused in mid-statement and *as if in disbelief as to where the thought had come from she said, "I think we will have a baby for you."* We all paused briefly, and then just as quickly resumed the original conversation as we proceeded to board the plane.

One winter morning during my prayer time, God revealed how He had planted a seed in my heart. I knew that like a flower bulb planted in the fall, designed to bloom in the spring, a desire planted in my heart in August would become a lively reality during the warm days of the fast approaching spring. Though I was not physically carrying a child, my struggling throughout the winter had been the growth of a child, not under my heart, but in it.

Prior to this revelation I had been searching all over the world, literally, looking for answers: calling international adoption agencies, child advocacy organizations and praying about what area of working in children's ministry God had for us to do.

Once again I had some puzzle pieces, but I was obviously not able to see what picture the pieces would create. Life does not afford us the luxury of our destinations all revealed in a beautiful picture. Still, my search had narrowed a bit. It was adoption of a child that we were waiting on God to orchestrate. That should have been enough, but that restlessness remained all too real. I didn't want to jump ahead of God and mess any plans up, but I could barely sit still and not try to find this child that I was sure God had for us.

Finally one day I could stand it no longer. I told John that I was going to take the older children to school and the younger ones to preschool, then return home to pray until I had my answer from God. *I had to at least know what I was to do next; there was an urgency I couldn't explain to have some idea of what was going on in the spiritual realm.*

Each time God has sent a child to our family, we have been completely humbled at the way He takes care of the intricate details, working His good for all involved. Those months of winter as I struggled so desperately to find God's direction were no exception. God had taken care of the tiniest of details. It would be months before I would know the extent to which our God moved in orchestrating the events that we would soon find ourselves caught up in.

I had been writing my prayers regularly in my journal. I wrote about all of my confusion, the questions I had for God, and most certainly my praises. I remember specifically focusing on the latter. I did not want to forget while I was groaning under the pressure of burdens I did not understand, how much God had already blessed us. I did not want my prayers to be selfish or self-satisfying; I truly was seeking the peace that can come only from the Holy Spirit. I was prepared to spend the day seeking God. I was determined to meet the sunset that day with some answers.

Not so far from where I was pouring my heart out, in an adjoining state, another mother also struggled for direction and answers from God.

Absorbed in climbing the corporate ladder, already single parenting another child and separated from an abusive husband, this lady now found herself in an unplanned pregnancy. Abortion was a consideration, but each time she seriously thought about it, or made an attempt to go through with the procedure she simply could not do it. Despite chronic nausea, extreme emotional stress and conflicting counsel, she knew she had to give birth to this child.

So, during those gray days of winter, she too had been seeking answers to a seemingly hopeless list of questions. There were no easy answers. Her directions came unexpectedly during a Christian television show one night. She listened as the director of a crisis pregnancy center in another state shared a vision of how, through their ministry, God was offering answers to the questions that are inevitable in an unplanned pregnancy. There were options and compassionate people to help birth families get through such tough times, one step at a time. This birth mother felt compelled to dial the telephone number shown and talk to Erin. After several phone conversations, an adoption plan was in the making.

As spring approached Erin began to earnestly intercede on behalf of the birth mothers, prospective adoptive families and the lifetime commitments that needed to be made for several babies. There was no room for human reasoning: only God's direction. There were now three babies due very soon, all of mixed races. There were no families that seemed to match the situations represented in the stack of paperwork on her desk. *As she prayed, our name kept coming before her, and finally she picked up the phone and began to dial.*

Meanwhile, I wondered about the race of this expected child. Was this little person East Indian, Caucasian or biracial? I felt if I knew the answer to that question I could somehow know more clearly where to search (as if I had to search to find the child God would bring to us!) A ringing phone interrupted my thoughts. *I distinctly remember as I headed to the telephone that I knew even before I answered it that this was to be a divine revelation.* I didn't have time to speculate who would be on the line, but I knew in my spirit it was going to be about adoption.

It was Erin. We had talked occasionally since that conference visit and airport conversation, but usually about things within her ministry and occasionally about babies who needed families. Because of my involvement within the community, it was not that unusual to get phone calls from ministry workers as well as prospective adoptive families.

We teasingly said we had an informal adoption hot line coming into our home at all hours of the day and night. I occasionally got to enjoy being a part of placing children with new families. Mostly, I just offered an empathetic ear and options that hopefully helped families in the waiting room of life, those trying to struggle through the maze of paperwork, social workers and bureaucracy that can be incredibly frustrating at times in the adoption journey. So, this request for families was no different than nearly a dozen other calls I had recently received.

Erin was calling about three babies who were due soon and needed families. *She told me that as she had been praying over these situations in the past few days our name kept coming to her.* She was hopeful that I might know of some families for these babies.

As she began to speak of the details regarding the first baby I began to cry and shake. She went on to tell me about the second child on her list, but I stopped her and began to ask more specific questions about the first child. Details are a bit jumbled because after that, my heart took over and my head unsuccessfully tried to follow things in a logical fashion.

Somehow, some of the most insignificant things she said spoke volumes to me, and confirmed that we were FINALLY on the correct path. For example, just a few days before, my good friend and I were out shopping. As always our conversation turned to adoption. I told her that if *someone called the next day* and said they had *a mixed race baby* and the *medical bills were paid,* then I would have to say yes to bring that baby home!

I could hardly contain myself when Erin said that the child had complete medical coverage. *There should be no medical bills!* This seemingly insignificant detail, along with the unlikely race of the child made me quite sure this was to be our baby. It couldn't have been clearer than if the message had been written on the wall! The race of this child was an unusual one: *It would be Black East Indian and Caucasian. Exactly the combination of races I had written in my journal just minutes before Erin's call!*

Given the huge number of potential racial backgrounds a child could have, this knowledge came against some incredible odds. I had to call John first and tell him the news before we could make any further decisions.

> *I prayed at a table all broken and torn,*
> *Once again confused, anxious, tired and forlorn.*
> *Was it a call to the ministry or adoption this time?*
> *Was I hearing God's direction or was it this strong will of mine?*
> *As I prayed and sought God on that valley of days,*
> *He assured me adoption was one of the ways.*
> *He would ask us to walk down a path with its fears*
> *Out of sorrow and pain would come joy, but first tears.*
> *Was this child Black, East Indian, or White?*
> *If I could only know, God, then I could see a light.*
> *The telephone rang, my spirit leaped at the time,*
> *The answer from God was about to be mine.*

When I called John and told him about the prayers and the phone call from Erin he said: *"That's our son; call her back!"*

I immediately called her back. I wasn't at all surprised to find out that an ultrasound had revealed that *this baby was a boy!* Erin had not told me that information in our original phone conversation. She agreed. This baby was somehow to be ours.

I was so excited I could hardly function the rest of the day. All of the long months of wondering were finally falling into some sort of plan and purpose. I wanted to shout to the world as I went down the streets to pick up the children at school—"We're getting a baby, we're getting our boy, and he's going to be perfect for our family!"

The next test came that evening when I faced the task of telling the older children. Jared's expression was disappointment. He had been hoping for a boy near his age, a playmate. I felt really badly about this, but believed that God had a plan far greater than the desires of a child for a playmate. It was unlikely that any child we would have brought home would have been what Jared or any of the rest of us envisioned. A new baby brother would be no threat to Jared's position. I knew Jared would come to accept this new brother with the same love he had unconditionally accepted the other girls with, but he too would have to work through the emotions of this recent announcement.

Leah, who had been in a bubbly, exceptionally talkative mood, turned from playing her cello and looked at me as if I were totally crazy. She pointed out that I was just beginning to feel good, just getting things done on the house that I had wanted to accomplish for months. Why would I mess that up?

I confess their honesty hit my inflated emotions pretty hard. Everyone retreated to digest the news. John left to teach his evening classes at the college, the older ones went to their rooms and I fed the little girls their supper. I was disappointed. I wanted everyone to be as excited as I was over the news. I wanted to celebrate, to pull out boxes of baby clothes, to paint a nursery, to go to the baby store! Instead I sat amidst dirty dishes, tired toddlers and a house that suddenly looked very small.

Then panic set in (stage two of any of our adoptions, at least for me). Stage one is always elation and excitement with no room for questions, just the anticipation of receiving another beautiful child. But when stage two kicks in I get really crazy sometimes! For me this is when the what-ifs start rolling through my mind like huge thunderclouds.

What IF we can't keep our bills paid?

What IF we have to take the other children out of music lessons?

What IF I don't have enough time for everyone?

What IF I can't keep the house clean?

What IF my entire family always resents this decision?

But, thankfully, during this time I could already tell that our faith about things working out was considerably stronger than it had been in past situations. After much prayer and considerations of my "What IF" questions, I knew that we were to follow the leading of the Lord and go toward this child step by step, day by day. I had no desire to give up the peace in my spirit for the logic in my head; I knew the latter would not last!

Stage three follows a typical pattern as well. In stage three the excitement returns, but this time in a more dreamy and mechanical mode, like we are acting out a movie drama and we all have parts to play, but we haven't read the script nor learned the lines yet. Life pretty much resumes the normal activities and we begin to individually imagine the new addition fitting into our daily routine. It's a retreat and regroup mode where everyone begins to prepare for the challenges and inevitable changes ahead. Much like pregnancy, at some point in adoption the reality that there really is going to be a baby sets in and the mental preparations begin in earnest.

Still the battles raged and I wrote in my journal: During the night a million fears came at me like fiery darts through the dark night sky. I became afraid of possible unemployment, unexpected illness, an unhealthy baby, or rejection of family members who would never understand our motivation to proceed with this adoption. I thought about the possible loss of normal holidays and weekend trips or vacations. And there was the very real fear that when I get to be 50 years old that I would regret the decision I made so quickly at age 35!

Feelings varied according to the people I was around. When in the company of those who thought getting another child was a great idea, I could see God's plan working ever so clearly. If I was with those who couldn't imagine why we would be doing this again, then I quickly became doubtful and unsure, sometimes really scared.

It is critical to carefully select the friends we surround ourselves with during times when God asks us to do something that goes against the logical or norm. I have learned that sometimes I must isolate myself if that becomes necessary to my staying focused on what God has asked me to do.

I longed to do what Jesus would do. I had to wonder if we had announced that we were going to sell all that we had and move our children to a remote mission field, would we then find that others would proclaim our heroism in missions?

Why then, if we have been led to give our lives to help parent some of

God's children do many people find that calling to be so peculiar?

I have often felt a sudden uplifting of a burden when I have decided to do what God would have me to do. Adoption of a fifth child would require a great deal of self-sacrifice in time, energy, finances and prayers, and yes in emotions.

But the week I was called about this baby, God confirmed through prayer and the Holy Spirit that we were to be obedient. In spite of the awesome responsibility and all the logical and financial reasons not to do so, I felt a great lifting of the burden to search that I could not explain prior to knowing of this child. Being obedient to God in this manner made me exuberant!

In my journal, I wrote: I realized anew this morning Lord, that all things worthwhile have a price. When we lift up our cross and follow You, we may not be accepted or understood by the world. You have even said that because of following Jesus, father and son, mother and daughter will be driven apart. I believe with my heart, though my mind does not understand, that You have called John and me to parent another child. There will always be those who will not even begin to understand why we would choose such an exhausting challenging lifetime commitment as adoption, but I know for us it is right. I believe nine months ago, during that first week of August, a child was conceived that was destined to become a part of this family for reasons John and I may never be able to totally explain.

As the preparations for the new arrival proceeded, I was continually amazed at how God had once again orchestrated events. This baby was to be born out of state. That was unusual because most birth mothers who came to the crisis pregnancy center were from our area. Occasionally, some traveled to give birth locally, but to my knowledge none planned to give birth out of state and then have the ministry place the child in an adoptive family.

On the baby's expected due date I wrote the following prayer: Lord, today is the due date for our newest family member. Be with the birth mother; help her to be peaceful as she struggles in these last hours before delivery. I know your timing is perfect Lord and that there is a time to be born. I have a great peace in my spirit about this whole adoption. I know You are in it and planned it from conception onward. I pray that You will guide all of the persons concerned in any direct or indirect way with regard to this adoption.

Several days later while Leah and I were out shopping for a gift for the birth mother, the call came that our son had been born. We were all so excited! The doubts and concerns of the early days after finding out we were going to get a new baby all seemed to disappear as we prepared to travel out of state to meet this new little one. We left the little girls in the care of friends and opted to take Leah and Jared with us.

> *The call came as divinely planned,*
> *And the son that was ours was White and Black from*
>   *an East Indian land.*
> *In a second in time, I knew our son's unique race.*
> *And that his adoption would come, but at a painfully slow pace.*

The trip turned out to be the beginning of an endless, emotional roller coaster ride. What should have been an exciting time turned into a nightmare. We met the birth mother briefly and saw the baby the day we arrived. Things seemed to be going well until it came time to dismiss the baby from the hospital, and then somehow things began to get confused. The state threatened to step in, and the reasons for these intrusions escape me, because in the months to come this part of the struggle would fade into a deep and distant memory. They were, at the time, very scary and caused emotions to magnify and tempers to flare.

Darkness was so heavy over the entire situation. John and I left Leah and Jared in the motel room and went outside to pace up and down the parking lot. We considered leaving the baby and just going home. After recent months of stress we weren't ready for yet another battle, one we might not be able to win. Leah was still in a time of recovery and adjustment. She and Jared were still skeptical about the addition of another baby.

Yet after just one small glimpse of their new baby brother they were outraged and disappointed along with us when things began to look like we might not get to take Jordan home with us. Perhaps God used that time to make Leah and Jared aware of how He had already made a place in their hearts for this new baby, in spite of their logical rejection of him.

John and I could not even think about what further damage this might do to our relationship with Leah if we had to focus so completely on fighting for another child while still doing spiritual and day to day battles over and with Leah. All of this left Jared without deserved attention and sapped energy that I would naturally give to Andrea and Trista. We felt so inadequate.

After crying hot angry tears in that parking lot and pacing until we were nearly exhausted we went back into the hotel room with few answers. The knowing in our spirit of all of the details that God had meticulously shown us over the past winter became the knots at the end of our rope, and we knew we had to hang on. We had to hang on to the knowledge that had already been shown us, the unknowns that were surely ahead of us, and the realization that we could not take care of any of the concerns we had, God would have to carry them for us, providing a safety net under that rough rope we would cling to.

Finally, after a delay of several days we traveled home with Jordan tucked into his car seat, between his big brother and sister. Our spirits were apprehensive, our faith shaken, our hearts full of love, but we knew our God was in full control.

Psalm 50:14-15 says: "Offer to God a sacrifice of thanksgiving, and pay your vows to the Most High; and call upon me in the day of trouble; I will deliver you, and you shall glorify me."

Once we were settled at home for several days during my quiet time I would take a portion of that Scripture and turn it into a personal line-by-line praise or petition. It was very helpful to me as I studied and wrote my revelations down. It never ceases to amaze me how the Bible can be so relevant at different times in our lives. Years later, while I wrote this book these words of Scripture ministered to me once again. We serve an awesome God.

Another detail God used to confirm this placement came in a rather odd way. As I mused back over events, I began to calculate how much time had gone by since that first offhanded comment made by Erin in the Knoxville airport regarding a baby for us some day.

Though only God knows the exact moment, sometime within hours of that airport conversation Jordan was conceived.

God had a plan from the very beginning. An inspired and seemingly insignificant meeting in an out-of-state airport planted the seed of a child in my heart. That seed would grow and crowd out the peace in my heart until I searched for relief from the overcrowding. When I went in searched I found the seed was the very spirit of a child still hidden in the womb. Though I could not begin to understand why God chose our family, or that child, I found great strength in the knowledge that we all had been a part of a picture much bigger than any we could have dreamed or planned.

There were months of uncertainty and deception that are much too complicated to explain. It was a very good thing that I knew for sure that this was the baby we were to get, or we would never have had enough strength to make it through the battles ahead.

We were still waiting for resolution on legal issues surrounding Jordan's adoption. As if things were not stressful enough, John got a call about a job in Arkansas. We had long talked about moving back nearer to our families. Was God opening the door for us to do just that? There seemed to be increasingly more challenges within the city schools, and we knew that our children were being exposed to things contrary to what we desired. Perhaps God was giving us opportunity to relocate where it would be safer and more spiritually appropriate for our family. Not knowing how long Jordan's adoption would take complicated our decision.

I wrote in June of that year: I have been so tired I could cry easier than talk. Literally my vision is blurred and my bones ache. I wonder if women with large households have been this tired throughout the centuries, or if I have some medical problem that is causing me to have chronic fatigue?

Later I found out I had horrible allergies while living in that house. The mold produced in the 50-year-old basement, and the insulation and dust that had accumulated over the years were causing me to be very ill most of the time. It was a miracle that I had even functioned as well as I had. I would also discover, that in comparison, my household was not yet that large, and that indeed, fatigue is a universal challenge to mothers of large families!

It had now been about nine weeks since we had traveled to get Jordan. We still did not know if we were going to be allowed to keep him or not. It was an awful time. Spiritually, we knew he was destined to be ours. I wrote: I still believe with every ounce of faith I have that Jordan is exactly where God wants him to be. I do not feel excited, but humbled by the calling to parent this child. I do not feel great, but ever so small. We are helpless to make this adoption happen. He may only be ours for a season; I pray we can accept that if it should come to pass.

Sunday, June 19th was Father's Day. We dedicated Jordan to the Lord that day. It was a huge step of faith as paperwork was still caught up in the system and mysteriously delayed.

We met his birth mother and saw Jordan for the first time on Mother's Day and then we formally gave him to the Lord on Father's Day. The four older children had prepared a song to sing. The kids managed to surprise John with their little ceremony in church that day. What a special Father's Day it was!

Not long after being baptized by John the Baptist, Jesus was allowed to be greatly tempted by Satan. I felt the same way. The manner in which God had orchestrated bringing Jordan into our lives was nothing short of a miracle. I had many spiritual happenings during the months prior to Jordan's arrival. Once we had experienced the receiving of this child, Satan was allowed to step in to test and question our faith in an all-knowing God.

A similar thing had happened to Jordan's birth mother shortly after she had given birth. She wavered in her decision to place him for adoption. Erin reminded her that she needed to stand firm on the decision she had made in the light, and not let Satan tempt her to change her mind while she was in a dark and difficult time. It seems from the early considerations of abortion, until after his arrival in our home, Satan had tried to stop Jordan from being where God intended him to be.

We had to wonder what plans God had for this special little guy, given the battles that were raging so fiercely over him.

John decided to accept the position in Arkansas.

We believed that in His timing, God would take care of the details of Jordan's adoption, the sale of our house and our move to Arkansas. Part of our reasoning came from the fact that the job had opened up without our solicitation and the fact that John had been offered free housing in Arkansas while we tried to get details of a sale on our house worked out.

We were even more excited when John met a contractor at the church he was attending in Arkansas. We were quickly pre-approved for a home loan. We selected house plans and had all of the initial paperwork complete. It was to be the house that we would build with expansion in mind. I was sure that if we waited long enough, God would work out the remaining details. When land became available and it seemed perfect for the house plans we had selected, I truly thought the doors were about to open wide on yet another relocation. We were very weary in the wait, but very excited about the prospective outcome of the events that appeared to be moving into proper order.

As if we didn't have enough to think about I learned of some biracial twins to be born soon and placed for adoption. I called John in Arkansas to tell him about the babies. I wrote in my journal: *This morning I know one thing for certain. These twins may not be ours, but the next addition to our family will be biracial twins.*

We talked long agonizing hours about the addition of twins at this point in our lives. We certainly didn't want to jeopardize Jordan's placement with us. How would we handle building a house, moving to a new state, and all that involved adding not one, but two newborns? The big question was: Is this what God is asking us to do? We had to be sure.

To complicate the situation even more, the twins were born prematurely. The birth father decided to step in. We would not have to make a decision after all. God shut the door for us. I was relieved, as was John. But, now, there was the burden of *wondering where our twins were!* It never ends!

I wailed to God, literally wailed! I had believed for ten months that Jordan was ours, but faith is all we had to go on, since there were still no legal papers in our hands. I had gone on John's faith since July that we were to move to Arkansas. The only signs to show us we were on the right path were free rent in Arkansas and some additional income John was generating working evenings after his regular job. Otherwise, we were weary of the separation, our phone bills were high, the credit card was stretched to the limit and no buyers were in sight for the house in Oklahoma.

Meanwhile, the stress levels were mounting, especially in the children. We were more than a little tired of Daddy being gone. The little girls were crying over anything and everything. I wrote: It is a zoo around here and I am trapped in a cage!

I could just feel the fiery darts of Satan all around me on some days. The battles were exhausting. Ever since we had picked up Jordan we had been in an intense war zone. We were even beginning to fear that we had made a wrong decision having John go to work in Arkansas. Who then, had opened the door? Was it God or the opposing forces? We knew we had not opened it; we had merely walked through.

I knew that God wanted us to give Him our burdens, to rest in His love. But rest was not to be found. If I took time to rest the phone would ring. If I tried to forget about trying to sell the house, someone would call and want to come and tour it. When I tried to nudge people to get the necessary paperwork through for Jordan's adoption I would find myself in more battles, ones I did not know how to fight. We did not want to hinder God's purpose in our lives, but we were finding it hard to not wrestle with all that was going on.

I finally hit rock bottom one night. John had called to say he wasn't coming home until Saturday evening and I had been expecting him at any moment, hanging on to my sanity until he got there to help share the load. I hung up the phone and ran upstairs crying. I was totally hysterical. I hurt so badly and was so upset I thought of doing totally irrational things. I cried for over an hour. Understandably concerned and unaccustomed to a highly distraught mother, Leah came upstairs to try and comfort me. I was ashamed that I had allowed myself to get in such a spiritual and physical mess that my young daughter had to pick me up and encourage me. God sends The Comforter in many ways!

The Lord must have prompted John, because at three in the morning he unexpectedly walked into the bedroom. He had never in our entire marriage come home in the night or changed his mind after he had told me he would not be coming, even in times when he knew I was upset at his delays. I have never been so glad to see anyone in my life! I felt like God had directly intervened and sent me the help I so desperately needed. It was quiet, as everyone else had finally settled down. I was able to tell John some of the things that were making me crazy. We finally realized we had to make some decisions or I was truly going to have a nervous breakdown. We agreed upon a date for John to come back to Oklahoma if things did not work out, either with the adoption or the selling of the house. Having a plan greatly helped and gave me new stability and purpose.

Finally in March, nearly eight months after he had left to go to Arkansas, John found a job in Oklahoma and moved back home. Jordan's adoption was still in question and since we had not sold the house we accepted that for a season we were to remain in our present location. We were very puzzled over the events of the past months, and to this day do not understand whether we were on the right path and man's free will changed many things, or whether we simply stepped off of the path and into the wilderness. What we did know was that God could and would redirect our paths once again, and we were peaceful in that understanding.

In June, when Jordan was 13 months old, I had a dream. *Jordan was in a one-piece knit play suit and I was taking him to someone. As I was going to this person, I knew I was going to have to give Jordan back and I was trying to be brave. Then I got to the man and put Jordan down. Jordan looked up at me so trusting. He then reached for me and my heart was hurting so badly in this dream that I felt the pain would choke me. I grabbed Jordan back into my arms and begged the man, who had a neutral expression on his face, to help us to do something! There had to be a way for us to keep Jordan. He belonged in our family and there was no reason for all of this agony. I was hurting so badly and pleading with everything in me for this child.* Then I woke up, exhausted from the battle that had interfered with my rest.

At nine that very morning John called to say that he had talked to the agency again and the attorney that had been holding things up had given the case to another attorney in the same office and it would be handled by a different person from now on. Things should now be moving toward our permanently keeping Jordan.

I have always wondered if the dream was really a battle in the spiritual realm, and that intercessory prayers on behalf of Jordan and our family were finally answered. *The lawyer, who had obviously not taken a spiritual interest in this adoption in spite of his professed Christianity, had finally released the papers that had delayed Jordan's legal adoption.* After three more months we finally received written confirmation that we would be able to finalize.

Just when we were about to rejoice —a call came saying that we would be getting a bill for thousands of dollars in additional legal expenses because of the complications and delays. The uncertainty of how this would all work out now hung over our heads: would this battle ever end?

The battle was fierce and the warfare strong,
The uncertainty crippling; the legal system long.
The years tumbled by us our hearts opened wide,
There were six of us to welcome Jordan, our hearts swelled with pride.

Finally we had a court date to legally finalize Jordan's adoption.

To celebrate, John had made hotel reservations and gotten tickets to a major league baseball game. For the first time in what seemed like forever we actually had enough money to enjoy a mini vacation and have a mind for celebration as well. We were all very excited to be traveling back to the state of Jordan's birth, and to have him legally a part of our family. We would make the trip to finalize the adoption and find out that a court date had not really been set. The agency caught us at the motel, telling us the news as relayed to them by the attorney who was to represent us in court. The trip was wasted and once again questions and frustrations flew through the air.

John missed a few days of work and we spent a good deal of money. The hardest part was the emotional let down. We had verified the date and time of the court appearance with the attorney's office just before leaving Oklahoma. It was difficult to enjoy the detailed celebration that John had so sweetly planned for us, when the victory had been delayed once again.

It is hard to describe the feelings swirling through a family's thoughts when so many months have been spent in battle and victory seemed sure, only to discover that you are all dressed up and have no place to go!

Several weeks went by, as we were thrust into the waiting room once again. Finally we had another court date. More cautiously and totally on faith, we made plans and prepared to travel. We hoped above all else that when we reached our destination, we would accomplish our greatest desire, which was to once and for all legally make Jordan a part of our forever family.

The battle was far from over and the enemy made one last attempt to stop this important court day. Battle weary spiritually, we had almost lost sight of the goal and emotionally we were exhausted from the delays, now more than 18 months in the making.

We were simply focusing on the legalities that had to be accomplished.

Because I believe that adoption is a spiritual thing, I was especially saddened to see the way we were attacked from so many angles. It was clear that we were going to be tested to the end.

With battle-worn senses, our survival modes kicked in to carry us through the motions of the mandatory, second out-of-state trip.

John and I were sick with sore throats the entire week before we were to leave for the court hearing. All of the children were sick, except the two boys, Jared and Jordan, who seemed to be feeling typically spirited and impish.

The weather had quickly turned from summer into fall early that week and we were experiencing torrential downpours of rain, hour after hour. These were cold, gray, autumn days, which didn't help the dismal feeling that the sore throats were creating. After a full day's work, John loaded our belongings into the car in the cold rain; but not before he swallowed as much throat numbing medicine as he dared, given the several hour trip ahead of us.

When we arrived in the destined city, the hotel that John had spotted when we were there on the previously foiled trip had a vacancy. We didn't have to drive around a strange city in the middle of the night searching for shelter; we were very thankful! We unloaded tired and sleepy kids in a downpour just after midnight. We were finally settled in, as much as children settle in the first night in a motel room after a six-hour drive through a dark and rainy evening. We gratefully turned out the light and collapsed into the strange beds around 1:30 a.m.

We had barely drifted into a restless sleep when John began coughing. He had an incessant cough that would not allow him to lie flat on his back. He resorted to sitting up in the hotel chair, covered with the bedspread. Not surprisingly, he ended up holding Jordan most of the night as well. The new sights and sounds, the closeness of the room and the coughing all contributed to the little guy's sleeplessness. At best we each drifted in and out of a fretful sleep, without rest that night.

The children were tolerant of our short tempers and cooperative as we went through preparations in strange surroundings. Groomed for the day, they were all so cute. In sharp contrast, John and I looked like sickened people after a rough night out on the town.

Supposedly, we were only about six miles from the courthouse. So close to the end of this long journey, and yet so far away. Some of our excitement was rekindled when we were all safely buckled into our seat belts and heading out into the cold rainy morning. We were finally on the last leg of the journey and determined to make a memory-it was an unspoken pact. A bit of apprehension set in when we realized typically zooming traffic was in reality moving more at a snail's pace and a slow snail at that. A stalled car on the freeway complicated rush hour flow.

Windshield wipers swished back and forth, unable to completely clear the glass as the rain ricocheted. We inched our way through the city streets, finding our destination one exit and turn at a time.

What a wonderful relief when we glimpsed the looming courthouse on the horizon. We began to breathe, just a bit! Still, we were running dangerously late. Knowing from past experience that judges have strict schedules and intolerance for late arrivals only added to our apprehension. John let us out in front of a large official looking building. He went to park the car, sparing us walking for blocks in the relentless cold rainfall.

We quickly learned that we were in the wrong building. Now, why wasn't I surprised? Nevertheless, the news did cause a quickening of my heart as I glanced at my watch. While juggling diaper bags, court papers and a toddler who was quickly coming out of new clothes purchased just for his special day, I tried to make swift and practical decisions. With much apprehension, I left Leah, Jared and Andrea just inside the building entrance. With bravery that would win wars, they assured me they would stick together and be totally fine. I headed with a fevered pace in the correct direction.

My maternal instinct balked at abandoning my children inside a public building in the midst of an unfamiliar city. They all looked so tiny as I scurried away. A quick prayer for their protection and safety and Trista, Jordan and I were through the revolving door and into the downpour once again. We had come this far; we just had to make the court appearance with all present and accounted for.

After climbing up flights of stairs and going down corridors that never ended, I finally found the correct place.

There was no attorney in sight. Just when I was about to panic, a lady emerged from the opposite end of the long, tunneled hallway and introduced herself. She had been sent to represent us as the attorney assigned to this case (whoever that was, we were never really sure) had a scheduling conflict.

Panic joined my frustration when John came rushing off of the elevator to join us...without the other three children! Having asked for directions, he had come straight to the correct courtroom, which meant he had never seen our children waiting apprehensively next door. John turned on his heels and sprinted back to the elevator to rescue the waiting children. I attempted to take some deep breaths to regain my composure and a normal breathing pattern.

John needed to navigate four floors and walk through two buildings to retrieve the children. We could only hope all would make it back in time for our appearance before the judge.

The court appointed attorney began to chat with me about some of his concerns regarding this placement. My mind raced and I had some moments where I wondered if we were about to be told that he was not going to recommend finalization. We had never gotten this close to a court hearing and had anyone expressing any doubts. This was a fearful conversation. Where was my husband? How could we ease this man's worries and get this adoption completed?

Distantly, I heard his voice recounting delays, details that had not been taken care of in an appropriate fashion (by the powers that be, not our family) and concern about a baby being placed in such a large family. Surely this was a bad dream! Surely I wasn't hearing reasons for Jordan to be taken from us after all of the other obstacles had been hurdled one at a time over many months. As he spoke I recalled phone calls telling of Jordan's birth mother's wavering apprehension because legalities were handled inappropriately and she did not want to jeopardize his safety if some loophole revealed a way to remove him from our family.

Slowly, my thoughts mingled with the attorney's words as I came back to the reality at hand. This man held our family's destiny in his hands. How then, could I convince him that we were a family, that Jordan was already ours, and that God had said this was His plan and we were simply trying to stay obedient to the call?

He had unintentionally planted seeds of fear and doubt into my mind and set the stage for serious panic when he proceeded to ask me to write him a check for a fee that no one had mentioned we owed. In fact, until just moments before, we did not even know there was an attorney representing Jordan or we might have called upon him in the preceding months to stand up and fight with us for this little guy whose life had been in limbo so long.

I thought surely this was where the road would end. We would be sent tripping back to Oklahoma without those coveted legal papers once again. There was not enough money in the checking account to pay this man. We were on our second major trip to the city in a few short weeks, which had resulted in missed days of work, causing a small paycheck to dwindle into nothing. We had also had additional expenses for medications for our relentless illnesses.

I just sat there with a blank stare of disbelief, silently begging God for several hundred dollars to just drift down out of the rafters, or at least allow me to wake up from this exhausting nightmare. I explained that we had no clue we were to pay him that day. I suppose it was a fact we should have known, but there had been nothing routine about this entire placement, and we had not known about this man prior to our arrival at the courthouse. He quickly assessed the situation and based on the history of miscommunications, agreed to partial payment that day.

John and the others exploded out of the elevator about the time details were beginning to be worked out. Now it was John's turn to practice normal breathing patterns to slow his heart rate. We had not been called into the courtroom yet. This adoption might just happen after all, and none too soon I might add!

Jordan's attorney seemed to settle down and really enjoy himself once he met our other children and talked to John and me a bit. He shared some information with us that we had not been privy to before. Apparently termination of parental rights had taken much longer than anyone had ever anticipated. Then there had been a visiting judge who didn't know what was going on in this complicated case so it had been put in a hold file for a period of time.

Unbeknownst to us there had been complications with interstate compact and for a while there had been some doubt as to the validity of the whole series of paperwork that had been submitted. Then there had been the court date the week before when our attorney did not show up. After so many delays, Jordan's attorney opted to change his schedule and get this matter resolved. This baby had been in legal limbo too long.

We were truly grateful for this gentleman taking the extra effort to show up on short notice, and told him how thankful we were. He quickly became a team player, the feared enemy dissipating into oblivion as we realized we were all on the right path.

At long last our name was called. One final inspection: I tied a few shoes, tucked in a shirt and fixed a hair clip. With heads held high, we marched into that courtroom with order that would have impressed an army general. Not one soul in that room had a clue about the skirmish we had just come through! Battle wounds were successfully hidden behind Sunday best clothes, pasted smiles and the knowledge that we were at the finish line!

Initially apprehensive about bringing all of our family into the courtroom, we were greatly relieved to see the pleased smile come over the judge's face as he watched us file in. Our united front seemed to ease not only the apprehension of Jordan's appointed attorney, but to also solidify the testimony given. The judge seemed like a giant to me, sitting high above us in that huge black cloak. I could only imagine how intimidating he must have seemed to our children.

With careful and kind words he spoke to each of the children and they answered in squeaky and fearful voices. But answer they did, and with appropriate words, thank goodness. After some remarks about our tough road to this date of finalization the judge quickly pronounced the adoption final and gave his complete seal of approval. No serious questions, no more delays, no more fear, Jordan Andrew was officially ours. I wish to this day I had had the foresight and the nerve to toss confetti and balloons all over that tension-filled courtroom. It was indeed a moment of celebration, in the courtroom and in the heavens as well!

When we returned to the motel room we called the agency as we had promised. We found out that at four that morning the secretary had suddenly awakened and remembered she did not include a very important piece of paper in the packet we had carried and guarded with our life for two days. She had called our house at five a.m., hoping that we had not left yet. Of course we were spending a memorable night in the coughing ward at the motel room when she tried to reach us.

All she could do was pray and wait to see if the oversight was caught and the adoption stalled once again. She was however able to get someone at the attorney's office at seven that morning and they had somehow covered the mistake as we crawled through rush hour traffic. We never knew anything had gone wrong, since our representing attorney had not mentioned a word. Until the very last minute there were battles going on over this baby. That call with the news of finalization was the best news that dear secretary could have received.

In spite of the continuing rainfall, the grayness of the day and our total exhaustion, it was time to celebrate. Since food is always a part of our celebrations, and having missed breakfast completely, we trudged through the downpour to the café next door to our hotel. But, this time our hearts were much lighter, and our destination sure.

The waitress treated us like royalty when she learned that we had just come from court. She treated the children to ice cream topped with whipped cream and a bright red cherry on top! They were thrilled, and I must say, deserved every bit of the special treatment she showered upon them. They had been good little soldiers, representing the army of God in that secular courtroom and their behavior had done us proud.

A week later I penned this in my journal: Today I am beginning to feel better. I know that when John and I finally get rested and over our illness we will feel a great burden has been lifted off of our shoulders. The Lord promised us He would receive the glory and indeed until the very hour of the hearing for finalization God had to continually intercede and direct the battles over Jordan. His promise was fulfilled and after many uncertain days and restless nights the victory is the Lord's. May we be worthy of the task set before us as we seek God's wisdom in parenting this child.

When Jordan came, we had to endure one of our greatest faith walks. All of the months of uncertainty nearly crippled our faith walk with the Lord. We do not understand why events were as they were, but we do know God was faithful and went to great effort to direct every inch of the path we were asked to walk. Our lives, ALL of our lives, have been eternally changed, through this fire we were refined and our walk will ever be changed because of Jordan's placement in our home.

An Audible Voice

Exiting the main highway for a subdivision of sprawling ranch-style homes, I wondered if we would ever find the home we seemed to eternally search for. This unexplored territory had that peaceful bedroom community feeling: quiet, safe and settled. I wanted that "Welcome home, you're going to be fine here", secure sort of feeling. I wanted more than anything to finally stop long enough in our wanderings to allow our spiritual roots to push their way deep into the soil of our own land.

We meandered through the narrow asphalt lanes, finding our way to the very back of the subdivision as our friend had instructed. Sure enough, just when we thought there was no place else to go, the asphalt fizzled into a gravel lane, which dropped, curved and bumped onto a quaint wooden bridge crossing a trickling creek. As we drove up the slight incline and the lane became a driveway, I had John stop the car.

Taking a minute to gaze over the secluded corner piece of property I told John, "Now, this isn't the style of house that I necessarily want, but this IS the 'feeling' that I want when we finally find our property. This has the 'feeling' I want everyday when we drive up to our own home."

He was already mesmerized with the whole scene, and I was not surprised. Completely different from every other house we had passed on our way through the neighborhood, this estate had been designed in complete contrast to the traditional ones we had seen. As if transplanted onto the land, there was before us, a huge stucco Spanish-style home, John's favorite style of architecture.

The kids spilled out of the car and began to gleefully run all over the huge yard. As we explored the vacant property we discovered an outside door unlocked and took the liberty of going inside to explore this new-found treasure more thoroughly. By the time we had toured half of the house we were sold. This would be perfect for our growing family's needs! I declared that I could live in this house, on this very land, for the rest of my life and be totally happy!

John wasted no time in calling the bank that held the repossessed property's title. We were soon in the midst of title searches, loan applications and quickly enough, a closing date! I spent a good deal of time in disbelief that we were actually going to get to move to such a huge home on such a pretty piece of acreage, and so near to all things familiar.

In disbelief I watched as the paperwork moved swiftly and effortlessly through the banking and mortgage company systems. The Spanish house on ten acres was soon to be our new home. Few things in our lives have fallen into place with so little effort.

Meanwhile the saga of selling the house in town continued into its second year. There had continued to be endless phone calls, lengthy conversations, and multiple nonprofit organizational and planning meetings. Countless people had assured me during that time that they believed the house had been updated and redecorated so that it could be utilized for full-time ministry. With that in mind, as I have said, we spent endless hours trying to work with a variety of charitable organizations. But, just when it would seem something was going to work out, crazy things would stop the grant money, or so many trials would come that those involved would just drop the baton and go on to another race.

After exhausting all options, not one of the humanitarian groups which had felt drawn to buy our property had been successful in securing funding. The months had been emotionally frustrating and we remained puzzled. Why did people keep approaching us to buy our house, and, if so many people were being prompted to consider it, why didn't it sell?

After John returned from Arkansas to Oklahoma we had ceased to try in our own strength to sell the house. It has been many years and I occasionally still puzzle over the way the story ended with regard to the house in Tulsa. I believe God provided that house for that season in our life. The entire time we lived there I could always feel the presence of God within the walls. We literally had the best of times and the worst of times while living there. In the end we allowed a couple from our church to assume our existing loan, with no cash down and on faith, hoping they would be responsible in making the payments and maintaining the property. When the family that moved into the house eventually disintegrated under the pressures of life and the house was lost to the mortgage company, I was completely puzzled. The house never became the light in the darkness that so many had envisioned the property would be. I still wonder why so many solid Christian people could feel so sincerely about a purpose and yet be so wrong.

Life goes on, and we were enjoying our new home tremendously. I remember feeling so completely blessed and humbled as we began settling into this new provision of God. Little discoveries would just delight me. The pond hidden from view by years of overgrowth would eventually become a haven for those rare and coveted quiet times. Giggles would soon echo through the grove of trees when toddlers pulled wriggling perch from the deep pool. Roasting marshmallows over an open fire and Jared trying to pull a huge grandfather catfish out of the deepest recesses of the pond would be fondly remembered in the years to come. Once the area was cleaned and groomed it also became the stage for Jared's sixteenth birthday party, as well as other memorable times.

I shall never forget the fun of bringing home a clutch of tiny chicks to the children one bright spring day. A small shed near the pond would soon become home to our first flock of clucking hens. The delight of gathering wonderful brown eggs, still warm and fresh from the straw nests never ceased. A stray cat meandered through one day and decided to take up residence under some old tires that had been tossed in the barn. That spring she would gift us with several fluffy kittens. There were always crickets singing into the night. I loved the huge ancient trees that had stories I begged them to tell. Their massive size showed that they had been there long before the interstate highway that backed the property, or the subdivision that touched the side boundaries. Best of all, a small school district was just down the road, a safe place for the children. I would never leave; I had found home!

We moved to the property in the fall that year, and by September there was an incessant, relentless obsession within me. Just when I would think that all were home, God would prick my spirit again and the restlessness would prompt me to search again for the next child destined to join our family.

My journal entry reads: I feel almost as unsettled as I did the week or two before we received the call about Jordan. I know we are very close to adding a child or children soon. I feel an urgency to get my house in order just as I always do before a child arrives. I think the appropriate term would be nesting. I have only in the past two months gotten to sleep at least six hours at night. What bliss! In spite of my wonderings, there is a incredible temporary peace over this household. Still, I do wonder how long before I will be asked to give up that blissful sleep?

I had been working at an adoption agency as the Director of Education. Busy with the recent move to our acreage, caught up in the search for our next child, and ever active in child welfare issues, I had not paid much attention to the birth mothers as they came and went from the office each day. Since we honestly thought we were going to adopt a little girl from Guatemala, I wasn't thinking about the situations that were literally right in front of me!

In staff meeting one morning I learned about a drug-affected baby. They were discussing placement options. I wanted to shout, "I'll take the baby— I'll take it!" But, in all honesty, I didn't have that mandatory confirmation from God that this was my child, and so I was still. Feeling as I had felt before Jordan was born, I recognized there was a space in my heart, prepared by God, that He was getting ready to fill. I was now in full-blown 'spirit alert', searching, trying to catch the first sign from the Holy Spirit of the direction we were to take.

Stage two reality set in. With five children already at home, I must be crazy at my age to even be entertaining the thought of a new little one to call our own. When would this need to fill the spaces in my heart ever stop? Always living in the waiting room was exhausting us! And most of all, it wasn't logical to even be thinking this way.

I went to an educational workshop one evening. It was presented by an adult adoptee, and was designed to enlighten all members of the adoption triad. There were a good many people present and I felt the meeting was going especially well.

During the break several ladies and I were visiting with a birth mom that I had seen in the office, but not officially met. Though she had been coming and going from the agency for the past few months I had paid little attention. Suddenly, she was standing in front of me talking about her hometown, her family, and her desire to find just the right people to parent her baby girl, due in mid-December. I felt really drawn to her and experienced a great deal of unexpected empathy. Hoping to help her somehow I vowed to myself to pay more attention to this young lady the next time she came into the office for an appointment.

After the break we all returned to our respective seats and the meeting resumed. I was caught up in what the speaker was saying and was not particularly thinking about anything else. So, I was totally shocked when I heard someone say, *"I want you to take (this girl's) baby!"*

God's voice in my mind was so audible that I turned around to see who had said such a thing to me.

I was overcome with a mixture of emotions, and was completely unaware that I was crying! Here I sat, in the center of the audience, bawling my eyes out and oblivious that I was reacting in any way. My friend leaned over to ask me if I was all right. I could only nod my head and imply that I was fine, though the doubtful look in her eyes made me know that I had not been convincing at all. It was a very unique experience and would take time to understand.

At the next break this birth mother seemed unexpectedly drawn to me. Of course now I was more than a little interested in her situation, at the same time being totally unable to say anything about my revelation. I needed time to comprehend what had just happened. The birth mother continued talking the rest of the break, shedding puddles of tears as she rambled about a multitude of fears. I would later understand that the power of God was working in her heart too. But, at that precise moment I don't think either of us had a clue that we were in the midst of a most divine appointment.

I thought the meeting would never end, and when my responsibilities were finally taken care of I slipped out to my car, full of questions and filled with unexplainable emotions. John was already asleep when I got home. So, I went to bed with all that had happened fresh in my memory and did not talk with anyone. *That night I wrestled in my bed with the Holy Spirit. It wasn't a physical battle I fought, but a spiritual battle, and the sin of doubt was working overtime!*

I remember struggling the most with the idea that this was an African-American child and I thought we were to pursue a Guatemalan adoption. In fact, we were about halfway though the international paperwork. All of the doubts of provision for this child, both culturally and financially, swarmed through my mind. What would happen if we were to take the wrong child? There was no rest.

The next day I called John and we met for lunch. Skeptically I shared the events of the night before with him. He suggested that I talk to the director at the agency once again. He instructed me to tell the story just as it had transpired, then see what happened from there. I thought the director would think I was crazy; hearing an *audible voice* in the middle of a crowd of people seemed very unlikely to say the least!

When I arrived at the office I went immediately and told her all of the details, including my doubts, and the spiritual battle I had fought all night. Thankfully, given her gift of discernment, she understood completely. It was her suggestion that we present the story to the birth mother and once again leave the outcome to God. I was comfortable with that decision and relieved that it would now be out of my hands.

The birth mother seemed at peace almost immediately about the Lord speaking to me. She asked to see some pictures of our family. I quickly put together a simple life book and gave it to her. Almost immediately she agreed to entrust her baby to us. The due date was just days away. This adoptive pregnancy would move through the stages in fast-forward fashion. We had our instructions, we had our birth mother, and we had a due date. When God speaks, mighty things begin to happen!

> *In a meeting I sat not so long ago,*
> *And once again God spoke, significantly low.*
> *Take this girl's baby for your own, was His word.*
> *As tears filled my eyes I began to question what I had heard.*

I came home from the meeting, my world in a spin.
The house was quiet and I began to wonder once again,
How could we take on yet another life?
The finances, the prejudices, the challenges, the strife?
I wrestled with God through the night in my bed.
When I arose to pray, I knew the logic in my head
Was in direct discord to the knowledge in my heart,
I knew what I'd known from the very start
The God that I served was much bigger than me.
His request He'd made clear, when on my knees
I'd prayed to my Father for direction and HIS will.
The answer came quickly, take her, pray and BE STILL!

A few days went by and my thoughts were completely absorbed in this newly understood revelation. We were not even totally unpacked from moving, and we had to have our home study updated as soon as possible. I shall never forget the day the social worker came and visited with us sitting amidst both full and empty boxes and glancing out bare windows awaiting blinds and curtains. It seemed strange, not having things in perfect order for such an important and life-changing meeting, and yet, peaceful.

I moved on sure of the plan, not feeling the need this time for any further confirmation that we were on the right path. But, for whatever reasons, God seemed to find it important to prompt me into more calculations and motivation to stay on the path in unusual ways.

For instance: *I had a dream one night that our birth mother went into the hospital. I dreamed her delivery was very difficult. In the dream the baby was born around 4 a.m. and John and I went to the hospital around 8 a.m.*

I didn't really have a clue what the point of this dream was all about. When I awoke I found the details intriguing and yet puzzling, and couldn't begin to figure out what this knowing was all about, nor what purpose it would serve.

I was totally shocked, when, around 6 a.m. the director called to say the birth mother had gone into the hospital around 4 a.m. and she thought it would be about two more hours before the baby was delivered. She promised to call me back as soon as there was news. That was just too crazy, since that was almost exactly the hours that I had been shown in the dream. I had no doubt we would have our baby by lunchtime at the latest. I promptly began making childcare plans and getting prepared to spend time at the hospital.

The story gets stranger though. The labor stopped, and around 8 a.m. they sent the birth mother home. After several trips to the hospital for what doctors termed false labor, the baby was finally born two long weeks later, under emergency lifesaving events. It was immediately obvious that she could have been delivered on the night two weeks prior when God had given me the dream. We never did figure out why the doctors kept sending the birth mother home. She was miserable and understandably exhausted, the first labor having begun on her original due date.

Once born, McKenzie had an Apgar score of one. Doctors scrambled to save her life. When we were called the news was grim, and totally unexpected. We were told that the entire frontal lobe of her brain was dark on the CAT scan, indicating permanent brain damage. She had Erbs palsy and was not sucking a bottle. In a few hours they would add deafness to the list of challenges. She was quickly labeled failure to thrive and put on a heart monitor and a variety of other machines that I never totally understood. The prognosis was not good. For the first time ever after the birth of one of our children, we considered saying no to this baby. We were truly scared.

One of the worst ice storms ever to bombard Tulsa hit that weekend. We were unable to get to the hospital as we had planned. Unfortunately that gave me time to struggle with what we should do. Extended family, visiting for the holidays, thought we had totally lost our minds. Considering the addition of a handicapped baby had to be just about the craziest thing we had thought up to do so far. It hurts when those you most want to love and accept you, appear to condemn you for trying to do something to help others, and more importantly, to be obedient to the leading of God. We had to remember their concerns were from a logical perspective, and this was a spiritual decision.

After more sleepless nights and wrestling with God over what to do, God showed us clearly that this child was indeed to come to our family.

In a way that only the Spirit can communicate to us, God reminded me that if I had given birth to this child we would never have considered not taking her home. We would have parented and loved her regardless of the medical unknowns. Why then, when God had assured me that this was a baby He had for us, would we even question bringing her home? Indeed! We asked forgiveness and quickly made arrangements, as soon as the roads allowed, to go to the hospital to meet our newest family member.

> *She was tiny and helpless, not healthy like the rest.*
> *We were humbled and hurting and confused at best.*
> *Her eyes were beautiful and she was ours at first sight,*
> *But the challenges before her were not to be light.*
> *Giving assurance where doubts had plagued our human mind,*
> *He offered help and peace of a supernatural kind.*
> *Unconditionally we brought her to our home to love,*
> *Guided by our Father, who smiled down from above.*

When I finally went to the hospital the nurses wondered where I had been. No one had informed me that our names had been put on the visitor approval list at the time of McKenzie's birth. We had assumed all we would be able to do was to inquire about the baby's well being, so, with the ice storm and the holiday, we had settled for making occasional phone calls to the hospital. All the while I was lamenting at home over my inability to make sure she was being cared for appropriately, I could have been helping to take care of the baby. Well, better late than never, here I was! Look out special care nursery; Mom had arrived on the scene!

Within two visits I questioned the duty nurses, wondering why McKenzie was not gaining weight, and asking why they were only attempting to feed her every three hours. She was not a normally developing infant; she obviously needed some extra time to eat, and more frequent and smaller feedings. They gave no satisfactory answers, and I was outraged that it seemed they were purposefully letting a newborn baby lie there hungry. Finally after persistent requests, they allowed me to start feeding her between their regularly scheduled feedings. It came as no surprise to me, that within a few days, she began to gain weight and show signs of more stability. It was obvious the difference more frequent contact and nurturing made in this small little life. It would be a long time before she was able to appropriately suck and swallow, but with patience she was able to eat, just not in the 'allotted time'.

We immediately put her on every prayer list we knew about. Miraculously when a CAT scan was repeated just before her dismissal, the dark place that had originally shown on the test was gone. No one could explain this unlikely change. I believe that God healed her, restoring life to the part of her brain that had been oxygen deprived. She would however, continue to experience some residual affects of the birth trauma. She was dismissed to us on an apnea monitor and a variety of medications.

God's presence permeated the air a few days later during the entrustment ceremony at the director's home. McKenzie's birth mother was weeping, yet standing firm in her decision to entrust this child to us. We have beautiful pictures of McKenzie gazing into her mother's eyes as they sat waiting for the moment when in a spiritual giving and receiving ceremony this special baby would be placed into our forever family.

All of our children gathered around as words of encouragement and prayers were spoken on behalf of all members of this unique adoption triad. Over the years I have come to cherish entrustment ceremonies and find them very assuring and uplifting, in spite of the intense emotions that permeate those brief moments. Entrustment lends opportunity for feelings to be expressed that are not socially acceptable in other settings, and gives closure to the birth mothers and a beginning to the child and the adoptive family. It is the hardest part of the adoption, and undoubtedly the most significant in my humble opinion.

In later years, the knowledge of that ceremony can be very positive in the life of the adopted child. In pictures they can relive the moment they were spiritually transferred from biological family to adoptive family and see the agreement that was evident in the decision. Knowing that their birth mother willingly and peaceably placed them in the arms of their adoptive mother must give a sense of roots and wings. The ceremony gives permission to move onward through life knowing they have been released to be all they can be in the kingdom of God. They see that they were destined for adoption-the perfect plan in the lives of many.

The warm glow of the spiritual entrustment quickly gives way to the realities of parenting- of the mundane, of life. As if it hadn't been enough that our family thought we were crazy, soon our doctor joined the list of skeptics. This man was an adoptive father and professing Christian, yet, when he saw McKenzie for the first time, he questioned why we would take on such a challenge. I was speechless. No clever thoughts came to me, just disappointment that anyone in the field of saving lives would wonder at the worth of a child, or even question why we would commit to her.

McKenzie was a very uncomfortable baby, requiring a great deal of care. Eating was a huge challenge for months to come, and to a lesser degree, continues to this day. The doctors warned us that she might never progress beyond the infant stage. No one could tell us what this child's life might hold. Others thought she might get to a five-year-old development and stop. We would have to accept the unknowns, taking one day at a time. That is what we chose to do. God had shown us His desire, and we planned to honor the request at all costs.

When McKenzie was about three months old, our family attended a pro-life meeting at our church one evening. Holding McKenzie, I was listening intently to the presentation by a family physician speaking on behalf of the local crisis pregnancy center. I don't specifically remember the words that were spoken, but as the speaker prayed, he was interceding on behalf of the unborn children in our nation. It was about healing, and about God having a purpose for every life. *At the closing of the prayer I felt a powerful bolt surge through my body, jolting on through the sleeping baby in my lap. Startled from the unexpected shock I watched in disbelief as McKenzie jumped and started crying when the noise of the final applause came at the conclusion of the program.*

The entire congregation looked our way. All eyes in the room looked on in disbelief when, with each little sound in the room, McKenzie startled! *God had restored her hearing.* I had never before, nor have I since experienced anything quite like that *instantaneous healing.*

> *She was healed, this baby of God's design,*
> *In the moment He chose, in His own good time*
> *The years had tumbled by us; our hearts were opened wide,*
> *There were seven of us to welcome McKenzie, our hearts swelled with pride.*

For reasons I can't exactly explain I feel McKenzie's adoption was one of the most unexpected that we have experienced. Though we were ever searching for our next additions I truly did not expect a domestic adoption to be the answer.

Though I would not likely have believed it had it not happened to me personally, I found out that God does speak in an audible voice if necessary, to correct or alter our path.

So many things about pursing an adoption were correct, even down to searching for a little girl. But, in the end we did not have a clue what the big picture was, God did. The difficult birth, the ice storm delays, the unknowns about her future and her health were all just tests of faith that only time could provide answers for. I was reminded that God is sovereign and often asks us to do things that few others understand; indeed sometimes we ourselves do not understand the call.

Today McKenzie is a beautiful young lady. With a dash of extra effort in day-to-day living, she is destined to be a great contributor in this life, for God indeed has a plan and cared enough to insure it, with an audible voice.

Twice Blessed

Sometime between Jordan's adoption and our move to the new house I had another dream. This time it was about twins. *I could see them clearly in my mind's eye as they lay sleeping in a small bed. The strange part of this dream was that I could not tell their race. They had dark hair in the dream, and they looked very much alike, but that was all I was allowed to see. Somehow in my spirit I felt like the one on the left in the dream was a boy, and the one on the right in the dream was a girl. I knew when I woke up that this was yet another revelation regarding children we would one day receive.*

When we learned about the twin girls while we were waiting upon Jordan's finalization, I was overly concerned about discerning if those babies were to be ours. This dream about the twins caused me to question taking McKenzie, since she was a single birth, and I thought we were to get twins. As it turns out I needed to understand that our timing is not always God's, and that just because He had allowed me a glimpse into the future, it did not necessarily mean the *immediate* future! I would not have wanted to know just how quickly the dream would become reality.

But, I am getting ahead of the story. McKenzie was born during the holidays. It was now spring and I knew somehow that we would be doing something significant with the agency in the fall. I was no longer working there very much, but I was still on the Board of Directors and felt a part of the ministry. I wrote: What does God have for us? I do not know. *But, August and September are going o be very significant with regard to ministry or another adoption.* I must begin to pray for specific direction and wisdom to follow the path God has for us.

After much prayer and conversations with John I began to feel that we were going to get the twins in the fall, and I held firm to the understanding that they would be a boy and a girl. I really thought they would be of some sort of mixed heritage; I was hoping that somehow they might be Asian, or Hispanic. From God's impressions upon my heart, I knew these children would be very strong-willed, and beautiful!

During this time God also impressed upon me that He had plans to give us several more children, handpicked for our family. Many would have a special anointing of God upon their lives and would be a part of unique ministries.

God showed me through much prayer and seeking that if we were to look carefully for the gifts and talents of each child we would then know how to pray for and parent each of our children. I knew that we would not be able to parent in a traditional way, and it would be imperative to seek God diligently for guidance and direction. This was not a job we could do under our own strength.

John joined the search for the next addition and became especially interested in a little boy who was in foster care and presently living with some friends of ours. John tried unsuccessfully to save that child from a lifetime trapped in the foster care system. He was very disappointed after talking to judges and social workers and any one else he thought could help with the case. We accepted that this little guy was apparently not to be ours, and found a peace when we had attempted to do all that we knew to do.

One day a friend of mine called from the agency to ask some questions about an upcoming educational workshop. The conversation rambled along and we began to talk about babies that were soon due, and new birth mothers who had come into the program. She told me that she had recently been told about a mother who was going to have twins. I was immediately interested in this new topic of conversation!

As we visited I decided that there were two things that would confirm the possibility that these could be our babies. One, that they were not Caucasian, and two, that they were due in August or September. My friend had no idea of the vision God had given me, or the thoughts that were zooming through my mind as she talked on. I took a deep breath and began to ask more detailed questions.

She told me that the birth mother was Korean, and the birth father was Black. What a perfect fit for our family! The races would be an intriguing mixture of Trista (Korean) and Andrea (biracial) all rolled into two new little bundles of potential. I would not have prayed for or even thought of such a combination! Without a due date, I would have to endure several more phone calls before I would have any accurate information on my remaining questions. Eventually I learned that they were indeed due in the latter part of August.

I was to be pleasantly surprised as the days went by how many of the concerns I wrote on my prayer list were slowly provided for or taken care of in ways I would never have imagined. It was like God was saying, "Got worries? Give them to Me!" And when I would do that, they were indeed taken care of.

I had thought for over two years that we would get a little girl and then twins. Well, though she hadn't arrived in just the way I had imagined, we did indeed have our little girl, and now, it looked like we might be on the road toward the twins, and what a trip it was going to be! Several times in the coming weeks during prayer time God would give me incredible thoughts that would be small revelations about what I needed to do next, or information that would be confirming when events would really happen.

In early August, my agency friend went to meet the twins' birth mother. We had decided to do another test of sorts, to see if we were actually on the right path. She took the profile of another family for this mother to see. After presenting the first profile to the birth mother, she then proceeded to tell her bits and pieces about our family. Though the birth mother looked at the presented profile and was interested, she requested pictures and more information about our family.

Without a doubt the profile of the other family more closely fit the initial requirements of the birth mother than our profile did. That was our humble, human assessment of the situation. God had the final say so, of course! We learned as a result of this meeting that the mother was actually Vietnamese, and the father Black.

Since we already had so many children, I fully expected her to dismiss us from consideration. When she asked for more information, we knew that the door was still open. While we waited for her to decide on the family she preferred, we learned that an ultrasound confirmed at least one boy, and that the medical bills would be paid by insurance. Of course that made absolutely no difference to us, except that I found it incredibly interesting that God once again was bringing into our family children who had roots in a far off nation yet were born within the United States.

Adoptive families are at the mercy of so many people, and often helpless to do more than just wait and see how the decisions of others play into the outcome of life. Still, my list of questions and concerns was dwindling as I saw God's hand upon the entire situation. All we could do was wait.

We opted to take a short vacation. Ever mindful that people are always watching us, we are very concerned about how our children behave. I have always prayed that our lives would be a witness to the love of Jesus, and that we would witness that fact without having to say any words. We were attending a music show one evening when a lady sitting behind us leaned forward and asked John if we were raising all of these children.

When he said that we were, she told John that she could see we were truly blessed . She said she could see the glow around all the children and their beautiful faces showed such love and joy.

We were blessed by her compliment and knew our prayers to be witnesses were being answered. In a time of doubting whether we could handle even those that had been entrusted to us, God sent a stranger to reassure us. Those times give us unexpected renewal of strength to continue on with the tasks set before us.

Back at home; rested from our vacation, I began to pray in earnest for the decision the birth mother of the twins had to make. I was glad to know that I was totally able to leave the outcome in God's hands and accept His direction. Still, somewhere deep in my mother's heart I had a feeling that those were to be our babies. There had been a multitude of confirmations in a very short time.

I noted Romans 11:29: "For the gifts and the call of God are irrevocable."

If God intended for us to have more children, then nothing but disobedience would keep them from us. I decided to try and catch up on my sleep; somehow I figured sleep might soon be in short supply!

Financially, it had been one of the easiest summers I could remember. Emotionally, it had been one of my most difficult. For some reason I had thought a lot about my grandparents, all now gone to be with the Lord. I knew that they would have found great joy in seeing the way God was building our family and I grieved over our inability to share our blessings with them. John was struggling with his newly established business and I found it hard to know how to support him and pray for him as our motivations and goals were so different in this particular area. It was also hard for me to comprehend that 18 years had flown by and our strong-willed, independent, Leah was ready to try her wings and leave the nest. She would no doubt flutter and fall a few times while she tried those new wings, but we knew we were not going to be able to contain her much longer. I knew once she had made the big step of independence that our family structure would never be quite the same, and there was a sadness that came with that knowledge.

Dealing with one about to leave the nest, and the potential addition of newborns all in the same few weeks was very hard to absorb. There were so many emotions, so little time to settle them in our hearts or the hearts of the younger children. As the eldest, I never thought about how a sibling leaving home so intimately affected those left behind. I wondered if it would be as painful each time a child struck out on his or her own. Oh my, this pain anticipated eight or ten times in the coming years was too much to bear! But, then, I was getting much too far ahead of myself! Yes Lord, one day at a time.

I have since learned that there is a certain sadness that comes each time a child reaches the age of accountability and flies out on their own. In a mother's heart each child is so special, and each graduation just as emotionally difficult as the one before. But, stop them from flying, we must not...for they are given to us for a season, to love and to train and to encourage toward the purpose that God has for each of them.

At last, after a phone conversation with the birth mother, her decision to place the babies with our family was confirmed. When she had opened the letter that I had sent to her via the worker from the agency, she said that she knew immediately we were to parent her children. She took some time to pray, finding an answer in her prayers and the verbal confirmation of other people in her life. She knew she had found the right family, and she was determined to do what she believed that God had shown her to do.

She had planned until her eighth month of pregnancy to parent the babies. God had been dealing with her and this adoption plan was in obedience to instructions she felt were directly from God. Of all the reasons for making an adoption plan, I sometimes think that this must be the most difficult. The sacrificial releasing of children to so many unknowns because an unseen God asks that of a mother has to be heart wrenching and the most giving sort of love there is.

Once again, for almost the same length of time that I had been struggling to find the babies that would fill the place God had made in our hearts and our home, this lady had been carrying our babies under her heart, nurturing, loving and making plans of her own.

The twin's birth mother lived in a distant part of the state. She had approached a crisis pregnancy center near her for counsel and assistance in making an adoption plan for her babies. They seemed unable to find a family to accept the twins. That ministry had called our agency and the chain of events that followed is documented above. To my knowledge the pregnancy center originally contacted had never called our agency before, nor did they after. No doubt it was another divinely orchestrated chain of events. I was reminded of the television program that ultimately brought Jordan to us, unlikely events had also brought the twins within our realm of existence.

It seems each time we adopt there is a different group of people who do not accept our decision to adopt. Sometimes it was our extended family, one time it was the church we were attending and *this time the Lord had impressed upon me that the opposition would come from within the agency*. I was a bit surprised, but when my friend told me that she felt God had shown her that information as well, we prepared for the inevitable.

Opposition would arise within the agency, just as God had warned. But, because of the forewarning, we were able to pray specifically and to understand that, in spite of the opposition, God would bring this placement about. All of the normal stage two horrible, awful, and fearsome thoughts began to rear their ugly heads. I had twinges of fear that I would have to ration food and eliminate activities to make our finances stretch far enough. What if I couldn't handle four little ones at home? I already had Jordan, just barely two, McKenzie just seven months and now two more newborns soon to arrive. We had children in high school, middle school, grade school and preschool demanding and deserving of my attention. This time I would join some of our biggest skeptics in wondering if we had lost our minds.

God had been teaching me over a period of time that I needed to go by what my spirit knew and quit living in response to my five senses. Many times I would know things in my spirit and let logic or what I could visually see change or alter my course. It has taken me a good many years to heed those instructions and go by what I call "gut instinct." It remains so much easier, to walk by sight and not by faith, at least for a season. So, in this adoption as I was reminded once again that my thoughts were condemning what God had shown me, I tried a bit harder to tap into those gifts of the spirit that God had so graciously given me. For me, this is still no easy task; old habits are hard to break.

The babies were to be delivered by scheduled Caesarean section. When the entire due date passed and no one had called me I could stand it no longer and called the family that the birth mother was living with. I was absolutely shocked to find out that there were TWO boys!

I had been so sure of a boy and a girl that I immediately began doubting if we had the right situation. The poor man on the phone misunderstood my surprise and thought that we didn't want two boys! Not so, we did, but there was no way he could have known or would now understand all of the long weeks of mentally planning for a boy and a girl!

When I hung up the phone I told John in disbelief that we now had two sons! When I expressed my concern over having the wrong babies he simply said, "Look around you, this acreage is a perfect place to raise sons!" Obviously none of the names we had selected were going to work. Maybe that's the reason I had not been able to settle on two names; we were supposed to be searching for two boy's names...

We had their names picked out within the hour. The next day I sent the names and an explanation of the meanings tucked amidst some gifts for the babies with the agency's director as she went to meet with their birth mother. I wanted their mother to match the names with the appropriate twin.

Three days later, all of us would travel in our van to meet the birth mother, her friends, and to pick up those long-awaited treasures. Their mother shared with me her amazement at how well the names fit! She knew immediately in her heart which name went with which baby. God's hand was once more obviously in this seemingly small detail! It is great fun to be reminded now and again, by the boy's actions, just how appropriate their names really are for them.

> *In prayer time some months before, God had revealed to me*
> *A clear picture of twins He'd allowed me to see.*
> *More children were coming our way, this we knew.*
> *Not one little blessing, but this time, two!*
> *With prayers and testing we humbly sought God,*
> *And when events fell in place they, to us, were not odd.*
> *The years tumbled by us, our hearts opened wide,*
> *There were eight of us to welcome the twins, our hearts swelled with*
>   *pride.*

I thought my heart would be torn in two with the joy of receiving and the pain of leaving. I can vividly recall the look on their birth mother's face as we pulled away with a van of full car seats and left her with empty arms.

God was systematically plucking children with heritages from all over the globe and replanting them in our hearts and home. Each child's uniqueness added to the beauty of our family like the variety of flowers that make an English-style flower garden so attractive to me.

In time we would come to realize just how much these boys needed a father figure above all else. As a single mother she could not likely have provided that. God knows the present as well as the future needs of ALL of us!

> *All children are treasures; they are God's greatest reward*
> *He makes no mistakes, for He alone is Lord.*
> *Nicholas Asher was sent, a gift from above,*
> *Nathan Alexander added to the circle of love.*

We tried in those first few days to give the twins space by placing them in individual Moses baskets. When they seemed fretful, I finally resorted to tucking them into one basket where they would immediately settled down, inherently knowing that they were back together again as it should be. I stood in amazement and watched their movements, so intricately intertwined even outside of the womb. They consistently faced each other, and simultaneously moved arms and legs, giving way silently to each other without so much as opening their eyes.

Some of my most delightful experiences have been to seize the moment, taking time to admire the miracle of life when we have been gifted with our babies. It was an especially miraculous sight to gaze upon the twins, sleeping snugly together in a bassinet, mirroring each other in a way that only twins are able to do.

The boys had been home about six days when I walked by the basket where they were peacefully sleeping. Shocked much as I had been when Trista flitted by the lace curtains revealing in a moment in time a vision given to me years ago, I once again experienced a moment of supernatural unveiling. *Lying before me were the babies that I had seen yet in another dream a few years before!* Another dream now replayed before my very eyes! There are no words to describe a moment like that! It is the most incredible experience, humbling, exciting and mysterious.

When I shared with a friend later that day about the wondrous event, I also expressed confusion about my misunderstanding that the twins were boys, instead of the girl and the boy that I had adamantly proclaimed would confirm the correctness of the placement. I had distinctly known there was a difference in the twins, yet I could not understand what it was that I had known, as confusing as that statement seems.

I continued to puzzle over it, but enjoyed knowing full well that these babies were certainly the ones God had revealed to me long before their conception. As years passed, I would slowly understand what I had known from the beginning but could not quite express in words. Somehow, in a way that only God knows, He had revealed to me the spirits of the boys. Each boy is very special and unique, at the same time genetically similar. But, their individual spirits are very different, and I believe that I had mistaken the more gentle way of Nathan for that of a girl. His spirit is simply different from that of his brother Nicholas. I remain humbled and amazed at a revelation by God within my spirit, that could have revealed such intimate details and yet been misinterpreted in my mind.

Knowing we were in a God-ordained plan, I moved forward boldly, determined to run the race that was now clearly before me -"Therefore, since we are surrounded by so great a cloud of witnesses, let us also lay aside every weight, and sin which clings so closely, and let us run with perseverance the race that is set before us" (Hebrews 12:1).

I sincerely doubt if training for the Olympics would have required any more physical labor than keeping up hour by hour with all the needs of so many busy bodies!

I would like to say that we settled into a comfortable routine and that life went on with few hitches. That was not to be so. There were many times the only thread I had to hold onto was the knowledge that we were doing what God had instructed and He would give us strength to get through ("I can do all things in him who strengthens me" Philippians 4:13).

Although the house was full of laughter and giggles, love and security, it was also cluttered and dusty. Even worse, I was tired and grumpy a good deal of the time!

The day would start out around 6 a.m. Nicholas and Nathan were songbirds from the very beginning, waking at the first break of dawn, energetic and starving. We'd change their diapers, feed them a bottle and let them sing song away. Jared, Trista and Andrea would be out the door to meet the school bus at the end of the lane around 7:30 a.m. McKenzie had chronic ear, nose and throat infections, and required a good deal of attention when she woke up crying each and every morning. Often she would have cried literally all night long, with me totally unable to meet her needs. Both of us would start the day off emotionally and physically exhausted. Most days I would not eat nor have my shower until just in time for the bus to return home with the older children late in the afternoon.

Trista was in competitive gymnastics at this time and trained six days a week for two to three hours a day. This required that I have three babies fed, diapered and loaded into car seats ready to make the 45 minute one way trip to the gym the second that the older children stepped off of the bus. We would drop Trista off, turn around and drive home. Usually Jared or Leah also had activities they needed to be delivered to. I would then drop them off at designated meetings and hurry home to unload babies, change diapers, give three infants bottles, start supper and begin loading the van all over again for the trip back to the city to pick up Trista.

Homework, bath time, bottles, more diapers, throw in a few loads of wash, try to clean up the kitchen and around 11 p.m. I would finally get everyone to bed. With three infants, as much as I tried to get them on the same feeding schedule at least over night, it was an impossible task. With so many people sleeping in the house, and certainly not wanting my hyperactive twins to wake up any sooner than they would under their own energized power, I was desperate to find a corner where the others would not be disturbed by McKenzie's crying. I spent most nights holding her and crying along with her as long and loudly as she did. When the fire in the fireplace would flicker out I remember how cold that living room seemed to become and I would be too tired to get up and put more wood on the fire.

There were many times in the night that I would sit on the couch, a baby on either side of me with a baby centered on my lap, propping two bottles and holding one while they all three ate. Usually though, I would feed one or two, only to lie down just as the remaining baby woke up demanding their own attention and nourishment. Sometimes when the older kids would wake up for the day, or John would leave for work around 6:30 a.m., they would find me still sitting in the living room!

One day I was at a stop light on the highway returning from taking Trista to the gym. Music played on the cassette player, babies babbled in the back, others scuffled and argued from being confined too long in classrooms and now seat belts. I was exhausted. I shut my eyes and momentarily drifted into a light sleep. I thought if I could only sleep while the light was red, I would have enough strength to get to the next intersection.

I was dangerously exhausted with no relief in sight. Not even John realized how little rest I was getting. Sleeping through the night, he often had no clue that I had never been to bed.

I was to learn that God's strength is sufficient but in order to do what I had been asked to do I was going to have to change my priorities. I had always taken pride in my clean home and enjoyed decorating and rearranging furniture. Now I had to learn to pick and choose those jobs that needed

doing in order for our family to run smoothly. Forget the extras like cleaning out silverware drawers and sorting blocks into different categories each
evening before bedtime as I had done with just four children!

For a season, we were blessed to have someone come weekly and help
me with housework. At least that way the bathrooms were clean and the
floors all vacuumed and mopped on a regular basis.

I did allow myself the luxury of dressing the babies in cute clothes and
I loved getting everyone dressed up to go places, such as to church. I had
fun finding twin outfits, and I managed to find bits and pieces of time to
sew for the girls.

With so many things to be thankful for, I remember the time after the
twins' arrival as a good, though bittersweet time. The boy's birth mother
gave each of them a note with a Scripture reference to their names.

To Nathan, she wrote: God's gift. "See what love the Father has given
us, that we should be called children of God; and so we are. The reason why
the world does not know us is that it did not know him" (1 John 3:1).
Nathan also means prophet or 'gentle' spirit.

To Nicholas, she wrote: "For God did not give us a spirit of timidity,
but a spirit of power and love and self-control" (2 Timothy 1:7). Nicholas
also means victory.

Nicholas and Nathan's arrival was foretold and anticipated. The greatest lesson I learned this time was the vast potential for misinterpretation of
the information God chooses to reveal to us. I allowed my interpretation of
a dream to almost delay the receiving of the twins. So, I learned, that regardless of the knowledge we are privileged to have before the fact, the
reality is, all adoptions, indeed all works for God, require faith.

There will always be those happenings, those events that we are unsure
of that require our complete dependence upon God for the outcome. The
boys were surely to be ours from their conception on, and I am grateful that
God used such a variety of confirmations to keep me on the path of rightness in this situation. They are growing into delightful young men, talented
in many ways, and yes, ever living up to the meaning of their names in a
most interesting way.

In one very significant entrustment, we were indeed twice blessed!

Burdens Blessings & Butterflies

*"But he knows the way I take; when he has tried me, I
shall come forth as gold" Job 23:10*

The business that had seemed such a blessing in the beginning had become
an albatross around our necks. We suffered loss of clients, increasing in-
debtedness and no relief in sight in spite of hours worked. We constantly
sent up prayers and prayers for wisdom and direction. Everything John had
worked for was gone. Finally he had no choice but to shut the doors. When
the end finally came we owed more money than we had made in three years
of business.

I grieved for John at the loss of a dream. As he brought in boxes of office
supplies he was a weary and humbled man. I didn't know how to help but
incredibly, I felt very optimistic and had great faith in what God would do
with us through the coming days.

I wrote: We are unemployed and owe more than we can repay in our
own power. So, in our weakness we are to be made strong! God will receive
the glory, in spite of what we have or have not done.

We sold mutual funds, cleaned out savings accounts and tried to sell
cars. We dropped our salary, canceled insurance and trimmed our personal
budget until we were buying nothing except diapers and a few grocery items.
We borrowed money to pay on past due notes, it was a downhill spiraling

mess that was only to get much worse.

John and I traveled out of state in order for him to take some classes, hoping the new knowledge would increase his marketability. During our hotel stay our vehicle was vandalized, adding insult to recent emotional injuries. John's golf clubs, his cell phone and some other personal items were taken. In the months that followed, another incredible loss occurred as well. While we were at church one Sunday someone entered our home and helped themselves to more items, which had more sentimental value than financial worth. An antique gun was taken, the only real gift John had ever received from his stepfather who had just recently died. Our class rings, John's wedding band and military medals were among the other items stolen. It just seemed to never end. Anything of value to John seemed to be threatened.

We remained in the trenches as far as the battles in our lives were concerned. John was looking worse and worse as dream after dream died and job challenges were thrust at him like the fiery darts of the devil. He was helpless to put out one fire before another was hurled his way. He remained battle weary, though strong, and we both began questioning why life was playing out this way. All I could do was pray that God would sustain us through these hard times and that my husband would diligently seek God's direction and receive mercy.

John persisted in exploring new business ventures. He worked hard at any odd job offered. He shingled roofs, painted fire hydrants, went on short-term computer contracts and taught at the junior college one semester. He and the older children spent weekends chopping and selling firewood. We had garage sales where we sold treasures I had intended to keep the rest of my life.

My friend Kris* who had been instrumental in helping us arrange Nicholas and Nathan's adoption had been attending a worship service one evening and felt that God wanted her to share this Scripture with us. It was to be used as a promise of God's plans and protection. I clung to these words many a dark and tear-filled night.

"He will deliver you from six troubles; in seven there shall no evil touch you. In famine he will redeem you from death, and in war from the power of the sword. You shall be hid from the scourge of the tongue, and shall not fear destruction when it comes. At destruction and famine you shall laugh, and shall not fear the beasts of the earth. For you shall be in league with the stones of the field, and the beasts of the field shall be at peace with you. You shall know that your tent is safe, and you shall inspect your fold and miss nothing. You shall know also that your descendants shall be many, and your offspring as the grass of the earth. You shall come to your grave in ripe old age, as a shock of grain comes up to the threshing floor in its season. Lo, this we have searched out; it is true. Hear, and know it for your good" (Job 5: 19-27).

The first time Kris moved in with us was around the time of Leah's wedding. I desperately needed the help with all the little ones. The financial pressures, stress of shuttling Trista back and forth to the city for gymnastics training each day and trying to ensure everyone remained involved in some activities was requiring an incredible amount of energy.

I was designing and making Leah's gown and making all except one of the attendants' dresses. Preparing the wedding completely ourselves was a joy, but with the responsibility of three infants under a year old there were not nearly enough hours in my day! Adding insult to injury, we had all suffered a round of the flu and so energy levels and patience were running fairly low.

In spite of all that was going on around us it became even clearer to my spirit that my desire to work in an orphanage or on the mission field was unfolding before my eyes. Though we had not traveled to the mission field I found that we were in the midst of a divine purpose and plan.

I noted in my journal: Last night while we were in bed John wondered how many children we would ultimately parent. It is an awesome thought; I felt I had all I could handle when we had three and then four children to care for. But, I know what John means, because I think the call on our life is way bigger than we are and much greater than we would dare to imagine.

"Therefore do not throw away your confidence, which has a great reward. For you have need of endurance, so that you may do the will of God and receive what is promised" (Hebrews 10:35).

One day in my devotional I ran across this quote, "When God's voice has been heard distinctly, there need be no human calculation." How true this had been in the preceding months of moving to the country, adding three children and now attempting to get a new business and a new ministry off of the ground. We had tried hard to heed the voice of God, but I remained puzzled by the warfare and inevitable problems that seemed to never cease. Calculations brought no answers, and if God was speaking now, we did not understand. It was a lonely time.

From the very first time I had crossed the bridge to the property I had prayed for protection from the enemy, and for peace of spirit for all who came there and the means to utilize that place for God's work. Throughout the coming months my prayers did not change. The home we were now in was a ministry, an orphanage, and a place to be used for service in God's kingdom. Our vision for a full time ministry would invite such attacks that plans could never be fully manifested in that place across the bridge.

There was one particular room in that house that taught us uncomfortable knowledge about the principalities and powers that we do not always see. Different children would be moved into the room and soon become victims of nightmares and vivid recollections of oppression and indescribable fears.

Eventually, in talking with me, each child described black clouds hovering in the upper corners of the room, without knowledge that their siblings had had similar terrors. Whenever the clouds appeared, fears and nightmares would manifest themselves.

Finally, I sent the children on a walk with Kris. I went timidly in my being, but boldly in spirit, into the room. I declared that the evil one leave, never to enter that place again. I then invited the healing power of the Holy Spirit, in the name of Jesus, to permeate the walls. From that time forward all slept peacefully in that room.

We also endured the impact of other people's decisions upon our lives. Though we were sheltered in what God had promised me to be a 'safe haven', others interacting within our circle of friends and business acquaintances were not so protected. As John dealt with different men in various business attempts strange and bizarre events took place. Just as legal and financial papers were about to be signed, one man's wife became critically ill, eventually ending that business proposal. Other times, holidays would delay acquiring necessary signatures on business financial or legal papers. During the delays, odd events would have transpired ultimately stopping the latest business venture. We were months recovering from the shock of the phone call telling us a man who would underwrite the finances for the new business lost his wife in an automobile accident on the way to the bank. He never returned to sign the closing papers that lay on the banker's desk at the time of the tragic call.

During these months I began to more clearly understand how Job must have felt. We were accused from every angle: of sinning, of not listening to God, of not tithing or in some other ways being disobedient. There must be some hidden sins; otherwise people reasoned, we would not be going through such hard times. I remember John and me searching Scriptures, praying and constantly reevaluating our lives. Still, I could find no blatant sin; I could see no outright disobedience all the while being painfully aware that "all have sinned and fall short of the glory of God" (Romans 3:23).

"As thou knowest not what is the way of the spirit, nor how the bones do grow in the womb of her that is with child: even so thou knowest not the works of God who maketh all" (Ecclesiastes 11:5, KJV).

The things that happened to Job were clearly allowed, even initiated by God and not as a result of any biblically revealed disobedience or sin. We know that Job did not understand what was happening to him and we learn that he too had beaten himself up at times and wondered aloud what he had done to deserve the calamities that were consuming his life.

I must confess, at times, I too joined Job's wife and wondered what John had done that would explain the circumstances we found ourselves in. John maintained that he was praying and seeking God. We knew that God was providing for us and sustaining us and He was a very real presence in our lives. Still, the hard times were being allowed to bombard us. Most of the time John prayed long and sought the council of others before making a decision, only to have the very thing that he felt God was showing him to do, fall apart. We could only assume God was allowing the testing. We prayed without ceasing, hoping we would pass the test with our family intact (more than Job was allowed).

There were many times when I doubted John's leadership, but God was quick to reprimand me and remind me that I was to be submissive to my husband regardless of how circumstances played out. It was John who had to hear God and I who had to follow my husband, trusting God for the outcome, even if in the midst of the battle I felt wrong decisions were being made. Under attack, it is so easy to find a log in the other persons eye and aim right for it! The last thing my husband needed was more judgment.

Meanwhile our food supply was running out. I will never forget the day I walked into the pantry and the only things on the once-stocked shelves were some seasonings and a bag of rice. Still, we never did go without food during this long time of testing. Leftover food from a church dinner provided a feast, and another day someone took us out to eat pizza. I vowed never again to take for granted a full pantry, paid utilities and employment. All can be gone in the blink of an eye, regardless of how diligent or responsible we think we are. Sadly many Christians just assume if they are living good and moral lives, and contributing to their churches they will have everything they feel they deserve. Much like life itself, these gifts are God's for the giving and the taking to distribute as He sees fit. No one person is more worthy than another and we should be careful to remember that each day and each luxury are temporal.

We struggled with feelings of inferiority, as our extended family grew more and more distant during these times. We appeared irresponsible to them I am sure. Also, just the pain they felt watching us suffer through something no one understood caused them to retreat. Relationships that were already stressed prior to this time had totally disintegrated at the end of this trial.

Life is full of mystery, even when we try to distinctly listen for the instructional voice of God. It was hard to know what God was allowing and what were consequences from poor choices. Sometimes things were happening so fast that John would be forced to make a quick decision and later come to regret it greatly. Other times events would happen that would be so totally God that we would stand amazed. It was a strange time.

We prayed together faithfully-it was our only strength. John and I agreed the valley would have been unbearable without God to lean on. If it was this hard with God on our side, we didn't dare to try and imagine this walk alone. I had recently read that God calls us to live a life we cannot live, so that we must depend on Him for supernatural ability. Supernatural intervention was going to be our only hope I knew that without a doubt. Psalm 5:8 states: "Lead me, O LORD, in thy righteousness because of my enemies; make thy way straight before me."

I wanted so badly to be growing and vital in my Christian walk, and I wanted that for my husband and children as well. I did not want us to miss the mark because of discouragement breeding fear and fear causing us to not be bold.

In a prayer time at the adoption agency a man had made these remarks, "A whole generation missed the destiny of God because they were too weak." Oh, how sad. We must not be weak; we must put on the full armor of God and move forward through the battlefields, expecting a victory. We could not allow weakness created out of fear to keep us from moving on. Stagnant things are so repulsive and Christians frozen in fear are no exception.

Soon God made it clear that Kris was to go to Romania once again. I was disappointed that my dear friend and greatly needed helper would be leaving so quickly, but I knew in my heart that God had a plan.

Late one night, in a rare moment of quiet time she and I talked heart to heart about our confusion, our desires, and about what God was preparing us to do—not together as we had originally thought, but separately, in totally different parts of the world. In spite of all the odds against it, I truly thought that during her time in the orphanage that Kris would find more children for our family. In fact, many times in the coming months events would seem to lend themselves to just such an event, and then the whole plan would crumble. Perhaps we still have some children in the Eastern Block countries just waiting to come home, as we never accomplished the task during her mission trips to that very poor area of the world.

McKenzie, Nicholas and Nathan seemed to remain in perpetual motion. Even with the help of a nanny, which God had miraculously provided when Kris left, there was always work waiting to be finished. I have never had little ones so unsettled and without purpose in their actions. They seemed to spin and bounce off of one another, the toys, the rug, the table, never stopping, never accomplishing a goal, never seeing what they were doing, just moving and going and running and reaching. I would later understand that with attention deficit and hyperactivity (ADHD), along with some neurological challenges, these children represent a very unique threesome, requiring incredible creativity and energy. With additional years of parenting we have come to understand few others will ever test us in a way that this threesome does. Without the delightful sunshine Marcie, a college student brought into our home that dark summer, I do not know how we would have survived. She was a shelter and buffer for our youngest charges and I know they never knew just what storms were swirling all around them and what battles the adults in their lives were fighting.

In midsummer I received a collect call from an acquaintance in Guatemala. Prompted by God to call us, she asked if we would be interested in an infant girl with spina bifida. We had not talked to this lady in over three years, so this was a very unexpected call. (She had been our initial contact in Guatemala before God clearly led us to McKenzie.) Ever optimistic I felt that if this child were to be ours, God would make a way. I hoped that if God were going to ask us to add a child perhaps this turn of events meant a resolution to our present situation. We would have to be employed to bring this child home for adoption. I told her that we would pray about the little girl.

Clearly few could understand why we would even consider the addition of children during such an unpredictable time as we were experiencing when we tried to get this little girl. We knew that logically there was no reason to make any plans, adoption related or otherwise, until our lives stabilized. Still, we knew that a walk of faith is seldom without many precarious challenges. We honestly believed that if God impressed upon us so strongly to do something, He would make the provision, regardless of how ridiculous it seemed to others. But, man's free will is always a deciding factor and both our own, and that of others no doubt altered the course of many people's lives.

Still, as we considered this new special needs baby, and especially under the circumstances, we wondered if our challenges and concerns represented a red light? Or, were they ways to test our faith, ways to allow God to intervene and to show His strength? It was so hard to know what we were to do. We walk such a different walk, few people understand it, and most think we are totally without logic or thinking skills. In all honesty, there are times we wonder ourselves what we have taken on.

The world looks in and says we can't do it, but we look at God, and from past experiences we know that with God we can do all things. Man's impossibilities are God's possibilities (with doors just waiting to be opened to reveal miracles beyond compare.)

John and I talked about what constitutes a valid reason for saying no to a needy child. How can we say no to any request made by God that has the potential to build His kingdom and to serve others?

We told the lady in Guatemala that we would try to get a medical visa and bring the baby girl to the United States for treatment. We knew that we could not adopt her at this point, but perhaps our mission was just to see that she could get the needed medical care, or perhaps after she was in our home for a season and things returned to normal, we could then proceed with an adoption. Whatever care I solicited for her would not change our present financial situation. All she would need from us were diapers and food, love and security. We had seen hour after hour the way God provided for our needs. If he sent this child to us, we knew that in spite of our worries, this child would be abundantly taken care of. Our children had not wanted for anything during this trial, it was we adults who were suffering with the unknowns and the questions.

I opted, with John's full encouragement, to follow the tiny light. I wanted desperately to bring this child to the States for medical provision and give her a hope for the future. So, I made phone calls, and prayed, prayed, and prayed some more. I tried knocking on doors of airline employees, doctors, and specialists, anyone who would be willing to help a child in need. We had walked this path so long, and knew without a doubt that help could come with only one phone call, or one doctor saying yes to a procedure, or one person agreeing to escort this sick baby back to the States.

Yes, the light was dim, but I just knew that God had a plan and that one day the door would swing open and a brightness only given by God would illuminate the path enabling this child to get to the United States.

I was exhausted, I wanted to cry, I wanted to run from the hopelessness of the task, but there was a child, and since I knew about this child, and not others, I needed to help her. I believed that God brought her to our attention for a reason.

"And one does not take the honor upon himself, but he is called by God, just as Aaron was" (Hebrews 5:4).

We knew of friends traveling to Guatemala on a medical mission trip. I asked-could someone pick up the baby and escort her back to the states on their return trip, since the mission team was going to be in the city where the baby was hospitalized?

I was told no, they had other children to minister to. The baby might cause a delay in their prearranged plans, with the agenda already set. They could not help me. I need to remind the reader: this was a medical missions team, going to serve medically needy babies and small children in Guatemala! Oh, the best laid plans of men, how vain they sometimes can be, even in the name of Christianity! Once again I was shocked when the church let us down.

I sought God again, what would He have me to do? Were we wrong in trying to find help for this little baby, or were others wrong in not being willing to alter their plans? I wouldn't dare to give an answer to that perplexing question. Free will is an area some of the greatest theologians are still debating. Ultimately we all have to do what we believe God is asking us to do. In our walks, we will make mistakes. I have learned the hard way that we will rarely understand the agenda of others.

What I did read and yet not fully understand was written in Job 23:14 "For he will complete what he appoints for me; and many such things are in his mind."

Another blow came when a longtime friend who could speak Spanish fairly well, impulsively called our contact in Guatemala and told her we were unemployed. We had not told our contact because we felt it was really irrelevant as we were presently attempting to bring the little girl to the U.S. to receive medical treatment. Yes, we were hoping to adopt her if circumstances changed, but the big challenge at the moment was her medical needs and the attempt to get her into the country on a medical visa. This friend called us early one morning to confess making the fateful phone call.

What this person told us shocked us and took us so by surprise that we did not know how to respond, let alone proceed. How would we call to explain or justify our position with our contact in Guatemala? There would be no way to explain our position after the phone call made by this person. Words could not now justify our motivation in trying to help this specific little girl. The language barrier had been our greatest challenge since the initial contact. We had not even considered we might be deceiving people in any way. We really believed with our whole hearts that we were acting in faith, believing that there were divine directions and purpose in our attempts. Ecclesiastes 9:18b says: "...one bungler destroys much good" (NRSV).

We will always feel that for a brief moment, when this fellow Christian was used to confuse even further the already murky waters, he unnecessarily damaged what credibility and self worth we had left. Perhaps, we did need to be stopped. More than likely God would have taken care of things without our having to deal with the emotional blows of a friend taking it upon himself to set our lives straight. Job 16:20 describes how I felt: "My friends scorn me; my eye pours out tears to God."

I wanted to run away from all of this unfairness, this judgment that people felt we needed to go through. I wanted to forget what our long time friend had changed in just one impulsive phone call, or what other Christians had decided was out of their comfort zone when called upon to help this child. Every time the accusing voices of those who thought we had no business getting this little girl would come at me, I would hear these words in my head, *"If you do not intercede on her behalf, she will be lost."* And, the profoundness with which God had previously warned me would become reality once again.

When the potential for an escort had deteriorated and employment was still not in sight, we had begun talking at length to another family about their willingness and ability to bring this little girl into the United States. When we fail in our humanness to fulfill His requests, God is able to send another man (family) to do the job.

Thankfully, when we could do no more, the other family stepped in and took all of the risks that we had been willing and yet unable to take. In short order they brought the little girl to the U.S. on a medical visa. Within their community were people, who, when asked, were willing to help and not judge the correctness or the family's willingness to take in a child that would be number 14 in their household. In reality, their financial situation was not all that much better than our own at the time. Taking care of God's children is an expensive and faith requiring business. Caring for the orphans is a call that typically seems senseless and irresponsible to those glancing in. The lady who welcomed the little girl agreed as we talked at length on the telephone that it seemed as if the Lord had desired the little girl to be a part of our family. Still, it was not to be.

Eventually, I would have to release this little girl spiritually to the other family and give my blessing to enable that all of our lives might move onward. The need to release her spiritually only confirmed to me that God had indeed placed her in my heart for a purpose and a plan much more complex than I would ever understand this side of heaven. At the time of this writing I still wonder if I lost a child or responded with obedience with the resulting outcome simply not what I anticipated.

We began to work more on developing a ministry that we felt the Lord had given us. It was a puppet ministry and included all the children. The message was about spiritual adoption, and combined the humor that only puppets can project and the seriousness of the plan that God has for each of us in a lighthearted presentation.

Our goal was to motivate Christians to consider adopting waiting children. A church loaned us their puppets for some of our first presentations. With the love offering we received at different programs, we eventually created our own puppet stage and purchased puppets of our own. We were well-received wherever we were able to perform. Though it was incredibly exhausting to physically prepare and present the program it was like fuel to our souls each time we gave our testimony. It seemed so right in the midst of all the battles to share and simultaneously be reminded of what God had already done in our lives and no doubt was still planning for us in spite of the present darkness. We believed that God was taking us through the storms of life to refine and prepare us for even greater ministry in the future. We continued attempting to make the presentation in spite of the battles we were constantly fighting. Eventually, in all the changes, we would pack away the puppets. Hopefully one day they can be brought out of storage and once again entertain and convict God's people.

Our house was about to go into foreclosure. We waited longer than perhaps we should have to ask for help. Pride was a part of the reason—it is so hard to admit defeat and ask for help. Also, we wanted to believe that God would make provision in spite of our failures. Finally we saw no options but to humbly ask for the needed back payments

On his way to a dreaded appointment, John stopped at a small cemetery bordering an old country road. Buried there is his first stepfather, who long ago badly mistreated John and his mother. Haunted at times by horrible memories, he had vowed he would never allow the way he was treated to taint the way he parented his children or provided for me as his wife. But, there were amends that needed to be made, forgiveness that needed to be asked. So, on this sunny August day, John decided to stop and make peace with the memories, forgiving someone who had been so cruel and asking forgiveness for the sins of anger and hurt that had festered in the recesses of his mind for many years. He told me later, that for the first time ever he had a peace and was able to truly forgive this man who had hurt him so much. It was a mountain top experience, a new beginning and a spiritual high that much of the world will never understand. But, the enemy was lurking close by and a reality test was soon enough to come.

The scene was horrible and as quickly as John walked in the door of a family member's home and stated his reason for coming, he turned on his heels and raced right back out of the door. He had walked into a confrontation almost as hurtful as the physical attacks of his childhood. Words best never spoken were hurled at John almost as soon as he entered the house. Without excuses, filled with rejection and fears, John fled without the financial assistance he had so dreaded to ask for. On his way back to our home he considered driving off of one of the many roadside cliffs, ending the testing, going home to the Heavenly Father who would accept him unconditionally.

Having been informed via a phone call of the ugly scene that had transpired, I knew I could not begin to imagine the depth of the pain John was experiencing as he drove toward home. I was weak with relief when John's car pulled safely into our driveway later that day. Wounds had been healed and just as quickly reopened in the short span of a few hours. Few words were spoken. The pain was too complex, with the wound recently exposed.

Somehow that evening we went ahead with a birthday celebration for Nicholas and Nathan. There was a heavy cloud hanging over us and yet there was healing in the ritual of the birthday party.

The older children sensed that something horrible and life-changing had happened that day, yet were wise enough not to question their devastated parents. The younger children were quickly caught up in sharing birthday cake and singing songs. I was thankful for the diversion and reminded by the simple trusting smiles on the faces of our birthday boys that in spite of our circumstances, God was with us and would carry us through this newest storm. The children that seemed to be the reason for our tests and challenge were at the same time the healing balm offered by our Lord.

I wrote in my journal: I do not consciously know what God is allowing –but I know it is major surgery. I keep praying for pills to swallow to kill the pain or take away the problems, which would be the easy way out. Just as driving off of a cliff would have seemed an easy way out of the pain for John a few days ago. Instead, with spiritual surgery, it is necessary to bring the problem out in the open, examine it, repair the bad part or remove it all together, then, somehow, put the whole body back together again. When this is over we will certainly need a time to heal, to rest and to recover.

Job 5:17,18 says: "Behold, happy is the man whom God correcteth; therefore despise not thou the chastening of the almighty; For he maketh sore, and bindeth up; he woundeth, and his hands make whole" (KJV).

We wanted to quit praying, for it seemed fruitless. John wanted to quit trying, for it seemed the right doors never opened. We wanted to scream at those watching us from the sidelines shaking their collective heads in disbelief. We wanted to prove we weren't purposing to be incompetent; we weren't putting our family through such testing on purpose or out of stupidity. We were simply trying, in our own way, to find God's will, and the results seemed irresponsible and incredibly crazy at times, yes, even to us.

We seemed to be incapable of making decisions that were acceptable or logical to everyone else.

Ironically when we did try to approach our challenges in a way that the world typically would, the door would still close. We were in a battle. Like Job sitting in the dust with sores all over his body, friends accusing and jeering at him, we were helpless to make our conditions any better.

In reality, God is the controller of all circumstances. Only when He allows are eyes opened, circumstances changed and blessings bestowed. And, though everyone thought they had the solution, or thought they could see the real problems, in reality they were not in the dust beside us, nor did they want to be.

Reluctantly our family had eventually given us the money to stop the foreclosure. We were humbly grateful. If we could have figured out anything else to keep a roof over our children's heads we would have gladly taken another option. We had a great fear of ending up on the streets with no place to go. I had always assumed people on the streets were there by choice, because they were lazy or chose not to work. We learned quickly that being willing to work, praying, even tithing and seeking God's will did not guarantee anything. Our manner of living could change in an instant. At the same time we frequently reminded one another that we did not need anything. Our material wealth was being eaten away in as many ways as God was providing for our needs; the good and the bad were equally confusing.

The roof over our head was now secure and we could breathe easier for a season. Still, there were relentless calls from bill collectors and daily fears that our utilities would be disconnected.

The air conditioning had long ago died and there were no funds to fix it. The septic system malfunctioned and the money designated for utility bills went flying out of our hands and into the plumber's bank account. The garbage disposal quit, the washer had to be repaired, things normally insignificant began to mount up and resemble huge war zones. When the dishwasher died, I collapsed at the kitchen sink and let the hot angry tears wash away some of my weariness. It was a futile attempt at release. I begged for this test to be over-for our blind eyes to be opened to whatever truths we were to learn so the lessons of life could be over for a season.

Instead of taking us out of the storm, the Lord chose to show His power and provision. I was upstairs crying because I knew that they were coming to repossess our van late that afternoon. It was the only means of transportation we had left. We had purchased the conversion van new, and only had six payments remaining. The phone rang and I tried to ignore the intrusion into my pity party. Something propelled me downstairs to answer the phone. It was a lady from our church. I barely knew her. She was telling me that her husband, who was a long haul truck driver, had just called her from a roadside pay phone.

The Lord had prompted him to stop on his drive and call her, instructing her to call me and see what sort of financial help we needed. I humbly told her about my praying and crying over the expected loss of our van. She instructed me to meet her at the church parking lot and she would write me a check for whatever I needed to not only make up the back van payments but to bring the insurance current as well! I could hardly believe my ears. Within two hours she and I had met, I had gone to make the back payments and I was home once again, transportation secure and humility firmly in place. We drove that van for another five years, then gave it to our daughter and son-in-law, who eventually sold it, still running smoothly after many more years. "Is anything too hard for the Lord?" (Genesis 18:14).

Soon though, I was in my room, hiding and praying once again. The prayers were frail and feeble; those of a foot soldier weary from battle, not knowing for sure just where the enemy crouches, waiting in the darkness. Finally, needing to find some light and to escape the confines of my room, I went outside.

I would later write the following story in my journal: After days of little sleep I walked to the pond and sat down on the bench. It was a beautiful, beautiful afternoon. There was sunshine after an early morning thunderstorm, and surprisingly low humidity, bright green grass, clean clear pond water, with late summer afternoon sounds. There were locust and a multitude of mother birds chirping to their young. Dozens of dragonflies flitted here and there, swooping to skim the surface of the pond water. Fish sipped at the top of the water-making a unique sound.

My mind wandered and I tried to find rest. I didn't know how to pray. I wanted so badly to have the pain, the burdens, the fears, and questions erased and for things to be better. I wanted to know we could keep our home, the home we had grown to cherish so quickly and that I really believed God gifted us with. I wanted to know John was making correct choices. That God was directing him and showing him the path, in spite of the inevitable mistakes. I wanted to know we would have a permanent job and provide abundantly for these children. I wanted to believe that we would soon be out of debt, in bondage to no man.

I wanted desperately to get up from the bench, to be physically well, energetic, the drawn look gone from my face, our life in order. I was desperate for assurance, I begged for answers! What I felt was numbness, an inability to figure anything out. Tears flowed down my cheeks without warning. I didn't really even realize I was crying for quite some time.

I sensed that God was intently watching me as I sat on the bench John had built for resting, for enjoying the pond and absorbing the pastoral feeling of the meadow. Suddenly I became very upset. This was not a bench intended for grieving; it had been built in love to give comfort and a haven on which to rest.

I tried to empty myself of all the garbage, crying away the fears, the fatigue, the confusion, the doubts and the anger. I tried to pray, but I didn't know what to pray for except, "Thy will be done." And "Please, please, God, don't ever leave or forsake us, it seems You have, but please God, hear our prayers, and send answers (the ones we want to hear) soon!" You see, I am sure that all along, God had been with us, hearing us, answering us, but we did not yet understand why His answers and allowances were as they were.

After a while acceptance began to creep into my thoughts. I realized that everything was nearly gone: the cars, John's dream business, our pets, unnecessary home decorations sold in yard sales along with numerous toys and extra furniture, and soon enough the house would even be gone. We were stripped. I was sitting with nothing before God and I asked: Where will You ask us to go, how will we protect the children You have entrusted to us? Can we preserve our marriage? How will we face the world? How will the world now perceive us? Had we blown any chance at a witness? Would they know and understand that we are human, we've made many mistakes, but we still believe in an almighty God though we feel we have lost so much?

I neither saw nor heard anything. No new direction, no new mission, not even a confirmation that everything would indeed be gone, or better still, that it would all be okay. So, I was still.

It felt like the volume on the surround sound music track of nature was being turned down. Entranced in my thoughts, I remained perfectly still, like a statue sitting on that rough wooden bench. Then, effortlessly and silently two delicate yellow butterflies played and skirted across the pond. High into the trees and back and forth across the water they dipped and dived, floated and fluttered. They were pure yellow and perfect.

Once, they were in cocoons, struggling in the dark, crowded in by their circumstances, not understanding what was beyond the darkness and struggling against the surroundings they were in. When their confinement became too much they pushed and struggled until they grew very tired. Thought they could not see out of the dark cocoon, God still watched carefully over them, and He knew where they were. When they finally renewed their strength and made a slight opening in the tangled wall of the cocoon, they peeked out and even might have been apprehensive in a caterpillar sort of way. There were big birds to gobble them up, trees to fall off of, rain storms that could drown them. And what if there was a drought and there were no green leaves to eat? Why did they have to leave the security of the cocoon that God had gifted them with? They liked it inside. It was warm and safe, and for a season, it was just the right size, just what they needed. To me, our present home was just that way.

Now they found themselves at a different stage of life. They had outgrown what had once been just right. They had struggled in their growth, resisted the place they found themselves in, and once out of the cocoon, they could not crawl back in. They had to rest a bit and then they must move on. Now, they flew high and lightly over the clean pond water, the green meadows and high into the bright blue summer skies, and they knew great joy! They didn't ask if God was going to take it from them, they just flew free and with great joy to new heights.

I knew God was saying to me again, "Be still and know that I am God" (Psalm 46:10). Rest and wait, I am YOUR God too. When it is time, you too will fly free and to new heights.

I didn't get any of the answers I sought during my time by the pond. Or, at least at the time I didn't think so. I walked slowly back to the house, and I knew that nothing I could do would change things, and just as He had in the past, especially during the additions of our children, via birth and adoption, God would make it known somehow what He wanted us to do next. If we tried to listen and if we tried to obey He would help us remain faithful.

If He allowed us to lose everything, then so be it. He gave it to us; it was therefore, His to take a way.

I was reminded once again that our hope, our only hope, is in God-not things, not people, not jobs, but God. In my spirit I know that as the world around us crumbles because of disobedience or lack of faith, or circumstances beyond our control, our only true peace and help will come in trusting and obeying God. Those lessons of waiting in obedience often come in the valleys of life or while in the confines of a cocoon and are not easily learned.

I wanted answers, I wanted miracles. What I was given were two butterflies flitting across my pond and with them knowledge about growing, and changing and moving on.

It was small hope to hold onto when Leah found herself separated and eventually divorced. There was much guilt for John and me as her marriage came to a sad and volatile end. We felt that had we not been fighting so many battles we could have been a more stabilizing force in their lives. When promises of a career with John failed, it only added to the increasing list of other broken dreams. The young couple did not have the ability to withstand the storms. Our other children were affected terribly too. Jared would have to leave his classmates behind the day after his high school graduation and start all over in a new state and without the security that remaining in touch with high school friends affords. Trista would have to leave competitive gymnastics for a long season. All of us would suffer incredible losses. The pain and the guilt seemed endless for John and me.

The day did come when John was able to get a contract job in another state. With employment secured we went to an attorney to see what we should do about saving our beloved home. We are certain that we received bad counsel when the attorney suggested bankruptcy and recommended allowing the foreclosure to proceed. Indeed, as the years passed and we became more knowledgeable about what we had done, we were shocked to find out that the bankruptcy had not taken care of our debt, as papers had been filed incorrectly, and we could likely have made a deal with the mortgage company once we secured a steady income. We were battle weary and defeated.

Not long after we had moved onto the property *God had clearly shown me that there would come a day when we would be given a choice. The choice would be to cross the bridge (move away) or to stay. God was crystal clear that if we crossed the road (the bridge) that things would never be the same and that we could only look back with regret. He was showing me that it would seem logical to (leave), but in reality that would not be in our best interest.* I wrongly assumed the vision was symbolic for a future day and time. I believe at this writing that it was a literal vision, a warning, foreknowledge of the choice we would soon have to make.

So, in spite of the warning we drove off of the property, back across the bridge, leaving behind dreams and hopes for better days. The hardest part was leaving Leah. She had decided to stay behind, trying to recover from the recent divorce and the loss of so many dreams. Moving to a new state seemed to only complicate things further for her. Everything within my being screamed that we were making the wrong decisions, but at the same time, we seemed helpless to stop the process. I hoped until the last moving truck crossed the bridge that God would mightily intervene and keep us from making what I was beginning to understand was a huge mistake. Instead, He watched as the trail of small moving trucks rolled down the lane and up onto the asphalt subdivision streets. We had pushed our way out of the cocoon, the familiar security of home, it would fit us no more, we could not return. I dared not look back; the pain was simply too great.

As I began to put the finishing touches on this chapter God opened my eyes once again to see in a different light what exactly had happened or been explained that day by the pond.

The cocoon did represent the house we were living in, God had told me the property would be a safe haven, and it had been throughout all of the trials. Just as the growing pupa turns into a butterfly while hidden in the cocoon, we too had grown and learned while in our house. Just as storms buffet the cocoon, the winds and the rains and the enemy attacks, so had those things been allowed to happen to us during that time…it was all part of the plan.

Though we cannot see how the butterfly develops while inside of the cocoon we know nevertheless there is growth and change going on. God showed me that though most of those looking at our lives from a distance could not understand our trials and our tribulations, our changes, we were indeed growing in spite of the confining boundaries that God allowed us to live within, in spite of the fact that others could not clearly see what was happening. We were being prepared for another stage of our lives, and ultimately the work that God had for us to do. Even if the butterfly should try to return to the safety of the cocoon he would not fit, he could not go back inside the safe haven, the place he had found comfort in, even as he outgrew the protective surroundings. Likewise, because of choices we had made, or perhaps because that was God's plan all along and we have yet to understand, neither could we return to the safe haven of our beloved home once the decision had been made to leave. Instead of repairing, enlarging or restoring what we had begun to build and had lived within, we had to move away, and start a new part of our life somewhere else.

Just as the butterfly rests for a while after his fight to get out of the confines of the cocoon, God allowed us a time of rest when we arrived at our new place of residence in Arkansas. Perhaps we have rested long enough and our wings at this writing are nearly strong enough to fly into the wondrous plans that God has for us...but more likely I feel that we have remained in a time of rest as we continue to live with the consequences of our decisions. Just as God provides food for the caterpillar, He has made wondrous provision for us from the time we left our cocoon, crossed the bridge and embarked on our trek through the dessert of life. He continued to sustain us during our time in Tennessee, and would protect us from many more human errors as we learned to wait upon the revelation of His plans for us. Hopefully soon we too will fly free, totally finding the plans that God has for us, past mistakes forgotten and clapping our hands in joyous praise much as the yellow butterflies seems to praise the Lord with the floating and fluttering of their wings.

My Gift

It was the last weekend in August. John and I had rented a cabin in the woods and were enjoying a rare time of retreat and restoration. I was so thankful to have such an opportunity after the previous months of challenges and testing. I was propelled from my comfortable bed to the porch swing overlooking the majestic Arkansas Mountains. John was still sleeping peacefully and I had this moment to myself.

As I sat in the coolness of the early morning air, the dream of just a while earlier began to drift back through my memory. I now sought clarity of the dream and craved more fellowship with God.

There is such a difference in dreams that are revelations, information for the future and for instruction, than in the dreams of the idle mind caught up in sleep. There are those who would argue that God does not speak to us in such a way. But indeed He does as I have previously shared in this book. I am ever humbled by the fact that God takes the time to show me certain future miracles in just this way. It is not something that I can will to happen; though the Lord knows at times I beg Him for just such a confirmation. But the dreams come when God chooses, in His timing.

Perhaps I have a lack of faith and God knows I will need such revelations to walk the path He asks of me. I prefer to think that it's because once revealed, the story becomes even more profound, and obviously God-or-dained. There is such confirming purpose and rightness in the fulfillment of dreams and revelations. The simple everyday things of life suddenly take on new and holy meaning. Most of what we experience is extremely important in the tapestry of life. I have come to understand that there are very few insignificant events in our lives. Even at this writing, there are many aspects of the dream that I do not totally understand. I will ever wonder if human error once again changed the course of our ways, or if I had misunderstood some of what God chose to reveal to me in that dream. One thing is certain: *God revealed the arrival of a little girl into our home in a divine and supernatural way.*

I wrote the following about the vivid dream that awakened me: *The baby has dark straight hair. She is wrapped in a pink blanket, and dressed in lightweight clothes. Would we receive her in warm weather? The baby must be a girl. (I would never put a baby boy in pink clothes!) From how it felt when I held her for the first time, I knew that we would likely receive an infant. In the vision, the baby is lying on her stomach on my lap and could just barely maneuver her head to look about. When John took her from me, he had to handle her carefully. She smiled a very crooked smile at him, which won his heart. I felt emotion in this dream in a very intense way. We were not exactly thrilled at the prospect of parenting another baby, but we had a peace and knew that we were doing what God desired us to do. I remember a distinct feeling of humility.*

I knew without a doubt when I headed to the porch that morning that I had just been given a glimpse of our future. I hadn't the slightest idea how long it would be to fulfillment, but I knew it was from God. When I shared the news with John, he was a bit disheartened, as we had been talking the night before of goals that admittedly did not include plans for any other babies. Predictably as the days passed, John was able to accept the dream as a special word from God.

Having the dream and realizing that God had not given up on us was very exciting! It was a huge encouragement in the ongoing process of healing of some very deep wounds. I had fresh strength to go forward and a purpose in getting details in our home in order. Our energy was renewed just knowing that God would soon use us. We had gone on this retreat to get a new focus, to set goals. We came home with a new purpose and anticipation of what God was going to do. That weekend was like a new commissioning from God, and I was so thankful that He would choose to use us once again.

We had "spiritually conceived" on that trip, and now we had to go through the "adoptive pregnancy and delivery" of that special child. There would be many more confirmations from God to keep us on the appropriate track. There were also many lessons to be learned, for adoptive pregnancy, as I have shared before, comes with a whole set of unique risks and potential complications, not unlike a physical pregnancy.

> *In His timing He would give me a dream in a very clear way.*
> *God showed me the child—even the weather of that future day.*
> *I knew not when this child would arrive,*
> *But God once again had a plan that would literally drive*
> *Us to search and pray and seek His perfect plan.*

We received a phone call from the new director of our agency the day after we arrived home from the trip. The conversation was in response to two letters I had recently sent. One was to one of our children's biological mother and another to a friend that I had assumed still worked at the agency. Apparently, the director had read both letters.

He assured me that though he was relatively new to the position, the original vision given by God for the ministry was still in place and the spirit of adoption was alive and very real. Even at the time I thought the phone call and these statements rather odd. I had not considered that the ministry had changed in any way. I vaguely sensed in that conversation that he was trying to convince me of the validity of present policy and procedure. Instead of reassurance, he planted a seed of caution.

We visited for a while and during that time I shared with him the confirmation that we had regarding adopting again in God's timing. I don't recall telling him anything about the dream, but I did tell him that we knew recent revelations were from God. He assured me that the agency would be very happy to place another child with us and would keep our willingness in mind. John and I both felt that because of the timing and unsolicited nature of the call it was confirmation from God that He was indeed orchestrating yet another placement for our family.

John and I struggled with this new revelation and our inability to justify our motivation in a practical way. This would be child number nine for us. Our ages were nearing the 45-year-old mark, beyond the age limit most agencies establish for the placement of infants. Still recovering from financial devastation involving the loss of both our home and business, we had recently relocated to another state to secure employment.

We lost a business and many earthly possessions we had,
There were tough times, dark times, life was tremendously sad.
We blindly drove off from our home and our friends,
I couldn't see how God would ever give us children again.

We were starting over at an age when we should have been making retirement plans, but, nevertheless, God had His own plan. Logic was not an option. For us, it continued to be a requirement to go against the odds and follow the Holy Spirit's leading to 'walk on the water'…

"And Peter answered him, 'Lord, if it is you, bid me come to you on the water.' He said, 'Come.' So Peter got out of the boat and walked on the water and came to Jesus; but when he saw the wind, he was afraid, and beginning to sink he cried out, 'Lord, save me!' Jesus immediately reached out his hand and caught him, saying to him, 'O man of little faith, why did you doubt?'" (Matthew 14:28-31).

As long as we keep our eyes on Jesus, as Peter should have as He walked on the water to Christ, we are fine. When we start listening to those around us, the logic and the fears threaten to swallow us up and prevent us from finding God's best for our family. So, once again we attempted to keep our focus on what God could do, not on our own ideas with their limitations.

In November I had another dream. The second dream was more detailed and yet in some ways a replay of the first one in August. *A nurse or maybe a secretary I do not know, tells us about a baby girl needing a family. She approaches us because she feels specific leading from God to do so. We are surprised and not particularly prepared to take on the addition of an infant. We were not in search of a child. We seemed to delay accepting the information, letting it settle in our hearts and minds, not referring to the knowledge nor discussing it with much detail for a season. We seemed to put the info on a back burner and go on with life.*

In reality, things began to slowly play out closely to the way they had been revealed in my dreams. In my spirit I had known for a long time that one day, in God's time, a prompting would surely come. I had no clue when that time might be. Most details God reserves for Himself. Then one day, we received yet another phone call. If we weren't going to step out in faith, God would just call us!

I was not anticipating any great spiritual event that day. A secretary from the agency called and asked if we were interested in adopting once again. As soon as she asked the question, I began to smile. We had conceived a child in our spirits during the time of the first dream. The understanding that there would be another child had grown with the phone call from the director and then a second dream. Now here was another phone call.

The lady admitted that she was following the leading of the Holy Spirit. We were not on the list of potential families that the staff had given her to contact. She had waited until other phone calls had been fruitless before calling us.

Until that moment, she and I had never met or even talked on the phone. She had no knowledge of my conversation with the director several months before. There was no way that she could have known of the dreams or that God was preparing us for another adoption. She just knew that her instructions from God were to *'call that family that moved from Oklahoma. So, indeed, a lady in a secretarial position did approach us. Her motivation came from a specific leading by God. Once again, just as He had shown me in the second dream.*

After our initial introductions and a bit of friendly conversation, neither she nor I were surprised that little progress had been made in her attempt to find potential adoptive families that day. She and I both knew that we were the family that God had wanted contacted.

A new anticipation crept into our household. Everyone knew that God was at work and the excitement was rejuvenating to all of us. God was using this time of the "adoptive pregnancy" to prepare the hearts of our other children, especially the older girls. Each time the phone rang, it was like a jolt of electricity raced through all of us.

When it had been weeks with no contact from the agency and no other obvious confirmations that we were on a right path, our faith began to waver. Walking in blind faith makes the path seem very dim at times. I consoled myself with the knowledge that our wait had validity, as do all events in life, even when we cannot understand why.

Finally, I felt released to step out and make sure that required paperwork was in place at the agency. We had extensive files already there; however, I was sure an updated home study was needed. I was anxious to get that in order. I did not want to be the one responsible for any delays if indeed we were called to receive a baby. Besides, I badly needed to be doing something productive during this first trimester of our ninth adoptive pregnancy! The only thing I could to do was initiate the paperwork shuffle.

I called the agency to arrange the update of our home study and inform them I would be sending a new life book. Life books are compilations of photos, stories and other memorabilia about a prospective family, rather like fancy scrapbooks. They are made available to potential birth mothers. These are valuable tools used in matching birth families and adoptive families, especially in open adoptions. I requested that the social worker review what was on file and let me know what they still required from us. Among other things, we were told we needed to fill out forms recently created and specifically developed for Caucasian families desiring to adopt across racial lines. At first, we were agreeable.

However, as we read through the questionnaire, we realized that this was an unnecessary evaluation tool for our family, since most of the questions were directed toward couples considering transracial adoption for the first time. In fact, the questions no longer applied to us, since we already knew from our daily experiences how we would handle the exact situations they were asking us to ponder.

We were extremely frustrated that the present social worker would not even consider our family unless we filled out all of the details on the questionnaire. (Especially since I had previously presented several workshops on transracial adoption issues.) Nevertheless, we dutifully filled out the pages of questions and submitted them, along with some other updated information. We made the completion of these forms a priority, only to find out that the social worker did not take the time to read over the urgently requested forms for several weeks! Days went by with no response to our express-mailed questionnaire, or our phone calls.

This was especially frustrating because the original questionnaire had been brought to our attention via a phone call with the social worker, then faxed to us. The worker had implied the papers were urgently needed. When birth parents are waiting to know about potential adoptive families, and families are living on the edge of every last nerve they have, anticipating the arrival of a child, then those behind the desks at adoption facilities should make reviewing and compiling the material provided a priority. At the very least they should acknowledge the receipt of requested information—that alone would be an encouragement to waiting families. We felt abandoned and unimportant, as if we were pawns in a game of chess. Our hearts were on the line.

Meanwhile, subtle battles among the staff became apparent as I tried to communicate with different people. There was apparently a power play going on in an attempt to control circumstance needing no control, only obedience to the leading of the Holy Spirit. Where was that spirit of adoption that I had been so blatantly assured of, or the spirit of cooperation for that matter?

Christians in positions of authority are especially vulnerable to deception and have to carefully seek God. I did not expect the enemy to attack from within the agency. Regardless, the attack was very obvious. God was quick to remind me that the only weapons that can overcome obstacles are prayer, application of Scripture parallels, and determined faith. I was reminded of how the enemy uses every tactic in his arsenal to prevent children from the safe haven of Christian families.

As I searched for what we were to do, God clearly showed me that the book of Esther was to be both strengthening and instructive. It was soon obvious that the lady who had originally called me from the agency would become much like Esther in the coming months.

During the months that ensued, "Esther" and I talked many times. We were developing quite a delightful friendship. Mostly our conversations were about the spiritual things that she and I were being shown independently by God. She felt God had given her a unique burden for, and wanted her to intercede on behalf of, a specific young birth mother and her unborn child.

Of course she was unable to reveal any identifying information or circumstances; we just shared what God revealed in such a way as to keep moving forward. One of the revelations was a vision of the family that was to adopt this birth mother's baby. "Esther" was shocked when she saw our family picture in an updated packet. It revealed that *we were the family in her dream.* She felt *we were to receive this baby!* The craziest part came when we received a newsletter from the agency with a picture of the staff on the front.

The lady that I had vaguely seen in my dream had a remarkable likeness to one of the three ladies pictured on the newsletter. *Of course it was her.* We couldn't wait to meet in person! In spite of the obstacles we faced on the communication end with the agency staff, this bit of inside information confirmed to me that we had to be on a right path.

In one of our enlightening conversations, I learned that God had impressed upon "Esther" some specific, encouraging words that needed to be spoken to this birth mother. Unbeknownst to me, *I had penned almost exactly the words that God had told her should be spoken to this birth mother,* enabling her to make an appropriate decision. Those words were in the "dear birth mother" letter attached to the updated application I had recently sent.

After that experience, I have become very serious about asking God for the words that I am to include in "dear birth mother" letters, knowing full well that they are intended to minister to a specific person and as God directs. I remembered the twins' birth mother had a confirmation in her spirit that we were to parent her babies as soon as she read the letter I sent to her as well. Still, this present situation was even more incredible, given that I had no specific person to direct my words to, as I had in the case of the twins' mother.

Apparently, "Esther" did tell her coworkers about her dream and the things that I had shared with her, but the staff never understood the full impact of the importance of the events that God was clearly orchestrating.

I eventually received a phone call from the agency social worker explaining a mother had given birth to a baby girl. However, according to the social worker, the birth mother had not scored high enough on the written evaluation, designed to determine adoptive readiness. Based on this tool, the staff had opted not to present the birth mother with any prospective adoptive family life books until they could be sure that she was ready to make an adoption plan. I quietly wondered how she could make a plan without families to visualize and situations to ponder as she envisioned her future and the future she wanted for her baby.

The worker proceeded to tell me that most African American mothers decide to parent their babies because it is culturally acceptable. This is a story that we have heard repeatedly during our years in adoption. Historically I would have to agree. In reality, we live in a different time, a different age, and I believe that as these young mothers are freed from the bondage of cultural tradition. God moves in a mighty fashion in the lives of all people. God is interested in our souls, while we are overly interested in the color of skin, at least with regard to parenting or spiritual mentoring.

I reminded the worker that our family was seasoned in all areas of adoption and would willingly take the risk of our profile being presented to the birth mother and even rejected. I so felt this young woman needed to know and visualize that there was a family desiring to parent her child. Visualization is so important in making such ominous decisions. The worker tried to console me by explaining that I would not understand cultural issues.

As I hung up the telephone I wondered why the worker even called me since her conversation revolved solely around the likelihood that this baby would not be placed with us or anyone else. In reality there was no logical reason for me to even know of the birth of this child.

In another conversation a week or so later, I expressed concern over the fact that the birth mother had made a special effort to come to an adoption ministry because she felt she was to make an adoption plan for her unborn child. My concerns fell on deaf ears. Still I persisted, and eventually shared parts of my dreams and other events that had indicated to us that we were to work with this specific birth mother. As I talked, the social worker did begin to recall "Esther's" similar dream. She began to express some interest in my story at this point, but remained basically pleased with the birth mother's indecision. It validated her 'opinion' that this baby should stay within her culture. I wept.

To ease my frustration and to keep the peace, the agency arranged a conference call so that I might openly express my concerns and allow them opportunity to explain their actions with regards to these situations. Just before the scheduled phone conference I was reminded of James 1:20: "For the anger of man does not work the righteousness of God." I knew that regardless of how much anger I was feeling, I would not be allowed to express it or even mention my feelings at all. God desired me to be carefully quiet.

Reluctantly and with heart pounding, I found a quiet spot in order to give my full attention both mentally and spiritually to this phone conference. I felt like a lawyer preparing to present closing comments on behalf of his convicted client. I honestly felt the destiny of a child rested on my communication and I had miles of telephone lines and limited time to convince others of the urgency I felt in my heart. There is a note in my journal that I wrote just prior to the conference call. I felt God prompted it. *If men listen to God, this baby will soon be yours.* I KNEW God could redeem previous actions and bring the baby back, if people would humble themselves. It could be a second chance to right a wrong.

It was with a heavy heart that I hung up the telephone. I knew I had failed in my mission to convince the staff to at least consider contacting the birth mother one more time. John, who had been listening on the extension phone, felt too, that a baby's life path had been altered. I spent long hours in prayer. It is not for me to know if that young mother struggled with her decision to take the baby home, or if she found the peace and rightness in her life that she longed for. I wonder if she ever looked down at the baby and knew afresh that she was destined to have been somewhere else? Or, did she perhaps look upon her sleeping baby and thank God that she had not followed through with her original adoption plan?

We tread upon dangerous ground when clinical decisions leave little room for spiritual guidance. Christian agencies have a huge responsibility to listen to God. Without spiritual discernment, they are no different than the secular agencies that line the streets of America

I will always believe that a clinical approach, rather than a spiritual one, was used for evaluation by the staff. Sadly, this was not the only instance of just such an evaluation, as I would discover in the coming months.

Of course I never knew the entire story, and in the retelling of the events that took place I can only tell what I know. This means, most certainly, that all of the facts are not available. Only God truly knows what was to have been and whether His perfect will was done.

Neither the picture of our family nor the letter I wrote was ever presented to the birth mother that God had given us a burden for. She never knew there was a family that God had seemingly handpicked to parent her child. She was never given the opportunity to make a decision, even when God had revealed so clearly the steps that would confirm the placement plan He had for this child. Perhaps it was all just a stepping stone down the educational path of life. Or, perhaps it was a path altered. Only God knows the answers to my human inquiries.

Ecclesiastes 12:14 says: "For God will bring every deed into judgment, with every secret thing, whether good or evil."

I believe there were some windows in time when the powers that be could have humbled themselves and attempted to correct the mistakes that might have been made. No doubt it would have required some difficult calls and a great deal of humility. But, it would have been the right thing to do. Helpless to make happen what we thought was God's will, life went on and John and I waited prayerfully for something to turn events and bring the baby back to the agency. The only reason I found a measure of rest during this time was that I had sensed in the dream *that we had almost gotten a baby and then had to leave the location where the baby was, for reasons I could not understand.*

In January the agency called to ask if we would like our life book presented to a new mother. John and I talked and agreed that we did not feel this was a right path. We told them no.

In March "Esther" called again. She was at the hospital and a baby boy had just been born. Although excited at the news and rejoicing at the birth of another baby, I remember distinctly thinking: '*This does not affect us, this is not the baby we are waiting for.*' With that knowledge it was very easy to listen with the ear of friendship, and not the heart of an expectant mom.

It was during this phone call that I began to feel that "Esther" was in the inner court. It would soon become a common thread of thought, as God would begin to reveal to me some of what was apparently happening within the agency, using the Scriptures in the book of Esther as a parallel. Just as the Biblical Esther was privy to information inside the courts, so was "Esther" within the agency.

She learned that the director had made a decision not to contact any other family, including us, until this birth mother had signed her termination of parental rights in front of the judge. From a business perspective, it was a logical way to proceed. In fact, within many agencies, that is policy and procedure, no exceptions. In this particular ministry, that had not been the case. In the past, openness between the birth mother and the adoptive family had been a huge part of the success of the ministry. Removed, it changed the entire process.

The Jews were released from the edict in the third month: "The king's secretaries were summoned at that time, in the third month, which is the month of Sivan, on the twenty-third day and an edict was written, according to all that Mordecai commanded concerning the Jews" (Esther 8:9). I knew without a doubt that the third months was significant because of the way God kept bringing my attention to specific dates and details in this Scripture verse—also because of the timing I had sensed in the dream and now because the words stood out boldly as I pored over the Scriptures seeking direction from the Lord.

On the very day the Jews were to be overtaken, (their destinies forever changed) they gained power over their foes (Esther 9:1). I wasn't sure how this Scripture applied to our present situation, but I felt the Lord clearly telling me to use it for instruction and confirmation. I assumed the Jews' situation paralleled the children we were presently aware of, and that somehow the right child would be released (to us in this instance) and overcome the foes that had previously oppressed and prohibited the placement. It would be a great victory toward the fulfillment of God's plan.

I continued to believe the baby girl born in December would somehow end up back in agency custody. I was content to wait on the three months period to pass, and assumed God had a plan to get the little girl back into a position which would enable her to join our waiting family. I had my heart set on a girl, and believed the desire to be from God. The older girls also had their hearts set on getting a girl this time, so we were finding it very difficult to believe that God intended for us to take this little boy. Still, we knew that we rarely understand events in life, and realized that God might well be planning on this little guy joining our family.

As we puzzled over what to do I was directed to James 1:3 "Knowing this, that the trying of your faith worketh patience" (KJV). As I was reading the 'vital statistics' listed at the beginning of this chapter in my Bible, I saw the reason the book of James was written in the first place. It was to expose hypocritical practices and to teach correct Christian behavior. So, once again I felt the Holy Spirit had led me to read passages that would help me specifically in our present situation.

John and I had agreed long ago to be willing to accept any child that God desired us to parent. This little boy would certainly be no exception. The love always comes. Still, the hours just before the dawn of understanding and confirmation are often very dark, difficult hours for me and to a lesser extent for John and the other children.

As I prayed and read my Bible, the story of Abraham was brought to my attention. I felt we were being reminded that when Abraham got ahead of God, Ishmael was conceived.

God allowed the conception, and for a season I am sure that Abraham thought Sarah's suggestion was going to be a fulfillment of the promise of God. Thus a warning, we might be presented with a child (or had we been in the case of the little girl several weeks previously?) that would seem to fulfill the promises made in the dreams and revelations, or one that might seem to replace another child. I knew that we had to proceed carefully or we would bring home an Ishmael and not an Isaac, as God had promised.

Finally John and I decided that if we were presented the option of the little boy we would delay making a commitment to him until we had passed the three months that I had felt were so important in the dream. The little girl that had seemed destined for our family would be three months old in just a few days and we felt that either God would allow the day to come and go as a confirmation that we were to consider other babies, or at the final hour the baby girl would somehow come back to us.

In my journal I noted several parallels to the Scriptures in the book of Esther. In Scripture, Esther is granted entrance into the inner court when King Ahasuerus places the royal crown upon her head and makes her the new queen. Eventually, she intercedes for her Jewish people.

Esther begged the king to avert the evil design that Haman had initiated against the Jews. Like Esther, on many occasions our agency contact had tried to open the eyes of the staff members to see the wrongs that were being done to all members of the adoption triad under the present procedures.

As God consistently directed me to read in the book of Esther, I began to see a parallel between the Jews in the Bible, and the babies and birth mothers who are also victims of the society in which they live. At least it seemed that is what God wanted me to see. Esther asked that the king revoke the original orders given against the Jewish people. I could only speculate what had been going on within the "inner courts" of the agency. Based on what we had recently been experiencing, we were seeing that many decisions made regarding birth mothers and their children were as wrong as those made against the Jewish race referenced in the Scriptures. Perhaps the director of the agency was not unlike the king in Scripture, depending upon those underneath his authority to make decisions and to give him counsel. Those in authority can be vulnerable for great deception.

In Esther 9, when Esther came before the King, he asked her what her petition was. Esther requested the conquering of the enemies of the Jews continue. I suspect that our "Esther" became bolder in her petitions to the director with regard to the biased decisions that seemed to be keeping children out of their destined families. The seed of change was being planted. I shall always believe that this was the beginning of restoration toward the original purpose of that ministry.

Just as the Esther in Scripture had guidance from God, I felt that He gave us a specific outline to follow. The first thing that John and I had to do was calculate the cost. We were not likely going to win popular votes with our insistence that our vision did not exactly line up with the plan the agency staff might prepare. We fervently sought God's will. Clearly we were to pray and seek direction and hope for obvious confirmations of what God desired us to do.

We were not to complicate anything by moving ahead of God. Our instructions were to primarily wait upon the Lord. There was the potential for error in our day-to-day walk, and there was also a huge potential for error within the "inner court."

Meanwhile, there continued to be discord within the ranks of the agency.

Esther had responded, "If I perish, I perish." I truly believed that our "Esther" knew she was taking chances with her position should she overstep her boundaries, which I am sure at times she did. We admired her obedience, doing what she believed God had given her to do within that inner court of the agency. I prayed earnestly for God's vision of what He desired to be done.

While waiting, I naturally went over the dreams of several months before. I replayed them many times in my mind, rereading numerous times the journal entries to ensure that we did not add to, nor forget any of the details written while the revelations were clear in my mind. *I was sure that there was a definite three month time period from the first notification of the baby girl and the actual receiving of a child.* I still did not understand what I knew, but that knowledge was very real. I also knew and found great comfort in the understanding that *once I received the correct child I would have no doubts.* It was an outcome to look forward to, one that kept us on the edge of our seat for many weeks.

It was a Friday evening and things seemed to finally be coming into focus. I was on my way out to shop for the baby I believed we would eventually get. Just as I was stepping out the door, the phone rang. Something drew me back inside the house. John was being told that his last day at his present contract would be the following Friday, one week away! He hung up the phone and the focus of just a few minutes earlier was lost. I called friends for prayer. We cancelled the home study. We stumbled our way through the weekend with not one clue of what was to happen. We were puzzled at this turn of events.

Having a contract end unexpectedly was hard enough, but not nearly as hard as wondering how this would affect the anticipated placement of a new baby in our arms. Or, was the timing just perfect? If we had known that unemployment was in the near future we would never have allowed the seed of love for the next child to begin to grow. Now it would be very hard emotionally to just stop the whole process. Also, only a few days remained on those significant three months.

What was God allowing to transpire? The wind was gone from our sails. We were trying to keep faith in a plan that we could no longer see. We tried to relax. We tried not to panic. I can truthfully say God was gracious and the peace that passes all understanding did indeed permeate our hearts and home that long weekend. Still, the questions floated incessantly in the recesses of our minds despite the peace that prevailed.

Within four days, John was offered a contract job in another state. This was a pleasant surprise and an incredible answer to our prayers. After the previous three years of odd jobs, business losses and fear, we had quickly prepared ourselves for the worst. Thankfully, this time the worst was not going to be allowed to happen. We were immensely happy and thankful for the job security, even if it meant a major move once again.

Maybe now things would fall into order for the baby. Gymnastic meets were ending soon, AWANA programs were finishing for the year, and school lessons were winding up. Everything seemed to be falling into a place that would make relocation a bit easier, except the anticipated adoption.

I wanted to pack up and move as soon as possible. Having experienced many job-related separations requiring single parenting skills over the years, I had no desire to be apart from John again unless absolutely necessary. As it turned out, we would spend the entire summer at that location, packed and ready to move at a moment's notice. I am thankful I did not know ahead of time how long it would be before we would be released to go.

Meanwhile I learned that the birth mother of the little boy was still requesting contact with us, and asking if we would come and see the baby. I would never learn why these requests were delayed, or denied, but I was greatly burdened for that baby and his mother. I wrote in my journal that I could not tell if I was more frustrated at the inconvenience our family had gone through since the birth of the baby girl in December, or in the knowledge of the great injustices that I was witnessing in regard to birth mothers and the destinies of the babies entrusted to the care of the agency.

It appeared more clearly than ever that the falling number of placements and failed ministry situations were the fault of the agency staff. Policy and procedure were causing the purpose of the ministry to corrode and crumble from within. The spirit of adoption was no longer in that place. I began to earnestly intercede, begging for the original vision and purpose to be restored. If it could not be restored to a more spiritual ministry, then I prayed it would officially be stopped, before there was more heartache.

During a conference call, the birth mother was adamant she wanted to place her baby boy. Her voice begged for closure, and I ached when I realized she would not likely get it under the present circumstances. The baby was several weeks old and she had consistently stated that she wanted her baby in an adoptive home. Once again forms and charts were being used to evaluate the mother's readiness to place. The birth mother lacked one point scoring high enough for the social worker to allow the adoption plan to proceed.

Once again it was obvious a clinical decision was being made for a spiritual need-I was so very saddened.

John and I were reasonably sure after the phone conference that though we were willing to take him, and would love him dearly, this little boy was not the baby God had for our family. We did feel that his mother was to make an adoption plan, so we decided that the way we could most minister to her was to make a trip to meet her. Of course it was too late on Friday when we finally agreed on a plan. We would have to wait until Monday to get permission from the agency to meet this birth mother.

As we adjusted to the knowledge that we would soon be moving and waited to know if we would be traveling to Oklahoma to meet this birth mother, the flu bug came in full force that weekend and caused several of us to be very sick. It made John's departure on Monday morning even harder on me. With no decision on the baby, sole responsibility for a household of eight sick people, a lack of rest, and complete unknowns about the future, I was truly tested.

On Tuesday, still tired from illness and emotionally weary from the roller coaster ride of the previous weeks, the children and I left for Oklahoma, where the agency had agreed we could meet. I was not prepared for the heavy, angry feelings I sensed when I entered the offices. The spiritual warfare in that place was strong and very unpleasant to experience. The atmosphere was radically different than what I had experienced in the past, as an adoptive parent and as a board member. It was a sad confirmation that the impressions God had given me in the spirit were reality.

Part of the staff and I went to meet the birth mother at lunchtime. We had picked up the baby from the foster care home as well. During lunch I was the one who held the little boy. I distinctly remember thinking that *I wasn't holding my baby, but someone else's.* Of course I did not speak those words. I remained quiet and attentive to what God would have me to do.

When we dropped the birth mother off at work, she looked me in the eye and asked me to take her baby home. I knew she was sincere, almost begging me to do this. I was sad that I was outside the inner court, and helpless to make things happen for her. Verbally I told her that we would pray about what God would have everyone to do, and tried to smile reassuringly as she walked heavily away from my van, leaving her baby once again in the care of others.

I called John after the meeting, and he and I agreed that for us to accept this precious baby would be wrong. As much as we longed for a placement, this was not the right situation.

I was clearly aware that we were now in the midst of what God had given me warning about through the Scripture regarding Ishmael and the future birth of Isaac. Not having a clue how to handle the present circumstances, I begged God for divine intervention.

The director and I had a long, serious talk. In a tense conversation, I told him that John and I did not feel the little boy was to join our family. After meeting the birth mother, I was convinced that she was to place her baby for adoption, but there had to be another family specifically waiting for this special little one. It would be very wrong for us to accept a baby that was intended for another family.

I was appalled at the turn the conversation then took. I was told in no uncertain terms that I would be going against policy and a promise made to a birth mother, if we decided not to take this baby boy. The staff had told this birth mother that we would adopt her baby, and we now had no choice in the matter!

I couldn't believe my ears! I was sitting in the midst of a conversation that now totally confirmed my worst fears.

Policy was once again going to far outweigh the spiritual knowledge given during the preceding weeks. We had never told anyone we would take this baby. We had never told the agency we planned to adopt him. We had in fact, told the staff that we felt we were to wait on a little girl. I had made clear my reasons for requesting a meeting with the birth mother- I felt I could minister to her, and I needed to confirm my feelings via a face-to-face meeting, in order to be sure we were making a correct decision.

I can still remember the disbelief I felt when the director told me that I had no choice but to take this baby if the birth mother signed the appropriate papers!

I felt violated and manipulated. How must young and vulnerable birth mothers feel when they are told that the most difficult decision they had ever needed to make was not culturally correct? Or that they had not passed a high enough score to be 'allowed' to make an adoption plan?

Now, here I sat, experienced in adoption, in parenting, and in walking as closely as I knew how to the Lord, and I was being told that I would be the criminal in this case if I did not do what the agency deemed the appropriate thing for their credibility!

I assured the director that I would in no way be a part of this plan. God would have to move in a definitive way before I would accept the word of man over the instructions I knew to be from God. Acts 5:29 states: "But Peter and the apostles answered, 'We must **obey God** rather than men.'"

I walked away, knowing full well that my boldness had likely shut the door for future placements from this agency. I had to wonder how we would ever get a little girl, and I had to wonder what God was going to do within that agency to stop this fraud. Late that night I left Oklahoma, arriving home in the wee hours of the morning with a carload of weary children, and a very heavy heart.

A couple of weeks went by and I nearly drowned in the thoughts swirling through my head.

From "Esther's" position within the agency's inner court, I learned that this birth mother was 'tested' once again. One point kept her from passing with a high enough score to be taken to the judge to sign termination of her parental rights. She would sign the termination papers as soon as she knew that a family was going to pick up her baby and take him home. She did not want him to stay long-term in foster care. She continued to be verbally adamant that she wanted her baby placed in an adoptive home. To our knowledge, no other families were ever presented to her.

I believe once again that if she had been assured there was a family for her baby, she would have immediately scored high enough on the test to be allowed to proceed with an adoption plan for her son. The one 'point' was the unknown future of her baby should she decide to relinquished him to the custody of an agency. She would then lose all power to be a part of any decisions made regarding her child.

These were very valid concerns and to me, she showed her love and maturity, not her inability to make a decision. I could never understand when the weeks went by and she remained committed to placing him, why the agency did not take her to the court to sign the mandatory papers, except that she was caught up in a vicious circle of inability to please everyone.

I am sure she had to wonder what happened to our family, and why I did not come forward to talk to her or commit to the baby. I don't want to know what she might have been told. I will always fear she was deceived.

Days later the director called to tell us the birth mother had picked her baby up. The staff had reassured her she could parent her son, along with the other children she already single parented with a great deal of effort and stress. Since, to my knowledge, the staff had not presented her with any other adoptive family profiles, I can only assume that she thought there was no family for her little boy.

Then the director briefly mentioned another situation that had unexpectedly presented itself. The state had called this agency to see if they had a family for an African American baby girl. It was a tough situation. If the agency did not find a family, this baby would go into the state system. Though it does happen on occasion, it is really very unusual for the state to solicit the help of a Christian agency in making adoptive placements.

This time God had miraculously placed a worker within the inner court of the state system. She was trying to keep this baby from being caught up, possibly for years, in a system gone crazy. The birth mom was a very young teen in a crisis situation. I remember little else about the conversation. The Holy Spirit came down over me in such a way that I had to contain myself from shouting *'That's my baby!'* I controlled my natural instinct and calmly reminded the director of the vision I had the previous December. Surprisingly, he allowed me to ask a few more details.

The baby in the dream was tiny, rather like McKenzie had been, only smaller. This baby was very tiny, only 4 plus pounds. The director told me that there would likely be medical expenses, and they did not yet have government assistance in place. Ordinarily that would have been a definite red light in our present transitional situation. However, in the dream, *we had to make a commitment to the baby without the medical bills being taken care of.* The baby was spitting up and not maintaining body temperature. Again, nothing to be alarmed about, perhaps because I had been shown in the dream *that she would be frail and not healthy at first.* If this was our baby, we would likely be traveling around Easter weekend; the weather would be lovely and spring like during that season of the year. *It had been warm spring-like weather in the dream.*

It had now been three months since the first conversations regarding the baby girl born in December. I knew three months was significant, but I had thought that the original situation might work out. Although this wasn't exactly the way I had thought things would transpire, it felt indescribably right. I was once again shocked when the director told me that he would find out more details and get back to me. I truly never expected this agency to work with us again after the confrontation we had a few weeks earlier.

When I returned home from errands that evening, Jared said that Leah had called. She wanted to tell me about a dream she had. Before I ever returned her call I knew it had to be about this baby girl. She told me that she had slept from about two in the afternoon until seven that evening. While sleeping, she had a dream. *In the dream she was mad at me because I had not told her that the baby boy's mother had changed her mind! And…that we knew about another baby that we were going to take!* She was dreaming about the events at the very time I was talking to the director on the phone! The following lines are what I penned just after that conversation.

Even in obedience we often do not have understanding of what we are doing. In obedience there is peace, even joy, but not necessarily the understanding that we seek. For that understanding of all things is for God to know. It is a sacred knowledge that even those closest to the Father are not often privileged to understand. It is at those times we must accept a Father who simply states to us, "Because…I AM." In order for our faith to be ensured, our love to be shared, and our lives to move on, it is time for us as a family to receive another child. Failure to get hold of this blessing will be spiritually defeating, faith wavering, and life altering, for every member of our family. We need God to move mightily, miraculously and clearly in this situation, NOW!

We traveled on Good Friday to greet the long awaited addition to our family. There were still many frustrations, as the agency required us to jump through more hoops and endure the holiday weekend before we could receive temporary custody of our new baby

In the dream *I knew that her name would be very important. Her life would touch the hearts of many. A testimony would evolve out of her story.* (This was also specifically revealed to "Esther" as well, so I know that this detail is an important one in a way we do not yet fully comprehend.) "Esther" and I had toyed with names off and on in our phone conversations. It was interesting how we often thought of the same names, though days would go by without our speaking to one another.

Victoria (fondly called Tori most of the time at home) was the obvious choice. It means 'victory in the Lord'. Indeed that was what we were finally about to participate in, a victory for the Lord! I had not been able to find a peace with any middle names that I had found. At the last minute, before traveling to Oklahoma, I ran to the public library in search of a name book. There was only one old, dusty name book left on the shelf. Disappointed I checked it out and went home, doubting that this outdated book would contain my answer. I sat down at the kitchen table with a glass of tea and opened the musty smelling book. I can still recall how, bold and black, one word on the page appeared. Naturally my eyes fell on that word-Aisling. The definition of Aisling (pronounced ash-ling) seemed to jump off of the yellowed page: Irish for 'dream or vision'! I never turned another page of that book.

Finally the day arrived. We were once again all dressed and polished, motivated, and very anxious to touch our latest blessing. It was hard for us to believe that something real might actually be going to happen after all of the disappointments of the previous months.

I sat on a couch in the office with John looking on, surrounded by all the other children. The social worker gently opened the tiny bundle of blankets and carefully handed the treasure to my eager, aching arms. The very first thing that Victoria did when she saw all of us peering into that cozy little *pink* blanket was *smile!* Remember, *the Lord had told us that it would be her smile that would win our hearts!* Well, with one glance at that crooked smile she melted right into the hearts of all nine of us. It was an instant bond!

While the worker who had presented Victoria to us looked upon this scene, she shared the following story. Although she had not been the social worker that we had been dealing directly with, this worker knew of the tension and long-suffering that had been a part of this placement. She admitted that logically she thought the baby should be placed with someone else. However, when she had arrived at the hospital to pick up the baby, God told her 'This is My gift to SuDawn'. She said that the voice seemed audible, and that she understood that God was clearly telling her there were to be no strings attached, no room for logic in this placement. Victoria was a gift. I was very humbled, as the worker had obviously been, when God made His desire so very clear. *The humility I experienced in the dream became a confirming reality as the worker spoke those surprising words.*

> *Finally, a call would come one day,*
> *We would travel the road to meet the daughter that God determined*
> *   would stay*
> *A part of our family as true to His word*
> *God spoke to a friend and these are the words that she heard—*
> *"This child is a gift to this family from Me*
> *No strings attached, no interference, you see?"*
> *The years tumbled by us, our hearts opened wide,*
> *There were 10 of us to welcome Victoria Aisling,*
> *Our hearts swelled with pride.*

I did wonder though, as the days went by, if indeed it had been God's will to place the first baby girl in December with us, as I had felt initially in my spirit. It is possible that the first situation was just a preparatory step toward Victoria. I doubt we will ever be able to know. Regardless, I was thankful this worker was listening with her heart even under adverse conditions, and I am sure God honored her obedience.

A couple of days later while filling out the legal papers, the worker mentioned that if this baby had as sweet a smile as her birth mother, we could expect to be blessed. She said that even in the midst of the sadness of relinquishing her baby, the birth mother had a precious, innocent smile. I shall always think that a smile is a special link in this adoption triad, a continuance from one generation to the next. Oh, my goodness, the details that God takes care of! The worker did not know that her statement was just another huge confirmation of what God had previously revealed.

We knew when we made a commitment to the baby we would know nothing about her. Our instructions from God were to take the risk and take her home. Those words from the dream were very helpful, since we knew less about Victoria than any of the other children we have brought home. Because the agency had little relationship with the birth family, and because it all happened in such a short time, there was little information to pass on to us. (It has been our experience that we rarely have as much information as we would like, but this time we had virtually nothing in hand as far as prenatal or family history). Also, her conception and delivery story were a new kind of risk for us and would involve many issues we had not dealt with before.

Victoria was *the tiniest baby* we had ever brought home. She weighed only four pounds and twelve ounces at birth, and little more when we first held her.

I know that each time we as parents hold our children for the first time we note every tiny toe and every precious wrinkle on their bodies. But, I still find it fascinating as I write this how God chose to reveal so many minute details about this child. I find it a huge testimony to the care that God has for our lives, and His attention to detail!

The details go on and on with regard to the way that the dream played out once we had Victoria. The day we actually received custody of Victoria was a confusing and tiring day, at least for me. There were difficulties in getting things notarized, papers misplaced, and people gone from offices that needed to supply mandatory paperwork. The enemy made one last valiant effort at foiling this placement. We were approaching the end of the business day, and of course it was a Friday! In the end, "Esther" was once again the lady that insisted we take the baby and assured us we were being obedient. She was determined, even when I was getting too weary to go on, that it was time for us to have custody of this baby. *Her insistence was of God.*

With a great deal of profoundness, the Holy Spirit once again entered my van and my mind as I drove toward Leah's apartment with that precious bundle safely snuggled in her car seat. *In the dream, the baby had been in the lady's car.* Just moments before we transferred Victoria to our van, she had been in "Esther's" car! Just as it had been in the dream, *the sun was hot, the day spring-like, the lady insisting that we take the baby.* I had been so caught up in the aggravations of the day that I had not even thought about the dreams for hours, maybe days. But, my goodness, when God brought these things to my attention, I was overwhelmed with spiritual confirmation and motivation to hold fast to this dear child's life.

There had been a sense of confusion in the original dreams about our family having been at some camp or place we were staying, something I couldn't quite define. Well three different times during the three months of this unfolding saga we had stayed with Leah in her efficiency apartment while visiting in Oklahoma. With Leah, her roommate, and eight members of our family staying in two rooms it could very well be described as 'camping' or staying in a 'cabin' or 'motel'. Inevitably there was lots of confusion and clutter and stress within the confining quarters of the apartment. *We were very tired of the circumstances just as I had sensed in the dream we would be.* It had gone on a very long time, there had been many tiring and stressful trips to the waiting room, and God had forewarned us perfectly.

Throughout Victoria's adoption I was reminded time and again of how the Bible can be used and applied as readily today as in times past. I came to rely on Scripture more than I had in previous adoptions, primarily because of the leading of the Holy Spirit to seek out stories such as Abraham and Isaac and the story of Esther. In reflecting upon that time I find it interesting the Bible seemed so utterly clear and instructive. Then, in rereading them in preparation for this text they were wonderful to read, but I failed to experience the same motivational surge or path enlightening understanding as I had during the time of seeking and crisis. I was reminded of how profoundly God loves us, and how He desires to direct us in many ways.

In her foster home, Victoria was referred to as Grace, which means kindly, patient, full of grace. The supporting Scripture was John 15:16: "You did not choose me, but I chose you and appointed you that you should go and bear fruit and that your fruit should abide; so that whatever you ask the Father in my name, he may give it to you."

We also learned that Victoria in Latin meant conqueror. The spiritual connotation-a triumphant spirit, and the supporting Scripture for that was Philippians 4:19: "But my God shall supply all your needs according to His riches in glory by Christ Jesus."

Victoria-gift from God, a promise fulfilled a victorious answer to prayers after miraculous revelation given in the form of a dream. When all hope of adding the children that I believed God had promised was lost, God gave us Victoria.

When I am frustrated or tired I have only to recall those words, 'this child is My gift to SuDawn.' The memories of those words give me encouragement that goes beyond explanation. I am empowered to move on in joy. In receiving Victoria, my faith was restored. Pain and questions from the past months faded, and I could finally begin to focus on the parenting promises that lie on the road ahead, knowing we could walk in His will on His path from this point forward— gifted with a new beginning, another chance.

Hidden for Glory

John had been working in Tennessee for many months and we were all very weary of the long distance relationship. Trips to house hunt had seemed fruitless and my faith was wavering. It was a hot Fourth of July weekend. With newspaper ad in hand, we had driven down the long asphalt lane to the property advertised as a three-bedroom ranch home. The setting was so peaceful and was a good distance off of the main county road. I told John that even if the house was a bit small I could live "back here." The house was set among trees at the back of several acres of property, and bordered on one side by a small wooded lot. It would be a perfect, private place for rowdy boys to run, jump and make lots of noise at play. I had a sense of sadness that it appeared so small from the driveway, because it felt very right as we drove up to take a peek. It was Sunday and the leasing company was only taking voice mail applications. The children and I returned later that day to Arkansas, disappointed that our two days of intense searching had failed to turn up a place for us to rent. John continued to search newspaper advertisements and even pursued rather seriously a piece of property in a more remote area of Mississippi.

Finally, one day late in August, weary of the search and of the wait, he called the leasing company about the house we had driven by over the July holiday weekend. Out of desperation, John decided to make an appointment to see the property. As soon as he walked through the front door and saw the view through the oversized patio door overlooking the back part of the property, he knew we would enjoy living in the house. Deceivingly small at first glance from the driveway, the house had an open floor plan and some bonus rooms that he knew instinctively I could recreate into living spaces that would make up for the lack of bedrooms that we needed. The leasing agent agreed to call the owners, took John's deposit check and called back in just a few hours after checking references, to say that we could move in whenever we desired. We officially moved to the state of Tennessee over Labor Day weekend.

In retrospect, we now believe that God kept that specific house available until we were desperate enough to finally call on it. It was a perfect fit for our family for more than five years. The bonus rooms had to frequently be changed around, accommodating the addition of new children, the moving in and out of adult children, and sibling rivalry, but it worked incredibly well for a three bedroom house.

Now, here I stood in the middle of a huge gleaming kitchen complete with pantry and adjoining laundry room. I was gloriously happy! Unpacking was easy with extra space and soon the formal dining room became a library, the office a small schoolroom and a basement family room a large bedroom for the boys.

Leah had called just days after we moved into the house in Tennessee to say that she was planning to get married again. We began to plan a small wedding in Arkansas, halfway between our new home and Oklahoma, where she still lived. Over long distance, while unpacking, I was trying to help her plan a wedding on a shoestring budget! The holidays were fast approaching as well, so we needed to figure into the equation all of the typical holiday get-togethers, shopping and decorating. From a summer in the waiting room, I found myself quickly thrust into the fast forward lane of life!

Then came the fateful morning when the phone rang and in disbelief I heard my sister-in-law say that my mother had suffered a heart attack during the night. Mom had just returned from a vacation and sounded rested and happy in our phone conversation the evening before, so I was not expecting this news at all.

By noon the older girls, Victoria and I had packed a few things into the car and were on our way to Missouri. We would stay for just over a month in a hotel next to the hospital as Mom's seemingly routine heart surgery turned into our worst nightmare. She never fully recovered and died the day after Thanksgiving that year. Numbed and fatigued, the girls and I returned to Tennessee to pick up the pieces of life and make attempts to establish a home in the house we had left abruptly a few weeks after moving in.

All too quickly, about two weeks later, we loaded up the entire family and found ourselves on the road once again. We headed to a bed and breakfast establishment in a small Arkansas town just a few miles from where my dad lives. After a short yet sweet ceremony, Leah and Hector were officially man and wife and we headed back to Tennessee just in time to get ready for the holidays. So much of life was crammed into such a few short weeks! I was sure that there would never be enough of me to physically and emotionally meet the needs of this family God had so graciously blessed us with!

Needing a fresh start and ready to reunite with the family after a couple of years on her own, Leah soon called to say that she and Hector were going to move to Tennessee to be nearer to all of us. Their U-Haul truck was backed up to our garage Christmas weekend and all of their earthly possessions unloaded quickly in order to return the truck before the Christmas holiday officially began. They would come to stay for a couple of weeks and live with us for over eighteen months as they established their lives together and we all tried to find our purpose in this new state.

In the spring Leah gave birth to Angelica Hope, our first granddaughter. Attended by a wonderful Christian midwife, Leah had Angelica at home as her proud daddy and I lovingly welcomed her into our special multicultural family. Her unique ancestry attributed to her liquid brown eyes and perky dark hair. She was indeed a treasure to behold, this child of Asian, American and Spanish heritage.

In spite of my attempts to stifle the knowledge that God intended to gift us with yet more children, my spirit could not deny the knowing that God had someone else for us. Our lives seemed so full and happy and busy, and now we had a grandchild. As is my nature, I once again began to question God. We had no connections with any Tennessee adoption agencies. I didn't have a clue where to start applying. On a very tight budget and with a full house of people, I couldn't see how this could possibly come about. But my limited vision has nothing to do with finally seeing and following God's plan!

Another holiday season came and went and I continued to know that God was working His plan to add to our family. We had filled our days with obtaining kid goats, baby chicks and eventually a small flock of sheep. Hoping to move onto acreage soon, we were gathering our farm supplies. Still, the nagging that there was another little person coming our way persisted, regardless of how busy or full my days seemed to be.

Holiday decorations would be packed away and we would be into the long gray days of winter before our God would prompt me once again. One day, around noon, I began to experience an awareness of a burden that I could not define. I continued to teach the children in the schoolroom while trying to discern what it was that I was feeling. I brushed off the thoughts for a while, even considering that they were hormonal fluctuations and reprimanding myself to get a grip on things and focus on the task at hand.

I refused lunch and trudged determinedly onward with grading papers and preparing for the lessons we needed to do in the afternoon. The feelings persisted and even intensified, so much so, that by early afternoon I was no longer able to concentrate and sent the children on to other things as I searched for answers to the roller coaster of emotions I was undeniably experiencing.

As I sought God's direction and prayed earnestly for understanding of such strong and yet indefinable feelings, I somehow came to a realization *that somewhere there was a birth mother either giving birth or agonizing over a decision to relinquish her baby and make an adoption plan. I could only have known this in the spirit; there was nothing within my realm of present circumstances that lent itself to the possibility of a placement or the knowledge of any birth mother. I knew little else, except that I felt like I was experiencing the same emotions that I would experience if I were giving birth and having to make a placement decision.* It didn't make any sense, but I might as well have been going through the birth myself. I was growing weary under the burden as the day progressed and the puzzlement over what was happening increased.

I left everyone home with Leah as I drove Trista to gymnastics that afternoon. I was in desperate need of some time alone, and I had an intense desire to find out what I was experiencing. After dropping Trista at the gym, I began to drive slowly home through the afternoon traffic. I could not control the tears that spilled over the steering wheel, and yet I had no clue why I was so burdened. I remember clearly the stop sign that I was at when the revelation came to me: *Somewhere, there was a birth mother who was giving birth, or who had recently given birth to a little boy and she was agonizing over the decision before her. God was asking her to place this child for adoption. Although she knew it was best, she was struggling with disbelief and all the questions that come from a decision presented without forewarning. I remember asking out loud, "God, what do you want me to do with this information, where in the world is this child, and what am I supposed to do?"*

I came home and decided that the only thing I knew to do was to call the agency in Oklahoma and see if anything was developing there. I had talked to them a few days prior with regards to something else and knew a birth mother had recently delivered but decided to keep her baby. I thought perhaps she had returned after changing her mind.

Our phone was being used when I got home, and by the time I had a chance to call the agency, they were gone for the evening. I left a message on the answering machine and tried unsuccessfully to call my friend, Carrie*, at home. All I could do now was wait for another day to dawn.

At 10 a.m. the next morning, our phone rang. It was Carrie returning my calls, wondering what was going on with me. I shared what had happened the day before. I had scribbled my feelings on a piece of yellow legal paper and tucked it into my Bible around midnight the night before. I had been prompted by God to get up and write down what had happened. Once again, those writings would give me a boost of faith when the path began to grow dim. I was truly surprised when she told me that oddly, they had received a phone call from a mother about midmorning the day before (about when the feelings first started happening). This was not someone they had been working with. The hospital staff had given her a list of agencies to call when she had decided to investigate placing her baby for adoption. The social worker was going to meet the birth mother in just a few minutes! Carrie promised to call me and let me know the results of that meeting before the end of the day, all she knew at this point was — the baby was a boy!

I never heard back from anyone. All weekend we wondered how the meeting had gone and if it was our son that the worker had gone to see. Finally, on Monday afternoon late I could stand it no longer and called to talk with the social worker. This was the same worker that had challenged me during Victoria's adoption.

I timidly asked the social worker if I could write down my feelings of the previous Thursday and send them in a letter to be shared with the birth mother. I really felt that this was what I was to do next. She agreed and I must admit, I was a bit surprised at her willingness to allow this step. In a frenzy I wrote down the feelings, visions and revelations of that previous Thursday and one hour later raced to a location where the letter could be faxed to the worker who was scheduled to meet with the birth mother in just a few minutes. Not only did the worker agree to present my letter, but she also delayed leaving for the appointment until the letter could arrive. I was encouraged and again, surprised at this change of attitude from our last placement.

Another night of unknowns and questions had to be endured. The next day, while I was shopping, my cell phone rang. It was Leah. While I was out running errands, a social worker from the state had called and needed to place three children before 6:30 p.m.! She told Leah that she would do whatever it took to enable us to take the three siblings. They were in desperate need of a home.

I knew no one within the state system, and I had not officially notified the state that we were searching for a child. I had met a worker at an adoption fair in November (it was now February) and briefly talked to her, but I had never had any further contact with anyone at the state. They had apparently talked to the worker from a private organization, who had recently updated our home study. Remembering our brief introduction at the adoption fair earlier in the winter, the state worker had decided to call us.

I was honest with the social worker, telling her I felt we were going to get a new baby from out of state and making it clear I would not intentionally do anything to jeopardize that placement. She agreed that the baby we had already received a phone call on should be first priority and that she would try to work with all the powers that be to make all of the placements work if that was what we opted to do. This was moving way too fast!

I was nearly speechless as I called John at work to see what he thought we should do. Willing to take in the children, he promptly said yes, but with one stipulation. They had to be placed as foster children, giving us a chance to see if they would fit into our family before making a commitment to adopt them or expecting our children to adjust to new additions without any forewarning or preparations.

While I talked back and forth with the worker from the state, Leah was at home trying to prepare supper. I had picked up children from piano lessons, delivered Trista to the gym and went home to pick up those planning to go to the church later for a meeting. The three foster children should be arriving at our house sometime just before bedtime!

While at home between taxi runs, the older girls asked me what I was going to do. I told them that I felt that God had clearly shown me we were to get a baby boy and that even though I had not yet heard anything from Oklahoma; I needed to make that situation our first priority. I had long thought we would get a sibling group of three. Maybe this was the right group-only time would tell. But, the only way I knew to do this was to walk down the path a step at a time, until God shut a door. My children were wonderful in their willingness to move over and add so many children at one time. I discovered what huge hearts and willing spirits each had. It made me very proud. They scurried about making a place in our home and their hearts, each in their own way. There were discussions on moving rooms and beds around, conversations about what toys and clothes to share, and even a pot of homemade soup simmering on the stove to feed scared and hungry children whose lives were about to be turned upside down when a social worker swooped in and carried them away to a new place.

Just as preparations were about ready, the state social worker called to say that a court order had not been secured and they would not be bringing the children until after school on Friday. We hit the brakes, skidded to a stop and tried to settle our own hearts down as we went from running a race to sitting in a waiting room once again!

I left to take Andrea to church, planning to simply sit in the quiet car during the meeting and beg God for some light on this crazy situation! I enjoyed a quiet 10 minutes, then I was jolted from my thoughts by the ringing of the cell phone once again. I was shocked to hear the voice of the social worker from Oklahoma calling me after business hours.

This worker was known for her nine to five schedule, at least as much as she could keep her day that way. This was also the worker whom I had waited days on to review my urgently requested paperwork in what finally turned out to be Victoria's placement. This was also the worker who preferred same-race placements and who truly did not understand our motivation to adopt so many children. This was the social worker who now spoke to me in the darkness of my car.

The words that she spoke sent prickly bumps all over my body and shot the Holy Spirit feeling from her office telephone right through the night sky to my cell phone all these hundreds of miles away.

She said: "This must be an act of God. I got up and came to the office to call you. I almost never leave in the evening to take care of business once I am settled at home. But, I really felt impressed to call you tonight. The birth mother read your letter and would like to meet with you tomorrow. The baby is still in the hospital, because he is too small to be released, but she needs to make a plan and feels that she would like to meet and talk with you."

There was absolutely no denying that God was directing steps and orchestrating events. I agreed to make the nine hour trip and made arrangements to meet everyone at the agency office late the next afternoon.

Do you see the challenges here? Now I needed to be in Oklahoma to meet the birth mother of the baby I had labored in the spirit to deliver and yet be in Tennessee at virtually the same time to greet a sibling group of three very distraught children who had appeared out of nowhere into our lives!

I called John at work. This required a 'staff meeting' of the highest kind! He had me call our social worker to see what we could do, and to talk out this strange turn of events. In spite of her probable inability to relate to the motivation behind parenting such a large number of children, she told me that all of the children could possibly join us as long as each step was followed closely.

When John and I finally arrived home, we talked quickly through all of the events that were unfolding. He offered to leave early from work the next day to greet the sibling group and then remain home with them until I returned from Oklahoma. Eventually, we decided that these sibs needed to arrive with a mother figure in place and likely needed my undivided attention. If we really did receive custody of the baby boy in Oklahoma, it could be as long as two weeks before interstate compact was cleared and I could return home with the baby. It wasn't practical for John to miss work while I was spending money traveling, on motel and adoption expenses. Tiredly we agreed to call the state and temporarily say no to the sib group. A decision already made, the older girls had begun to pack Victoria and me for the trip to Oklahoma. If the sib group really was ours, then they would be available when I returned from Oklahoma. We were sure I was to go and meet the birth mother out of state, so we went with what we knew God had shown us and remained open to the situation we were unsure of.

It was one of the hardest decisions we had made in a very long time. I made plans to stay with a friend while in Oklahoma, left several children in the capable hands of Leah and the other older girls and bravely headed toward a completely unknown situation.

I apprehensively drove up to the agency on Saturday. This was indeed a walk of faith. There had been very little light shed on the path, and I had no clue what I was walking into. I did feel I was on the right path, which was some consolation. About two minutes into the conversation with the birth mother, I began to realize that she had not been told how many children were already in our family (no small thing)! At first, I was frustrated that she had not been told. Later, I realized it was wise, giving both the birth mother and me a chance to walk into this uncharted territory without preconceived notions about one another. We were just getting acquainted when without any prior warning the birth father walked into the office! Nesha* (not her real name) had not seen this man for over eight months and was clearly surprised when he entered the room.

Nesha had desired a two parent Black family who lived in the same city as she did, hoping they would be willing to share in an open adoption. She was presented with a two parent White family with a crew of children, living in another state and more comfortable with a semi-open adoption. With social workers present, Victoria playing on the floor, and both birth parents there, I was begging God to give me just the right words, just the right smile and just the right reactions to this incredibly volatile situation!

After meeting for some time, I took Victoria outside to run in the grass and left those who held my heart in their hand time to discuss what the next move would be. In a while Nesha came outside and we had a wonderful visit. It was quickly apparent that the Spirit of God was present in our midst and He had given us kindred spirits. We both knew quickly that we were to share the destiny of this child. We also knew painfully well that a battle over the very soul of this child was imminent and that we had to band together.

> *A few months later alone in a room*
> *God would speak to my heart, and from another's womb*
> *Would birth a child meant to be ours from the start.*
> *In a moment in time this child stole my heart.*

With the agreement of both birth parents, I was taken by the social worker to see the baby. As the nurse greeted me and then handed me the baby, I felt the power of God come over me in an incredibly humbling way. I sat and held this baby, cradling the treasure as if in a mist. The activities of the special care nursery seemed to dim into the background as did the occasional smile of the social worker as she busied herself with paperwork. The whole scene was so dreamlike, and yet my apprehension and joy assured me I was very much experiencing reality.

How does God orchestrate such events? How does He bring children and adoptive parents together, and why? How in this world could I ever be worthy of the task of parenting yet another child? Did I dare allow this little raisin of a man-child to creep his way into my heart? Oh, so many children presented and snatched away over the years, so many scars, bucketsful of tears, and questions beyond measure when things didn't work out. I couldn't cry over the loss of another child. Still, I must take the risk, for in walking away I would be surely disobeying the God of the universe, and that was something I simply could not do.

> *The conception had been hidden even from his birth mother you see,*
> *And now God had chosen to reveal a plan to me.*
> *The choice was ours whether to fight the battle or flee,*
> *But to follow God's instructions would reveal a destiny.*

There were many battles to be fought over the next few days. There were dark times when I was truly afraid that the free will of man would once again change the destiny of a child and our family. With the return of Erin* as agency director, I knew that the agency was being restored with a spirit of adoption and sincere attempts at seeking the will of God. This gave me a measure of confidence that was most certainly lacking in Victoria's placement.

One day as I was driving alone down the freeway toward the hospital, I was suddenly overcome with fear and doubt. I knew that I was going to visit the baby under the watchful eye of hospital security because they had concerns regarding the birth father. I knew that God had asked me to come this far, but I also understood the desires of a birth parent's heart to have control over the destiny of their child. As angry as I was over his sudden intervention into this plan, I was also empathetic with the birth father and understood his need to control circumstances, which in reality were so utterly out of his control.

God clearly encouraged me to keep moving forward and to be strong and to stand on the limited knowledge already given me. Yet I felt that God also allowed me to consider walking away-it was about exercising my free will. However, He was also pleading with me in the Spirit to be strong for this child. God showed me clearly that He had hidden this baby from all of us for a season, for His purpose and for His glory, which was yet to be revealed. My singing is not a pretty sound (I am so thankful that God knows my heart and doesn't judge me on my lack of talent in this area), but I began to joyfully sing— praising God and renewing the faith wavering in my spirit.

Eventually the day came for me to pick up our new son. The name our family had selected seemed to fade into the recesses of my memory as God made it clear that He had selected the name for this child.

His mother had named him Gabriel, and I had to agree the name suited this tiny little man of God. The name's meaning included: "God is my strength", and "having spiritual consciousness." The Scripture that supported this name was taken from Joshua 1:9: "Be strong and of a good courage; be not afraid, neither be thou dismayed; for the Lord thy God is with thee whithersoever thou goest" (KJV). For personal reasons and to keep up the tradition of our boys having middle names that start with the letter 'a', we agreed on the middle name of Addison. The name's meaning included: worthy of trust and God's helper. The supporting Scripture was from Ezekiel 36:27: "And I will put my spirit within you, and cause you to walk in my statutes, and ye shall keep my judgments, and do them" (KJV).

During the days we waited on appropriate papers to be signed and on the baby's release from the hospital, Nesha and I had time to develop a really sweet friendship. I learned that she had not known that she was pregnant. Early in the pregnancy she had felt that she had a flu that lasted a very long time, and she attributed her weight gain to the holiday indulgence of overeating and lack of exercise. Perhaps she had denied the pregnancy.

But more than likely, in the realm of understanding and realization, God had chosen to hide this baby, and I shall tell you why.

Nesha shared with me that she had once had an abortion. She feared that if she had known about Gabriel she might have been tempted to make a decision for abortion again. She tearfully told me that she was certain God had hidden this baby from her in order to protect his life. Of course by the time she placed Gabriel in my arms it was with the sincere love only a mother can have for her child and with great purpose and confirmation from God that she had been a part of the plan for Gabriel since his conception.

The entrustment ceremony was such a beautiful and incredibly enabling ceremony, giving closure to the preceding days of uncertainty. There were several people present as Carrie led the ceremony. Nesha and I uttered moans from our spirit as Carrie read the following words from Isaiah 49:1-3: "The Lord called me before I was born, while I was in my mother's womb He named me. He made my mouth like a sharp sword, in the shadow of His hand *He hid me*; He made me a polished arrow, in His quiver He hid me away. And He said to me, 'You are my servant, Israel, in whom I will be glorified" (italics mine, NRSV).

Carrie had prayed for a special Scripture to include in the entrustment ceremony. None could have been more fitting or more confirming that God had indeed had a plan from long ago.

While seeking encouragement from God for the battle ahead,
He showed me clearly to act upon just what He said.
The years tumbled by us our hearts opened wide,
There were 11 of us to welcome Gabriel Addison,
Our hearts swelled with pride.

Once again, Scripture was especially confirming, as the final hour of entrustment from birth mother to our arms became reality. Using Scripture to enlighten those present at the ceremony, God showed us that hiding Gabriel even from his birth mother was all in His Holy purpose. Once again I was humbly reminded that God's ways are much higher than our ways, and to attempt to walk in obedience is to truly walk on 'higher ground'.

As I thought about the ways that God has hidden all of our children at various times, and for a variety of reasons, I realized again how intricate are the details of our lives, the day- to-day living, the mysteries and the challenges-all for a purpose. At one time or another, I suppose we have all been hidden from someone or something. Some of our children have been hidden from us until God opened the doors and allowed us to walk down the path to those special children. Presently, I believe some of our children are being hidden in a positive way until they can fulfill the destiny and find God's path for their lives. Many times we are most certainly protected and kept 'hidden' from the enemy, the one who would do us harm.

All of us at one time or another are certainly hidden for glory—God's glory!

Not the name of the individual

Running Scared

An unexpected call came from a friend who lived in Oklahoma. Cee* now worked for an attorney, assisting birth mothers with their adoption plans.

She was calling from her cell phone, as she drove to pick up a baby boy. God had brought our family to mind and she wanted us to pray about this child. She felt that he would fit perfectly into our family. I was totally surprised by the phone call, having had no contact with her for a very long time. In fact, I did not even know that she was working for an attorney; it had been so long since we had spoken.

John and I agreed to take the baby and went into fast forward motion with plans for a trip to Oklahoma on Christmas Eve. Making plans to travel was a tough decision because Christmas is an incredibly important holiday in a household with so many children. Now we were going to have to leave most everyone home in Hector and Leah's care while we traveled through unpredictable weather to pick up yet another baby. Since part of the motivation for the birth mother was a desire for her baby to be with a family for the Christmas holiday, it seemed very important to make the effort on behalf of this child. As we loaded the car, John and I swiftly made decisions on who would accompany us. We took the boys and left the house before daylight the next cold and frosty morning.

The roads were slick and the weather forecast grim as the radio announced school closings and threatened dangerous travel conditions for the next 48 hours. We stopped for breakfast not far from home. Making an unusual decision, John announced we were turning around and going back home.

He felt we would be taking too many chances on such unsafe roads. We were traveling to pick up a legally "risky" baby, leaving behind our other children on this special holiday. The boys and I were numbed and quiet; absorbing the change in plans as we carefully picked our way over the ice and climbed back into the loaded car. The rest of the family was equally surprised when we tumbled back into the house just as they were all getting up to greet the day. Turning back turned out to be a very wise decision.

We called Cee to tell her our change in plans and to assure her we would leave as soon as the roads cleared, probably the day after Christmas. She understood and agreed with our decision. As it turned out, we would never see that baby. Once the emotions of the holiday passed, the weather cleared and the mother had a few nights' sleep, she opted to keep the baby. We would have made a very dangerous trip for no reason. God had spoken to John and spared us a great deal of expense and grief.

But now, where was that baby that God seemed to be insisting we would find?

I remember I spent hours on the Internet, searching the waiting child sights, ever wondering if by some miracle a child, or sibling group would appear before me on the screen and I would know in an instant that I had found our next addition. Meanwhile I joined a Christian adoption e-mail list and found great support and friendship there in cyberspace. Now and again someone would post a message about a special needs child awaiting a forever family. Usually I just read the posts with interest, deleted the messages and went on with life.

However, there was one post about a little boy with cerebral palsy that just kept getting my attention. The first time the post was made I was pricked in my spirit by the message, but logically I thought, "no way", and hit delete. Some time went by, and I remember having fleeting thoughts now and then about that little boy, but nothing that I would have considered especially spiritual in context. Eventually the little boy was posted again, and this time I learned that he was in the same state that we were presently residing in, and that they were still searching for a family for this little guy. I hit the delete button quickly, because this time the urge to find out more about this child was stronger, and I simply didn't want to 'go there' as far as taking on a physically handicapped child, even though *I had been plainly told by God that we would receive a child like McKenzie, only opposite.*

Since the stories of our children's arrivals typically span over a long period of time, let me digress a bit before I proceed with the present trail of thought. *Strangely, for many months I had an unusual sensation when I would drive by a specific location in our city. In spite of radio music, talking children and crying babies, each time I drove through this area I would unexpectedly have a 'feeling' that we would one day get a child through a particular agency that had facilities nearby.* It was a very odd experience, something I had not felt before, and I usually just brushed off the feeling as ridiculous.

Meanwhile, through a series of events that turned out to be God-ordained, I eventually met another like-minded mother/adoptive family who lived just over the state line about an hour from our home. Only God could have orchestrated our meeting, in a number of different ways. This family worked with an adoption agency not part of their denominational preference, for assistance with their ongoing home studies and frequent domestic and international adoptions. I was intrigued, not only by the fact that they were working with an agency of another religious affiliation, but I was also intrigued when I learned the worker seemed accepting of large families and also of the placement of children of different racial backgrounds with Caucasian parents.

I recall thinking that if we decided to adopt again I would like to contact this social worker as well. *Indeed, I had called on two or three occasions inquiring about their placement policies, and telling them of our availability to adopt special needs or transracially.* My phone calls had received cordial but noncommittal responses. In other words, the doors had closed. I couldn't get past a light conversation with a receptionist or a social worker. I would just shrug my shoulders and assume that God must have our next placement coming from somewhere else.

When I learned that the little boy posted on the adoption e-mail list was being overseen by this agency, I assumed my request for information would once again fall on deaf ears. When I could deny no longer that God was working on me to make a call of inquiry regarding this little boy, I dialed the number. Secretly, I was hoping that the call would be unsuccessful and I could then say I had been obedient to call and inquire about this little guy, but we were unable to get him. To my surprise I was immediately put through to the worker on the case, which turned out to not only be the worker that my friends used, but with the agency that *I consistently had the strange feeling about when I passed by an affiliate facility near my home.* Still, I wasn't to the stage of putting together, let alone accepting, the God coincidences at this point in the situation.

After initial introductions and formalities, the worker proceeded to inform me about why this little boy, now nearly one year old, was available for adoption. Truthfully, his challenges were greater than John and I desired to knowingly take on, so I was very relieved when, toward the end of the conversation, the worker told me she thought they had a family for this little guy. If it didn't work out, they would contact me. Years of experience in adoption allowed me to heave a big sigh of relief. I know when I have been politely dismissed, and frankly, this time I was entirely relieved that my phone call had been fruitless. I had obeyed the prompting from God, but apparently He was just testing me to see if I would follow His leading, and wasn't going to really ask us to take this complex child. I slept very well that night.

> *He's created these children in a way not our own,*
> *And stopped at nothing to create just the home,*
> *Where there's no room for logic, prejudice, or despair*
> *But a NEED for our God and His competent care.*

I had to sit down when I answered the phone early the next morning and it was the worker once again! She told me that she had been thinking about our phone conversation, and she really felt like our family might be a better match for this little boy, Austin, than the family she had referenced yesterday. She wanted us to talk more seriously about the possibility of our considering this child. I was shocked, scared, and completely reluctant now that I had time to mull over the facts the worker had shared with me in the conversation of the previous day.

It was quickly arranged for John and me to meet Austin. He was just a few miles from our home, so this was easily coordinated. We met the worker for the first time on our initial visit to see Austin.

I immediately felt that Austin had untapped potential, but denied openly to John on the way home any real spiritual or maternal confirmations regarding this little guy. I simply did not want to take on the awesome task I sensed was lying lethargically upon my lap during our interview.

As we drove toward home after our first visit, our lives began a journey not unlike Jonah running from Nineveh. I sincerely wanted to be released from the opportunity it appeared God was giving us. There was no excitement; no immediate confirmation such as we had gotten accustomed to having when God made clear His request regarding our other children. The instructions were quickly understood, but in our humanity, John and I wanted to run far away from this challenge. Consequently, we spent some pretty gruesome hours in the belly of the whale.

Jonah 2:1-3: "Then Jonah prayed to the Lord his God from the belly of the fish, saying, 'I called to the Lord out of my distress, and he answered me; out of the belly of Sheol I cried, and you heard my voice. You cast me into the deep, into the heart of the seas, and the flood surrounded me; all your waves and your billows passed over me' " (NRSV).

We spent the next few days struggling with the option now before us. We did not want to take on this task, and yet deep within both John and me there was an inability to say no to this child. John offered to call the agency and say no, and I would cry. I offered to call the agency to say no, and John would hesitate. We prayed to God late at night, early in the morning and without ceasing, hoping to be relieved of this call. The storm seemed all around us, scaring us, the unknowns of how things would turn out-almost drowning us as the sea had the potential to do to Jonah. Although saying no to taking this child would have given temporary relief from the fears floating through our minds, we were incapable of doing so.

Just as God was in control of the stormy seas in Jonah's life, He also was in obvious control of the events that followed in the next few days. Regardless of how many arguments we gave, of how inadequate we tried to portray ourselves, workers who would usually shy from a much lesser confession of inadequacies seemed to not hear a word we spoke and intently went about making this placement happen. I confess I have never tried harder to stop a placement in my life. Though Jonah repented and was spewed from the whale's belly to go back to Nineveh, he still did not like the outcome. Likewise, for a while we were not excited that the instructions we received were contrary to that which we desired.

In record time we found ourselves approved to adopt Austin. If we did not take him, supposedly the only option remaining was to institutionalize him. As badly as we didn't want to take on the challenges, we didn't want this child (who seemed to have potential hidden in the crippled and almost autistic body) to be caught up in the world system. But, admittedly, we questioned God, we cried, we denied the call, we argued, we faced opposition from our children, our peers, our church family and more again from within ourselves.

Finally, when I simply could not say no, the workers of both the placing and receiving agency (which now represented us as well) proceeded with a placement plan. We have never had a child literally dropped on our doorstep, but this time one was literally brought to our door. Not only did they deliver the child, but all of his earthly possessions as well and there were many, including a crib, clothes and several days' worth of formula and diapers. Along with those things came a list of his schedule, his therapists, doctor appointments, medications and a daunting list of resources. When the foster father and the worker retreated down our lane and I stood holding this rigid, unresponsive child, we were simply in shock at the way things had transpired in spite of our verbal protests, our insistence that we were not qualified for the task, and most of all, in spite of our fears.

I knew in my heart that God loves all people. I would be the first to stand in front of the toughest crowd and profess my belief that all children deserve life and a forever family. I would however have to repeatedly be reminded He will equip and enable us to do that which He asks us to do (in spite of ourselves). Often the call of a missionary requires time in the trenches, or the belly of a whale. These times keep us humble and remind us of our inability to do that which is presented to us under our own strength. In desiring to serve God we must continue to adjust our dreams and visions to fit those that the Lord seems to have for us.

Thankfully, just as God didn't reject Jonah because he tried to abort his mission, He has not rejected me, but has shown great love and patience and forgiveness as I have failed miserably in the tasks presented to me. The lesson for me has been to understand in a new way that to love God and truly glory in that love, we must also learn to accept all those whom He loves, and all of us are unlovable at times.

Many would think that numbers of children would be the hard part of parenting our family. For us, Austin has presented the greatest challenge. Over the next few months we would see our privacy invaded and our family dynamics changed so radically that John and I frequently wondered if we had made a huge mistake.

We soon found out that trips to fast food restaurants, one of the few diversions our large family enjoyed, could no longer happen, at least if we were going to take Austin. Any new situation totally distressed him, and he would act out and become totally uncontrollable, making a scene and drawing a good deal of unwanted attention from people whenever we were out in public. Even trips to the park turned into nightmares as his relentless crying and pouting put a damper on the simplest of outings.

With Austin's arrival, there were endless doctor appointments, phone calls and fights with the Medicaid system. Home schooling became almost impossible with the intrusions of therapists at random hours during the day. Having other children with learning disabilities and problems with attention deficit only magnified the challenges, as the slightest interruption in their routine was almost as devastating to their learning environment as our lifestyle was to Austin's existence. Committed to home educating our children because we felt that God had asked us to, there seemed to be no options but to trudge through the endless interruptions and hope that some-day soon things would settle into a more comfortable routine.

Austin slept lightly and so could not be in a room with any of the other children. Consequently, he ended up in our room. This quickly affected our relationship, as the only place in the house that John and I had been able to find solitude was now gone. Not only that, Austin made many un-usual noises while he drifted in and out of his light sleep, so my ears, many years fined tuned to hear the noises of children, found it impossible to shut out the unique sounds of this new child. Soon I was getting little to no sleep at night, which only magnified the challenges I was now facing.

In our heads we knew that he could not help his behavior or change his special needs, but at the same time we felt helpless too, since the world as we had known it before his arrival had changed radically.

Suddenly I could not go to church because he was so miserable and would take a day or two to settle down even after an hour in a worship service. I couldn't cuddle or hold this child, both because the cerebral palsy caused him to be difficult to hold, but mostly because of my own weak back which would soon have sharp pains piercing through it if I tried to hold this child any length of time. None of the younger children could hold him or interact with him, and at the time he appeared totally unresponsive. Austin could not suck a bottle or take food properly, so his basic needs could not be met, causing him to be continually unsatisfied and grumpy. He screamed through many feedings and soon one feeding time was running into another and then another. His constant unhappiness was affecting our normally happy family.

I had to give up going with John and the other children to places like the zoo, or other youth activities at church, because Austin was just too upset by anything outside of our home. I was saddened by the thoughts that I might miss wonderful memories with John and our other children. I was thrown back into that sinful state of self pity that I so despise in myself and others.

Some, perhaps even most, of our fears will prove to be unfounded-only God knows the outcome. But the days after Austin arrived were difficult times indeed. This was the first time that acceptance and agreement had not come soon after the addition of anyone into our family...and it was a very hard situation for all of us to deal with, a humbling time for sure.

The heart of Jesus wanted to accept, love and even enjoy this new addition, but unwilling human flesh found the task nearly impossible. So many families that I knew were so gifted at taking care of these children, and seemed blessed by the privilege of being entrusted with a handicapped child. I felt guilty that I was not measuring up to my own standard of how I should be feeling and what I should be able to do.

I suppose at any time we could have had them come and pick Austin up. But truthfully, I was very concerned how that would affect our other children, especially the younger ones, who in short order had learned to accept and accommodate Austin in a way those of us older and more set in our ways were incapable of doing. Nathan was especially connected to Austin, even in the early days, and as the months would go by, to our pleasant surprise, Andrea would find it within her heart to minister to Austin and eventually take a load off of me that would save the placement and ensure happiness for our entire family. God did and continues to have a plan, I knew that in my heart of hearts, but it did not change the reality of living day-to-day with this very complicated, but beautiful little boy.

As if all of our challenges weren't enough, adding insult to injury, I hit an all-time low one hot summer day:

The intense Tennessee heat had slowly infiltrated walls and furniture as we went into our sixth week without air conditioning. To complicate the situation, the house had no alternate airflow. For reasons I never understood none of the windows on the south side of the house could be opened. North windows had typical screens and storm windows, as did the three tiny windows on the west side. Their assistance in producing airflow was nil without the cross flow benefits of either south or east openings.

While renting the house, we had many aggravations when it came to requesting repairs on even the simplest of items. It had not been unusual to wait six weeks for burner eyes on the stovetop, or a thermostat on the oven. This was no exception. The air conditioning had simply not kicked on one day, and now six weeks later, we were still waiting on a new heat pump unit. I was exhausted, not only in the wait, but also in concerns over a handicapped baby which were only magnified by sleepless nights.

Challenges that seem overbearing to the average-size family can be killers to those of us with nearly a baker's dozen at home! The boredom of summer was upon us, vacation to the beach a dim memory, school in the distant future and needed relief from the heat an unknown. Stress levels were pushed into the danger zone.

I couldn't seem to meet anyone's needs, and surely my own were far from being met. Our two fans were on constantly, one focused solely on Austin, since he was unable to move about and just lay in a lethargic state upon the floor wimpering mindlessly most of the hot days. I was concerned that what little progress had been made in his development was slowly being melted out of him with each additional day of relentless heat. Austin was incapable of taking enough fluids, sometimes taking all day to consume eight ounces. Because of his inability to swallow properly and the fatigue of the heat, he couldn't consume solid foods. (Later I would wonder why at that point a feeding tube was not suggested. That option would come much later.) I was more than a bit worried about his health and well-being. Besides health concerns, I was worn out from his constant whining and complaining. He was typically awake about 18-20 of the 24 hours in a day. If you do the math, it is easy to see that there was little relief from the frustrations of the overall situation.

When I looked around the room of bedraggled children, killing their afternoons in front of mindless television programs or sprinting outside to play in sprinklers for brief interludes, I thought I would scream! This was NOT the way that summer was supposed to be! We were supposed to be enjoying swimming and outdoor activities, catching up on hobby projects and resting from our home schoolwork. Instead we were in what we have termed over the years, "survival mode", and that mode had far exceeded its time limit for the crew grumbling on the living room floor. The enemy seemed to perch on my shoulder, reminding me that if we didn't have Austin we would be able to go somewhere cooler, at least to eat a hamburger or visit a museum—some diversion, just for a while. Also testing me even further, the air conditioning had gone out in our van and couldn't be repaired for several more days as well. To travel would have been worse than to stay at home.

There are only so many 'easy' meals to cook without a stovetop, which I was waiting upon a repair for as well. There are also only so many games to play in the garden hose, especially when my frugal mind could just see the water bill moving into the triple digits, along with the outside temperature readings.

Finally, when I was told we had to endure another week before the air conditioner would be repaired, I surpassed my normal limits of endurance (and my limits are broad compared to many parents I have talked to). I can endure great stress and manage many crises, but even I had reached the end of the rope and found not one knot left to cling to.

I went to our bedroom and closed the door, leaning against it and slithering to the floor as I turned the lock. I dialed the social worker that had delivered Austin to our door eight months earlier and begged her to rescue me. I felt I had to have some respite care for Austin. I had to relieve some of the pressure and he was the most likely valve to release.

He had moaned in his low-pitched way for hours and not one attempt to try and get fluids or foods down him had been successful. I knew Austin was close to dehydration. Selfishly, all I could think about was the push that would send this family over the edge if I had to admit Austin to the hospital. I would then have to be away from the other children, requiring John to likely miss work while I was taking care of a baby that wouldn't or couldn't accept any help.

It was a valley; it was dark, and it seemed endless. There was no light in sight. All of the activities that I would typically do to alleviate the stresses for my family seemed impossible. So, I called. This was the first time I have ever called for any help in all of my 27 years of parenting, fostering and child care. I did what I thought I would never do in a crisis; I called, of all people, a social worker!

Now, I knew full well that making this call might jeopardize not only Austin's placement with us, but might even prompt an investigation into our ability to cope with our present circumstances. I felt beaten, defeated, and trapped. I was concerned that I was going to collapse out of total exhaustion and frustration. Later our worker would term that time as a total meltdown.

Our social worker was finally located on her cell phone. She promised to try and find a foster family to take Austin for the weekend for me, just until the air conditioning was fixed. Maybe if I had a break from the constant crying, maybe if I could get some sleep, maybe if I could focus on my other toddlers, maybe then I could see a light out of that tunnel.

Deep within my being I think that I really figured that if I was able to go through with sending Austin out the door to a stranger, I would never bring him back through the door. This was an easy way out for me. The other children could understand Austin's need to be kept cool and have someone try to get fluids into him. They would understand his leaving under these circumstances.

Some reprieve, at least mentally, came after making the phone call. I swallowed the guilt; I refused to acknowledge the failure I felt because all I could think about was the sticky heat that seemed to be suffocating me. Like Scarlet in *Gone with the Wind*, I would have to think about that tomorrow.

A good deal of time crawled by. I imagined what I would pack for Austin, making sure mentally that I would send the few things that seemed to bring him some measure of comfort. I thought about how much calmer it would be without him and reviewed again how I would explain why I was sending him away during this hot, testing time.

I wasn't proud of my inability to cope. But, much like a trapped animal, I could only think of one thing, and that was getting out of or changing my current situation. I couldn't even think about what I would do after I escaped. Still, if this was the answer, why did I feel so badly?

I mentally went down the list of all of the reasons we were struggling in the first place. I needed to justify my reason for making the call to the social worker. I realized that though it was all truth, and a valid list, it didn't release me from the commitment we had made to God when we agreed to take on the addition of our children, and more specifically Austin. But, still that suffocating feeling remained, and I kept a close watch on the clock, praying that my answer was going to come with the next ring of the telephone. If I had made a mistake in bringing Austin here, surely this would give God an opportunity to correct the error and bail us out.

I told the older girls that I had made the call to the social worker. In their own states of heat-induced stupor, they seemed surprised at my actions, then, maybe, a bit relieved that he might leave, and yet not believing either. They had heard repeatedly over the years our emphatic statements of commitment to a child once it arrived in our care. They knew that though we had struggled immensely with bringing Austin into our home, we were in it for the long haul, and days like these were what made it a long haul indeed! Maybe I saw just a bit of disappointment in the faith they had in my ability to handle the most pressing of situations, and in that flash of emotion across their lethargic faces I found more guilt.

Still, I'm human too! Why did everyone expect me to handle so much more than others had to deal with? Of course, that is another lie of the enemy, but we were on the front lines that day as I would later find out; fiery darts flying so fast that we could not possibly have dodged them all, no foxhole was deep enough and I wanted to run from this battle.

The phone call came, but the relief did not. Our worker couldn't find anyone to take Austin. She told me that she was leaving on vacation and if things weren't better by next Tuesday, then she would try to help me find someone to keep him for a few days.

Now, I must tell you, I learned many lessons that day. I cried for help in a legitimate situation, yet relief was not forthcoming. I learned more about my endurance. I have more of it than I know or care to test in the future. I quickly realized that once again I had asked God to get me out of a situation and He had clearly not provided the key to unlock the door so I could flee. That realization certainly changed my future days with Austin as the reality that He was right where God wanted him to be continued to seep into my soul.

The girls were just as shocked as I was that no help would be offered. I was given the name of another social worker at the office that I could call if I needed to talk. It was suggested that I call the state for respite, which I am fairly confident the social worker knew I would not do. I would be especially careful with whom I left a helpless child. No, the options presented were not solutions at all.

I was trapped. Well, it seemed that way to me.

I have learned over the years that when I feel trapped I can continue to fight the situation, or resolve to rest. If God had closed a door, then He must know that I could handle what was on my plate. He was with me in this storm.

Thankfully I have a God who stabilizes me while I am on the windy sea. Thankfully I have a husband who is in this ministry side by side with me in the good times and the bad. Thankfully I was an older parent, and understood after the initial shock of refusal that I could and would get through this time, that this too would pass.

As John, Andrea and Jordan were preparing to leave for a week at church camp; John told me that I could call the attorney in Texas and stop the adoption proceedings. John knew me well enough to know that calling a social worker for help had been a radical decision for me. He understood my exhaustion, he knew of my doubts, and of my need to take some control of the challenges I was trying to face. We agreed that we would put the

finalization of Austin's adoption on hold for a few weeks. When John returned from camp and we were more rational and cooler, we would take
some time to talk once again about the situation that we found ourselves in.
We promised to pray for each other while we were apart, and to peacefully
endure.

I commented to one of the girls during those sweltering hours that the
battle we found our family in felt very similar to the ones that we typically
experience just before the placement of a child in our home. We have become very familiar with the attacks launched against our family prior to a
placement. We have come to readily expect the fiery darts of the devil. I
imagined during those dark hours that the battle in the spiritual realm was
more than I could have dealt with if I had been able to visually see the
arrows that were flying about. I was well aware that "our struggle is not
against enemies of blood and flesh, but against the rulers, against the au-
thorities, against the cosmic powers of this present darkness, against the
spiritual forces of evil in the heavenly places" (Ephesians 6:12, NRSV).

The warfare was manifesting itself to us in broken air conditioning,
crying babies, sleepless nights, unsettled emotions, sibling rivalry, and doubts
about adoption, parenting and life in general.

I felt we were not done adding children to our family via the adoption
route, but I was very doubtful that God would be sending us any more
children under the present circumstances. Still, *the feeling of a battle over a
child or children was very real to me throughout that entire week.* There were
moments I expected the phone to ring and someone on the other end to
have another child for us, totally unsolicited and unexpected…but the call
never came. So I puzzled over what was really going on

Somehow having the permission to call the attorney and stall the adoption proceedings gave me a plan and some momentary relief. I don't think I
ever thought we would really stop the adoption, but I guess I needed to
know that we had some control, and could stop it if we decided to. When
will I ever learn that in our walk with God we rarely can make a decision
based solely on our own logic?

By now it was Saturday afternoon. The campers were safely on the road
to church camp. There was a slight reprieve in the hot summer tempera-
tures. Fewer people in the house meant at the least a change of routine, and

at the most, fewer people to cook and care for.

When some of us are gone for a fun thing, we give those remaining permission to plan little things that change the routine and make those left behind feel like they too have some respite. So, giving myself permission to slack on the housekeeping until the air conditioning was fixed, picking up some rented videos and purchasing fun comfort foods started to ease the tension and there seemed to be a cease-fire in the battle over our household.

I did not realize how exact those words were for a few more days. But, in a cease-fire was exactly where we found ourselves that weekend. At church, there were extra prayers for our situation. We were offered a window air conditioning unit so that I could at least cool a bedroom and have one spot in the house where we could rest. I didn't take the person up on their generous offer, but it was greatly appreciated. Another friend insisted that I use her air-conditioned mini van while John was gone with our big van to camp.

At least if I did figure out some place to go, we could travel in cooler comfort. I was overwhelmed with the offerings of help. I came home from church armed spiritually and encouraged physically. Not exactly the solutions I had looked for, but God's answers for sure. A subtle reminder that we must learn to live one day at a time, the big picture is simply too huge to embrace.

Monday morning we welcomed the unexpected intrusion of the repairmen who came to install the long overdue heat pump. By mid-afternoon the air blowing from the vents was beginning to cool down the heat-saturated house and I felt hope in the air! I felt like I could finally think straight enough to call the attorney to see where the paperwork process was regarding finalization of Austin's adoption. I really don't recall having a plan as to what I was going to say or do. I just remember that I wanted to know what they were doing, and had in the back of my mind John's permission, even encouragement, to slow down the finalization process for a while.

To my complete surprise, when I talked to the paralegal she was just delighted to tell me that during the preceding week they had finalized Austin's adoption and that I should be receiving a copy of the final decree that day in the mail! I was speechless. I would later find out that on the VERY DAY that I slid to the floor and called the social worker to pick up Austin; the attorney was representing us in a court in Texas to finalize Austin's adoption.

Even with more than 27 years of involvement in adoption work, I have never known an adoption to finalize without at least one parent appearing before the judge. We knew that the attorney had intended to file a hardship plea with the judge. Living so far from the county in Texas where finalization would take place, and with the level of care Austin required, especially while traveling, the request was valid. Different states allow different things and sometimes parents do not have to appear before the judge, but I don't think that either John or I ever thought that they would finalize the adoption without our even knowing of the court date! Obviously God had taken matters into His own capable hands once again. The decision had been irrevocably made. Austin's place in our family was secured.

I went back into the living room where the speech therapist was working with Austin. I was reeling with the information I had just received. It was like I had just crested a hill I had been climbing for days. While talking on the phone, the knowledge and understanding became reality. Quickly I saw the reason we had spent the past days in the trenches. When I relayed the news she just looked at me and asked if she should congratulate me or cry with me! Indeed I wasn't sure.

After a few minutes I began to explain to her that I now understood why things had been so intense over the past few days. This therapist had been with Austin the day I had called the social worker to rescue me. She had stayed longer than usual that day, trying to get Austin to take in some fluids, fully aware of my concern over Austin's potential for dehydration. She told me that she had gone home after that session wondering how she could help me. She had the responsibility of her grandchildren that evening and didn't feel she could take care of Austin too, so she had just extended her stay on her own time and then went on home. I had been so caught up that day in self-pity I had not even noticed the extra time she spent with him. I was glad she brought it to my attention so that I could express my thanks.

I began to try and explain to her that when God places a child in our home the enemy seems to immediately begin to plant seeds of doubt and confusion, using many obvious or sometimes more subtle situations. We have come to expect such a battle. However, this time I had been deceived. Though I had considered that the battle was over a child or children to be placed, it never occurred to me that it was over a child already in our home!

The days preceding Austin's placement in our family were some of the most stressful and confusing that I can recall. We should have realized then and there that if the battle was so fierce, the child must indeed be incredibly important in the kingdom of God…in spite of what present circumstances and our human weaknesses could see. So, regardless of how we tried to justify not taking Austin, it seemed things just kept moving in that direction, and one day they literally delivered him to our door!

The confusion that had been over this household the few weeks before the finalization and very specifically the 24 to 48 hours surrounding the legal finalization were obvious now that I knew that likely while I was fighting a battle within myself over whether to even keep Austin, the attorney was standing before the judge requesting that nothing ever legally stop this child from being a part of our family. I aptly dubbed this time "the devil's last stand."

The therapist didn't understand that the strains of the past few days only made me surer that Austin was to be in our home. If there had been no battle I suppose I could have accepted that God had just allowed a painless journey to finalization. But, on the other hand, what I now saw was the huge potential for disruption on the day that I tried calling the social worker. God had once again kept me from disrupting this placement and had kept Austin right where He wanted him to be. I finally saw clearly what had been going on.

I believe that the whole story opened the eyes of the therapist too. She commented on how she never really thought about the battle that goes on over our children, and how very real it is. The battle is fought in a variety of realms and ways. I pray she left our home with the scales lifted off of her eyes, seeing anew the intervention and divine planning of an almighty God. I pray that in my weakness I did not blow my witness, but opened her eyes to see God in a more tangible way.

Finally, that day I understood where we were with this adoption. Regardless of where Austin was to be in God's perfect plan, he was now with us. In spite of our weaknesses, or rebellion, or our real or supposed inabilities, God seemed to insist our home was a good place for Austin to be. I God so divinely keep doors open to something that I doubted so much, something I begged to not be a part of.

At this writing, Austin is three years old. As he makes progress in various areas, sometimes quickly, sometimes almost unnoticeably, we are reminded that God has a plan and a purpose for this child's life and indirectly our lives intertwined with his as well. Each day we are all finding new measures of love for Austin. As he heals from past hurts and rejection, and slowly accepts his limitations, he too is becoming more happy and productive.

We are all daring to give and receive a new version of God's agape love. Austin is still difficult in many areas, far from healed, but we are all growing together and becoming better people in a spiritual sense because of his place in our family. His inabilities make our abilities seem especially important, special gifts from God.

Even in the writing of this book, God is growing me up, opening my eyes, revealing His plans and confirming our steps-those traveled and those yet to be taken. He is reminding me once again how patient we must be with one another, for God isn't finished with any of us yet!

In visiting with the social worker I have been humbled to learn that after Austin's placement in our home she began to reconsider her options when presented with other special needs children in need of adoptive families. It seems that she had typically opted to not place the very difficult children, thinking that there was no hope or future for them within the families that she usually worked with. Seeing our younger children give of their love and service so willingly and unconditionally to Austin encouraged her to reconsider the options. Several children are now in forever families as opposed to the state system or institutions because of Austin's story. So, in an indirect sort of way, Austin's placement in our family has already changed lives. That is an incredible encouragement to me as I struggle in the trenches of life ever seeking to be pleasing to God and a humble servant to the least of these.

I had often wondered if I had missed the dream or vision that should be a part of Benjamin Austin's story. As I penned the other children's stories and relived the hand of God guiding us along, I continued to puzzle over Austin's placement. One of our older sons reminded me during a searching conversation that Austin was almost *exactly opposite of McKenzie—she being a girl, he of course a boy. She is black and he is very white. Both arrived in our family with incredible unknown medical questions.* The only thing missing was the placement of twins that quickly followed McKenzie's unexpected placement in our family. (Soon enough the latter would become reality— but again, I get ahead of my story.)

God had given me words that foretold how Austin would be, *comparing him to McKenzie in a dream many months before his arrival.* In fact, that vague revelation had prompted the search for a special needs child, which had resulted in the original phone call to Austin's social worker. Still, more than a year after Austin joined us… in my weakness, I needed additional confirmations. In my meandering through boxes of stored journals I unexpectedly found what I had been searching for. It had been there, in written form long before Austin had been presented to us.

His story would become yet another example of knowledge hidden about a child destined for adoption-hidden from my understanding until God saw fit to reveal more of His plan. I had penned the poem sometime most likely in the 1980's. Now that Austin was home and had lived with us for a season I was amazed at how the poem, written so long ago, could so completely describe him. Even more exciting was the accuracy with which God revealed details of Austin's story. The final line in the poem gave closure to my questions. I share these words with you now, praying you will see God's purpose and plans once again.

Special Child

God had in mind a special task.
He said, "Please, will you do as I ask?"
We wish to obey You in all that we do.
"Then, My children, I'll help you through."
A special child is to be born one day.
One labeled handicapped, or so they will say.
The woman who births him will enable My plan.
Then you must nurture the babe to a man.
People are selfish and won't seem to know
The lessons in love this child will be sent to show.
You must teach that all are conceived for a plan.

I hold everyone's destiny in the palm of My hand.
This child may be crippled, or slow, or too small.
He may be blind, or deaf yet he can hear My call.
Expect no praise for this wearisome chore,
But eternity waits and for you so much more.
When asked to parent this special guy
Most will say no and spend much time asking why
I would allow such a thing to happen to this baby poor,
In fact, there will be those who just slam the door.
The door that will shut is to their very own heart.
Unconditionally accept him, for that is your part.
Protect him from persecution, rejection and scorn.
Understand completely this child was to be born.
Open wide the door to your lives.
Share milestones and tears as he struggles and tries
To reach his potential and be all he can be.
I assure you his purpose is known only by Me.

A few days before Austin came to our home I was traveling down the road to visit him. As I argued with God, adamantly listing all the reasons that we could not do this child justice, God clearly spoke to me. He impressed upon me that *Austin's handicaps were not what they appeared to be, and He seemed to assure me that there would be an unexpected outcome at some point in the future.* I am still not certain as I pen these words just what those words mean, but I am trying to be content and wait upon the Lord for the understanding and the works that He plans to do in the life of Benjamin (favored son) Austin and our family. I am now certain that God has great things planned. But, for a season I ran scared.

*Not the name of the individual

Burned Out
While in Search of Our
Promised Land

I suppose deep inside all of us there is a longing, a homing device, something that drives us toward a certain location, country or city. Sometimes we are profoundly aware of the drive; sometimes it is almost imperceptible. A lucky few find home early in their lives and are privileged to put down roots that grow deeper with the years and produce many memories. Most of the earth, however, is on the move, ever searching, ever longing for their promised land.

In my humble opinion we have moved too many times in our marriage, causing a great deal of insecurity in our lives and those of our children. Each time we leave a home, part of our heart and soul remains behind. Memories echo down the neighborhood streets, in the walls of the houses we occupied for a season and in the hearts of friends and members of our church families.

While I longed to plant trees and see them grow to maturity, and to see bedrooms turned into playrooms for our grandchildren, I have been asked to live a life not unlike a nomad of biblical days. I have often wondered: did Abraham's and Moses' wives yearn for perennial flower gardens and trees that not only sprouted roots, but were a part of their garden long enough to produce plentiful fruits? Did they get weary of packing up their tents just about the time they had a routine established? Did they understand that they were a vital part of the history of the world as we know it?

But, had I had the opportunity of planting trees and seeing them grow, would I have perhaps missed the privilege of parenting these wonderful children?

I suppose it is the comfort of a familiar routine that is so hard to relinquish. Packing up possessions and treading toward the unknown is a very frightening thing for all ages. As the heart of the home, I feel I shoulder the emotional burdens of each family member from the adult child that is left behind, to the infant who must adjust to new surroundings.

John carries the burden of the logical, financial and physical work of change. But I must carry the heart of the family from place to place, prayerfully keeping emotions intact for our family.

As our family members increase via adoption, marriage and births of grandchildren, the moves are ever more complicated and the needs increase. The giants in each new land always scare the scouting parities of our family. After our concerns are voiced and petitions to God are made, we must then move in faith toward the unknown territory. Uncharted territory is what life is all about.

I have few answers. Just as God had a destiny for our children within our family unit, He also must have a plan for us in our moves. One has to wonder if the influence of others within our neighborhoods did not need to be in place in order for us to find the children God desired that we should parent. For it was in each city and each state that God brought together the people who would become part of the story you just read.

Perhaps we will be more flexible, more useful somehow in the kingdom of God for all that we have experienced.

In the Philippines, we received the commissioning from God that would forever change our plans for our lives as we adopted our first child. Later in Missouri, we conceived and had our only biological son.

From Missouri, we moved to Oklahoma, where with each new house we added a child.

I thought when we crossed the bridge to our acreage in Oklahoma; we had found our promised land. I looked forward to planting trees and herb gardens and seeing the seasons of life change. Whether from disobedience or because we did indeed need to leave in order to fulfill our mission, today we still find ourselves searching for a place to call home. A place to pitch that tent, expand the cords, to build with expansion in mind the home that God has instructed us to build.

For a season we searched most weekends for acreage and old homesteads to restore and call home. Ever hoping to simplify our lives we prayerfully explored the plain lifestyle. For a season Leah and Hector lived without plumbing or electricity near a Mennonite community. It was never our intent to neither mimic nor totally immerse into their chosen lifestyle. We sought after lessons and skills lost, and an intrigue with how others within our society chose to glorify their God.

The lessons learned were invaluable and have become an integrated part of our family's thinking just as other life experiences have been woven into the tapestry of our lives.

A good deal of time, money and effort was spent while in the state of Tennessee searching for just that perfect place-our promised land. The longing for a piece of land was dominant in my thinking and I was shamefully motivated by little else except planning and pursuing that which I thought God would lead us to find.

Finally via Internet, we located a 130-acre mountain homestead in Eastern Tennessee. Several attempts to work out a deal with the owner failed. Puzzled, we dropped the idea, even though it seemed a perfect way to fulfill our life long dreams for our family. Just when we settled into searching elsewhere the owner approached us once again.

Believing the door had been reopened by God and after verbally working out the details, John, Hector the older boys and a friend spent the next two wintry months traveling the 12-15 hours each weekend to the property. They cleaned and prepared it for our family to move into. We were all very excited, since we could finally begin to make long-term plans and put down roots.

There was a large home for us, a nearly new mobile home for Hector, Leah and Angelica, and room to build a place for Jared or the others later if they desired to be near us. It was our plan to move completely between Christmas and New Year's Day.

In total disbelief I listened to the marshal speaking on the other end of the static-ridden phone line. He was at the new property and was inquiring if anyone was staying in the trailer or would have been in the house. Not exactly knowing where Leah and Hector were in their move I couldn't answer for certain. I felt like they were probably in route with the last of their belongings.

The marshal went on to explain that he was at the property and as he spoke the trailer was in the final smoking stages of burning to the ground. The house had failed to catch fire when the diesel fuel tossed inside by an arsonist had fallen on flame retardant curtains and went out.

Like a scene out of a movie, he described the cross that was lying across the front door of the main house.

We were shocked. We had researched the area and talked to people, even made sure that people of color lived near there long before we prayerfully went about trying to purchase the property. Obviously we had not been told total truth.

That fire changed the course of our lives completely. Not only did the geographical location change, but from that moment forward every decision, every acquaintance, everything in our lives would be tainted and altered by that cross tacked to the front door of a house we thought stood on our promised land.

We had many things to be thankful for. God had spared our lives. Delays had kept Hector and Leah from arriving at the trailer the night before the fire was set. Ignorance in how to start a fire had resulted in the fire set in the house fizzling before we lost many possessions. Our pride and our faith in people were shattered though, and this event would create scars that would never totally be erased.

We were made painfully aware of the hatred and prejudices that remain in this land.

We also grieved over the loss of assets the owner who dared to help us had to experience. He is the one who shouldered the loss, but together his family and ours learned some tough life lessons.

There had been and continue to be occasional signs of prejudicial reactions towards our family. We have learned to handle this ignorance with a guarded spirit and hope to change hearts and minds by our examples of love and acceptance. Still, I pray none of our children are ever again exposed to such a blatant and dangerous act to soul and body as the torching of that property was.

Make no mistake; prejudice comes in many forms, not simply racial. We are judged by the world in ways too numerous to state here.

Our family is larger than the cultural norm. Though many may think that most prejudice is against Blacks in our nation, we need to think again. The influx of Hispanics into this country is creating a new ripple of unrest. Then there are the subtle prejudices against those who learn differently or are born with physical handicaps.

The prejudice I fear the most is the silent war against basic Christianity that is permeating this great nation much as the smoke of a killer house fire seeps under the door sill to unsuspecting sleeping family members.

Yes, prejudice abounds. The closer we get to what God has for us to do, the greater the spiritual attacks become. But, we must persevere. Immigrants from all nations have persevered and come into this land in search of religious freedom and basic human rights. Now, in this generation, as in no other before it, there is a great movement of God's children from all nations of the world. He is mingling the people into beautiful pieces of tapestries called adoptive families. Perhaps it is a call to nurture and train up a remnant of people who will be a part of a spiritual revival and truly restore this nation as one people, under God, indivisible, with liberty and true justice for all.

So, while I learn about patience, prejudices and provision, I have created my own dream where there is a huge old barn, a bubbling creek and a house that just overflows with God's children. There is a lush garden full of organic fresh foods to restore the body and thus enable the soul. There are herbs falling out of clay pots, plucked daily for health and culinary delight. Sheep graze peacefully in a meadow, with baby lambs to delight the heart. Fresh milk flows to nurture babies, both the human and animal alike. There are tire swings, slides and a swimming pool for taming the energy of overactive boys.

It is a safe haven, as God promised, a place where love is unconditional, discipline fair and within the boundaries of God's direction. In this place children understand that parents are human and not without fault, but that love is unconditional and without end. It has a pond, and a meadow where we can wander while in prayer, perhaps stopping for a rest and dropping a pebble into the clear water, allowing the rippling water to renew in my mind the analogy of love given away. It is a haven where children are prepared to become the pebbles of love, capable of changing the world because they found their purpose in this place. It will be the promised land where they will be preparing for their eternal destinies.

Perhaps this is not exactly God's plan for us, so I try to find peace in the things He so graciously and abundantly provides for us. But, it is a beautiful dream, and one that brings peace and purpose to my meandering. Only time will tell if this is a desire that God has planted in my heart and therefore plans to gift us with, or simply a dream to serve no other purpose than to rest the soul as I muse upon the thoughts — thoughts to help ease the memory of being burned out while searching for a promised land.

Hidden Once More: Our *Baker's Dozen*

"Maternal love: a miraculous substance which God multiplies as He divides it." – Victor Hugo

Our small trailer was packed with baby gifts, a dozen suitcases, and bedding for as many pallets. Caden Graye, our first grandson, had made his debut into this world earlier that morning, and we were on our way to give him a grand welcome into our ever-growing family.

Rather than staying on familiar road, we decided to take a shortcut to the hospital. The rain was coming down in sheets and it was nearly impossible to see the road signs, causing us to make a quick decision at a dark intersection which unfortunately resulted in our taking the long way to our destination. As we drove, the torrential rainfall became relentless and would eventually delay our arrival time by more than two hours.

Cell phones allowed us to stay in touch with our son Jared and his wife Amber as we crawled down the rain-slick roads, otherwise I am sure there would have been great concern for all as the hour grew later and later. Resembling a bedraggled squadron returning from a night of field training, we finally trouped through the small, quiet hospital sometime near midnight on the day that Caden was born. What a sight we must have been! Disgruntled from more than 10 hours packed in a van designed for fewer people, rain dampened and very tired, still we trudged in with delighted anticipation in search of the birthing center.

Official oohs and ahs over the baby, delicate touches, amazed glances, tired smiles and grandparent congrats later, we trooped once again out into the cold rainy night. In the wee hours of the morning we finally made our way to Jared and Amber's apartment, where we unloaded our belongings, rushing to and fro through the cold continuous rainfall. The trailer had leaked, so the carefully wrapped gifts were rain dampened, as were much of our clothing and bedding, including pillows. I was extremely thankful that night for the luxury of a tumble dryer!

Saturday morning brought trips to the hospital in shifts, to allow more quality time for each admirer. We crammed in visits with friends that we had not seen in years, and even some academic testing for three of our children. Later, more visits with friends, picture taking sessions and more turns at holding Caden. It was a joyful, and exhausting day.

It seemed strange to gaze at a baby that so closely resembled someone we had held not all that long ago! Caden looked remarkably like Jared had as an infant and it was great fun making comparisons and recalling when we too had held our first (and only) birth son in our arms. John and I had waited so long to experience birthing a child, but now it seemed the eight or so years waiting to conceive Jared had been longer than the 23 years that had now passed since his birth. Time goes by much too quickly; that day I vowed to make a greater effort hour by hour to enjoy the moments and memories of all of our children and grandchildren's lives.

Sunday midday, as we were preparing for our return trip home, my cell phone rang. It was Leah, who had stayed at our house in Tennessee with Austin. She excitedly told me I needed to call the agency that we had worked with so many times in the past. Thinking that my friends had gotten word we were in town and just wanted to touch base for a visit, I told Leah I would call them later, perhaps from the van on our way home.

Leah insisted that I needed to return their call immediately. Apparently they had a baby to place. The family that had been matched with the birth mother had a change of heart and so the agency had called us, (on a Sunday morning no less,) and wanted to know if we would be interested.

Shocked that they would even call us, and on a Sunday morning, and even more incredibly, that we were just miles from their office; I skeptically dialed the number to see what the rest of this surprising story was! Having believed for the longest time that our next placement would be a girl, or maybe even two girls, I questioned the situation a bit when I learned the baby was a boy, and a single birth.

It appeared God was really working out every detail since we were already in town and wouldn't have to travel to do the needed paperwork, meet the birth mother or most importantly, meet the new baby! We were visiting at that very moment with a friend who quickly offered me the use of her apartment as she was planning to be out of town for two weeks. Quickly John urged me to say yes to this little guy! He felt if God was so radically opening doors, it was important for us to walk through them.

Three stages of adoptive pregnancy happened in the span of three short hours. We soon had plans to meet the birth mother, take our family to the hospital to greet our newest addition and then to send everyone home with John, while I remained to take care of the baby, the paperwork, and to wait upon Interstate Compact Approval for travel back into our home state. Details too numerous to mention seemed to quickly fall into place; we were tossing around possible names when the phone rang once again.

Apparently, after leaving the baby at the hospital, the birth mother had talked to extended family who had put a guilt trip upon the birth mother and convinced her they would help her take care of the baby; though they had been of little or no help prior to this birth with assistance in parenting the other children she already had. She had been making an adoption plan for this little guy for many months, coming to the agency for counsel, support, and other necessities. Then, in a few short hours the free will of men, perhaps tainted with some cultural conditioning, had once again changed the destiny of a little child.

We conceived, bore, named and lost a child in one short afternoon! Physically and emotionally exhausted, knowing we had been obedient and willing to be used by God, we reverted back to our original travel plans and began to make our way home.

The entire return trip John and I puzzled over why certain events are presented to us in this life. We realized anew we never know from one minute to the next what the lines of script in our lives are going to be. There are so many variables, so many options, and yet God is somehow able to use all things for good (see Romans 8:28). We tried to absorb the magnitude of that knowledge once again. (In retrospect I now believe that God was preparing us for a boy, but we couldn't have known that at the time.)

I suppose the most mind-boggling part of those few hours was the realization that we were about to pick up a son exactly the same age as the precious grandson we had just enjoyed welcoming into our family. The responsibilities being presented to us once again seemed staggering.

A few days later lying in bed, *I found myself replaying a dream I had experienced just before dawn.* In the mistiness of my still sleepy mind, I had to wonder if the dream was one intended to keep my mind occupied while my body physically rested, or if this was yet another God revelation. Shrugging the details out of my mind, I stumbled toward my morning shower. With the stinging of the hot water and the wonderful smell of shampoo and soap I soon forgot the dream and plunged into the day.

I'm not sure just what triggered the memory of that early morning dream, but I was soon to realize in my spirit, that indeed I had been given another tiny bit of information that was to become another prompt on the stage of life. Suffice it to say, John and I began to toss around boy names where before I had been adamant that we would likely be getting one or two girls in our next placement.

Two weeks after Caden's arrival, I was working on this book when another unexpected phone call came from the agency. This time the connection was with a crisis pregnancy ministry in an adjoining state, and revolved around a baby to be delivered by scheduled Caesarian section the following week. Once again, everyone involved thought this just had to be the situation God had been preparing us for. (That would prove to be only partially correct, but I'm getting ahead of the story!)

Because I had been praying and seeking God when the phone rang, I felt very intensely that we were to say yes and take a chance on yet another placement. John was quick to agree and within a few short hours the necessary arrangements were well on their way to being completed. This was certainly another step in faith since the sex of the baby was unknown, and because I had felt so certain that we were to get a girl. I was also fairly certain we were to get two babies, either related, or in placements that came unusually close together. I asked the worker on more than one occasion if they were certain there was just one baby.

In the few days that followed the frenzied gathering of paperwork and baby supplies *I repeatedly kept envisioning the backside of an infant, curled as if yet in the womb. I felt that hidden within the curve next to the front side of this baby was another infant, hidden completely from view. Two separate lives, encircled within one another in safety and secrecy. I couldn't understand what I was seeing, but I felt it was significant to our next placement.* I really thought that this birth would produce twins, but of course, I would have to wait to see if that was correct.

When the call came and the worker assured me that there was just one, almost ten-pound baby girl, I was very excited and yet puzzled. In fact, I asked her twice if she was sure that there was only one baby! Later I would tell her why I kept asking such strange questions, but for now, all we could do was travel down the road, which I must say, felt extremely right in spite of the missing pieces.

Now, let me take you back in time, to at least three years previous to this blessed event. Yet another dream, full of details had been given to me, and documented carefully in my journal. In fact, when we had agreed to take Austin, I had been so sure that we were to quickly get two little girls that I would not commit to Austin unless the placing agency agreed to let us take another placement, should one be presented, before we finalized Austin's adoption. They thought they were working with a crazy woman, but to appease me in my adoptive hormonal state, both placing and receiving agencies agreed we could take another placement before we finalized Austin's adoption. We drew up an agreement that was a compromise for all, but allowed for what I thought was inevitably going to happen.

In my dream: *John and I and several of the children were at a location I did not recognize, planning to pick up a new baby. When we arrived at the location, (the description of which I have documented in great detail in my journals) there was a second baby. In the dream we were asked to quickly make a decision if we would take both babies or not. We were totally surprised, but as might be expected, both in a dream and in reality, we agreed to take both babies!*

The dream continued and, before we had seen the babies, I went to a store and purchased car seats that matched and a few other necessary supplies. I recall distinctly thinking we needed little else except the car seats. Somehow in this dream I understood the placement would not be as open as some of the adoptions we had previously experienced. This was symbolized by the birth mother's back being turned toward us as she lay in her hospital bed when we first saw the babies. I also 'knew' that the babies were tiny, but I wasn't clear if they were related or not, which had caused me over the months to wonder if we would go after one child and maybe arrive and discover the placing agency had a second child for us from another birth.

There were many ways to interpret this revelation, and I puzzled over every possible option over the months that followed, trying in vain to figure out what God was going to do.

More than six months had lapsed since talking to my friend in another state. I was pleasantly surprised when I heard her voice at the other end of the phone line one morning while I was in the midst of home schooling. We chatted awhile and then she hesitantly began to tell me about the purpose of her call.

A few nights before, in a dream, God had shown her *that John and I were to get more than one child in a future adoptive placement.* She was afraid I wouldn't grasp the validity of the dream since it seemed so unlikely that we would receive more than one child at a time. And, she wasn't sure if we were even considering adoption again with so many children already entrusted to us. She had pushed the knowledge back in her mind until the promptings to call us were relentless and at God's insistence she phoned.

I was practically squealing by the end of our conversation as she shared detail after detail just as God had shown me in my dream several weeks before! We were both incredibly encouraged when we began to grasp just how important this placement must be if God had gone to such great lengths to give foreknowledge of its coming and to confirm it to two different people in two different states at two different times! When my faith would really begin to waver I would fall back, not upon my own revelation, but the even more incredible confirmation from my dear friend.

Those dreams launched an all-out effort on my part to search to and fro over the earth for the children God had planted within my spirit. I wouldn't have wanted to know the length of this adoptive pregnancy at its conception! I confess much of the time I allowed myself to be robbed of the peace that should have come during this time.

I wish I would have been better at just nestling in God's love and not wrestling with what I was to do. But in the classrooms of life, we are, even as adults, ever learning, ever yearning for what it is that God would have us to do!

Of course, no matter how hard I tried to figure out what was going to play out, only time would reveal the mysterious answer. I am certain God enjoys keeping us on the edge from time to time! Even with what I knew, I confess it seemed so unlikely with the number of children and our ages that even with three confirming revelations I still muttered my disbelief as I mused what God was purposing to do.

My fears about receiving Austin had been well-founded and had great validity since the time when McKenzie, Nicholas and Nathan were infants was one of the most physically challenging times of my life. I knew far too well how hard adding three babies at one time would be. In fact, I am certain without the knowledge so clearly given by God, that we would have completely run away from the placement that was about to be!

I could totally relate to Jonah as he ran from God and Nineveh and indeed I spent time in the belly of the whale in the weeks between learning of Austin's availability and his ultimate delivery to our home. I didn't want to run anymore, I wanted to be able to willingly go wherever it was that God chose to send me, or unconditionally receive whomever God chose to send to us.

It had been well over a year since Austin joined our family and many months since we had finalized his adoption. Typical for me, my faith was wavering, and I was questioning what I believed God had shown me. At the same time I was eagerly waiting to see what it was that God would finally make happen. As much as I wanted to settle into a routine, I was always searching, always wondering where these mysterious babies were and where they would ultimately come from.

In my obsession, I had shared with our social worker various details of the dream several times. She just kept assuring me that if it was God, nothing could stop it. If it was not God, then nothing I could do would make a placement happen. I think the social worker was a bit skeptical of my insights, but we had not known each other long and she had not experienced firsthand how God had so divinely manifested His plan in the other placements. The stories surrounding our children's arrivals almost have to have been experienced to fully grasp the impact that God has had in the destinies of our family members.

Now, back to the rest of the story! The single baby girl out of state was now awaiting the final approval to travel from the Interstate Compact offices. We had selected a beautiful name for her. We discussed travel plans, and washed baby clothes. My longtime friends could not believe I had not gone immediately to be with the baby as I had done at considerable risk in most of our previous placements.

All I could reply was that I didn't feel I had traveling permission from God. I truly felt God would show me when I was to go. John completely agreed. Still waiting to travel was incredibly out of character for both John and me, who are always eager to 'lay claim' to our next child. We knew waiting on our next set of instructions was the correct thing to do by the unexpected peace that God was supplying in this highly emotional time!

When the baby girl out of state was about two days old, our local worker called with some very intriguing information. *It seems she had just left the hospital where a scene had unfolded that was so similar to the dream I had told her about that she found herself unable to resist dialing the cell phone and sharing the events of the afternoon.*

Earlier in the day she had been unexpectedly called to the hospital, where a woman whom she was to meet that very day for lunch, had gone into premature labor. Paperwork in hand, she prepared to continue with the placement plan for the little boy the birth mother anticipated. What she found was clearly incredible. It had been necessary to perform an emergency Cesarean section as the baby appeared in distress. When the baby girl was born, the attendants rushed away to begin typical newborn care, only then did medical attendants realize there was a second baby, and a boy was also quickly delivered.

The little girl had been hiding behind the little boy in the womb! In short, the 'feeling' I had that there would be twins when a single birth was expected and also the 'feeling' about a baby hidden by another in the womb had happened, against all human odds!

Once again God had hidden a baby in the safety of the womb for reasons that will undoubtedly bring Him glory. Later as we found out more details, I would recall that on the day this birth mother had first contacted the social worker I had been prompted by the Holy Spirit to call the agency. The worker had assured me that she had not received any new information about babies. She continued by telling me that she had talked to only one birth mother, who was having a boy. The worker reminded me that I was adamant that we were to get a girl, so this obviously could not have anything to do with our next placement. You have probably already guessed the birth mother the worker had spoken with that day would soon be the mother of twins, at the time, no one had a clue.

With the logic of a seasoned social worker, she denied for a brief time what she knew in her heart. As clearly as the scene had unfolded, she still could not justify placing twins in our large family, especially not now, with the commitment we had made to the baby girl out of state! Still, as she left the hospital parking lot she found herself dialing her cell phone. She was shocked when she realized she did not consciously even recall our phone number.

As she began to tell me the events surrounding the birth of the twins she had just left at the hospital, there was a witness in my spirit that only 28 years in adoption experience and walking with the Lord could comprehend. Confirmation that we were hearing about our babies was verified when I hung up the phone and relayed the incredible development to John.

He immediately wanted me to call the worker back and ask her to wait before considering other families. We needed time to figure out what was really transpiring. John was very sure that we were to pursue these babies. I could immediately feel a difference in the urgency of his voice than I had seen for example just after the call about the baby boy or others we had heard about from time to time.

Still, *we could not deny that we 'felt' that we were on the right path to the little girl born just two days previously.* As a family, we really felt that we were to get all three, but the odds of that happening were slim and completely out of our hands. We prayed for doors to open and close quickly, babies were waiting for the love of our forever family, and we were impatient to bring our next additions home, whoever they were.

All we could do was pray as our social worker insisted these babies could be ours only if the birth mother of the little girl out of state changed her mind. There was no way that we could pray for that to happen, so we had to pray that God would clearly show us what we were to do, or work in the heart of the social worker in an even greater way, as we were more than willing to take all three babies. This worker had helped us submit application papers just a few weeks previously for triplets, so John and I had already worked out in our minds the logistics of receiving three little blessings this time. I had even ventured to buy some triplet outfits and we had mused how we would provide and care for three new babies. We just had to wait for the social worker and others in authority to catch up to speed on what God might be orchestrating!

We rode an emotional roller coaster for several hours, and had few answers for the multitude of questions posed to us by the other children, and well-meaning friends. It was a bit like watching a tied ball game that has gone into overtime. We were all on the edge of our seats knowing that one play could change the entire outcome!

I began to feel in my spirit that we would soon have an answer. Sunday afternoon in a phone call to the worker out of state I listened in stunned silence as she regretfully told me that the birth mother had appeared at the home of the foster family and demanded her baby back. With no legal reason to stop her, the worker helped the distraught birth mother strap the fragile newborn into a toddler-size car seat as she moved empty beer bottles and piles of trash out of the floorboard of the borrowed car.

Watching the vehicle disappear in disbelief as the birth mother sped away, the worker prayed for the baby, the birth mother, and God's will to ultimately be done. She told me that she felt in her heart that the story wasn't over yet. She couldn't explain it, but she didn't feel that the outcome had been correct and she just wanted us to know that she felt like there was more to happen. Still, ten days and several hundred dollars later we found ourselves empty-handed and struggling with mixed emotions over the loss of a child that had seemed destined to be a part of our forever family. The waiting bassinet seemed incredibly cold and empty as I walked into the room. The baby bottles waiting to be packed drew tears to my eyes when I wandered by the kitchen sink.

Our shock was somewhat buffered by the knowledge that the odds had just remarkably increased with regard to our being allowed to adopt the twins now laying in separate isolates somewhere in the city. Still, the path seemed gray and foggy as we slowly walked along that day, trying to understand just what it was that God wanted us to be ready to do.

Allowing ourselves a few hours for the rapidly changing events to seep into our souls, we finally decided to call our social worker at home. It was Sunday evening, so our conversation was brief. She was decidedly moved and possibly even a bit stunned when I told her the unexpected change of events. She told me we had our answer; she could now consider placing the twins with us.

I really didn't expect an answer from her at that point; I simply wanted to let her know what had transpired so she could proceed accordingly when she went to the office on Monday morning. I had full confidence that God had a plan in the drama that was unfolding, but I learned long ago to not count on anything, since man's free will is such a powerful tool. Still, I knew we had made the right phone calls that day, as unexpected as the outcomes had been.

Monday afternoon I finally heard from our social worker when she called once again from her cell phone to describe in detail the baby boy that she was now delivering to the foster family. Again on Tuesday afternoon a similar phone call came while she traveled with the baby girl to yet a second foster home. There was no firm confirmation that she would place the babies with us. It was obvious that we would have to wait until after the birth mother had signed her surrender papers before we could talk seriously about a placement plan. Seasoned with years of waiting room experience, I did a bit better this time with all of the unknowns. Still, it was hard to know how to handle the wave of emotions that seemed to relentlessly beat against us.

We told the children that the birth mother of the baby out of state had chosen to parent her baby girl. There were some tears, some questions and a lot of sadness, but they were troopers, seasoned themselves from years of change. John and I chose not to discuss openly the situation with the newborn twins, not wanting to get hopes high or have to soothe hurt feelings if yet another placement failed.

Meanwhile, without warning, the programming contract that John expected would extend through the summer ended abruptly. John was without a contract once again. He did have options however, and we began to earnestly pray about what God desired him to do, practically begging God to act instantly. An additional waiting room seemed more than we could presently bear. This turn of events had the potential to stop the placement of any babies in our home; we had to have a new contract immediately!

Historically, we have had job losses simultaneously with adoption plans. The enemy finds ways to jeopardize placements, and for us this is just one of the many tools used against us, robbing us of peace and causing confusion and extended waits.

Thankfully, within hours, John secured a job out of state, and in a location that we had longed to relocate to for many years.

We had remained in frequent phone contact, but finally one particular afternoon our social worker gave us the answer we had longed for. She explained how she had talked to her supervisors and other people: all agreed, the twins must come to our family. God had a reason and it could not be denied!

Conflicting plans made setting a placement date difficult. Finally I knew that I was going to have to pick up the babies without John, who was already out of state working. It seemed so strange. I had often traveled out of state to pick up our newest additions, but I had never brought anyone home without Daddy there. Still, it seemed God was prompting us on, both to get the babies reunited from their separate foster homes, and to reassure our family that indeed, we were about to be gifted with not one, but two more blessings!

I decided that Jordan, a 13-year-old at the time, would be the one to accompany me to the agency to pick up the babies. It will be a memory he and I will cherish. Jordan was given the job of dressing one of the babies, and of later presenting them to me, when after an all too lengthy delay, the social worker finally announced her approval of the entrustment of these long-awaited babies. *I KNEW the minute that Jordan placed them in my arms that these were the right babies, the ones that God had so meticulously shown me, confirmed to me and encouraged me to find.* It was a day of rejoicing!

Now, if you can stay with me a bit longer as I relay this story, let me fill in some of the incredible details that I have purposefully left out up to this point in the drama. If they amaze you only half as much as they did me, you will see that these babies were indeed destined for our family.

In the original dream: *We had arrived to pick up the baby and been presented with two. So, I had to hurry out and buy two car seats. Also, the decision to take the two babies had to made in a hurry, as opposed to having several months, which would be typical of either a birthing pregnancy or an adoptive pregnancy.*

In reality we did have to make a decision relatively quickly. We found out about the babies, not during the pregnancy, but on the very day they were born. Then, when the time came to get them, because of conflicting schedules, I had to make a decision while on the phone with the worker about when we would actually pick up the babies. It had to be within two days, or wait well over another week before I could even see them. As we know, I opted for two days! *That forced me to rush out that very night, after the confirmation of placement, and purchase two new car seats!* It was just hours before the babies actually came home.

Another part of the dream: *I felt like we were on our way to pick up one baby and found out there were two babies.* In reality, my bags were packed and preparations had been made to travel out of state to pick up the first baby girl. We were 'on our way' so to speak when the call came about the twins. (I suppose we will never know if we were indeed to have gone to pick up the baby out of state, or if God knew all along that we would willingly go down a path that would ultimately close. However, as the story played out, the dreams and visions were incredibly accurate). There still remains a remote chance that one day that little girl will come back to us through unforeseen circumstances. She would certainly be welcomed.

That evening, after the excitement of bringing home the twins had settled a bit I had time to muse back over the events of the day. *I realized the building we picked the babies up from had a circle drive with a covered walkway, spring green trees and profusely blooming pansies along the roadway curb!*

Entering a side door to the complex there was a sliding glass window in the reception area. I was amused when Jordan and I began recalling the maze of hallways with multiple closed doors at the agency. *If we had entered via the front door, we would have walked through several corridors to find the exact room where the babies were the day we picked them up, just as I had seen in the dream!*

The birth mother's back turned toward us in the dream with the two babies laying in isolates was symbolic of the closed adoption agreement we were now participants in. The babies had been in not only separate beds, but separate nurseries at the hospital, which would have accounted for my confusion over whether they were siblings or not, since they were not really together after birth until they were reunited in our home some two weeks later.

Another confirmation of the correctness in this placement was *seeing two baby girls in the revelations given by God would also be correct. We had been on our way to pick up one baby girl, and then in the midst of that plan had found out about another baby girl, who had been hidden yet part of a set of twins, which would explain seeing two babies side by side in the first dream.*

The more recent dream about a baby boy that prompted boy name games would also become reality when one of the twins was a boy.

I had to wonder why God would go to great lengths to reveal His plan to us. First, I had a dream. When I my faith wavered, God prompted a friend to call, replay, and confirm the details God had so incredibly revealed.

As I waited anxiously for the fulfillment of the remainder of the revelation I would journal at least two more dreams which would prove tremendously confirming as the story began to unfold, not just for myself, but for the social worker and other key players in the drama of life.

Why did God give so much to light our path? He knew it was a path that I would find difficult to follow, and that others would not see if the way had not been somewhat mapped out beforehand. There was great potential for unbelief and resisting the will of God.

With the memories of such hard times when McKenzie and Nicholas and Nathan were small, it is not likely that we would have willingly thrust ourselves into another special needs or multiple child placement.

The irony was that those looking into our glass house thought that John and I somehow just proceeded through these placements without any rational reasoning or thought as to what we are getting ourselves into. Contrary to what others think, we proceed with a huge portion of understanding gleaned from the threshing floor of life.

Only those who have shared similar experiences can totally comprehend-those called to adoption as a ministry or those sensitive to the leading of the Holy Spirit in a world comfortable with logic, material wealth and non-confrontational lifestyles so norm in America today.

In my weakness I am made strong: "But he said to me, 'My grace is sufficient for you, for my power is made perfect in weakness.' I will all the more gladly boast of my weaknesses, that the power of Christ may rest upon me" (2 Corinthians 12:9).

The day I arrived home with the twins I had to wonder if we had made the correct decision. Though the younger children were ecstatic and eager to greet and hold these latest bundles of joy, the older children were more reserved, cautious, and skeptical. Their skepticism came from experiencing life, of knowing the reality of the responsibility and the sacrifices that were inevitable in the addition and responsibility of two more little lives. The older girls knew all too well that they too were being asked to take on sleepless nights, more confusion and a good deal more responsibility. I was sorry for the sacrifices they would be asked to make, joyful at the gifts being bestowed upon our family and experiencing so many emotions that I remain to this day unable to express them meaningfully upon paper.

God is faithful. Within days, the babies made their way into all of our hearts. We named them Aaron Ashon and Abigail Grace. Aaron had been one of the names on our lengthy list for boys, and when we learned the foster mother had been calling him Aaron we felt it confirmed just the right name for this wee little one: Aaron-"One of light." The Scripture we found was Psalm 27:1 "The Lord is my light and my salvation, whom shall I fear? The Lord is the stronghold of my life: of whom shall I be afraid?" Ashon means "seventh son" in an African language and was exactly right as well.

Abigail means "source of joy." The supporting Scripture was Psalm 51:12 "Restore to me the joy of your salvation, and sustain in me a willing spirit" (NRSV). I needed more than ever to have the joy of my salvation restored and for my normally willing spirit to once again be pliable in the hands of God.

The supporting Scripture for Grace was Psalm 84:11 "For the Lord God is a sun and shield; He bestows favor and honor. No good thing does the Lord withhold from those who walk uprightly." With these confirmations, we felt sure that we had just the names that befitted our newest angels.

As it turns out the babies have been a healing balm to our weary hearts. God has gifted us with little people that bring quick smiles to dreary days, return hugs of stupendous proportions and encourage us once again in the ministry God has given our entire family.

In spite of our fears regarding their lack of prenatal care and premature birth, they have surpassed all of our expectations, reaching milestones in quick and effortless fashion.

Only God knows His purpose and plan for these latest additions to our family; indeed the greatest mysteries of life are hidden from our physical eyes. Thankfully at times we are allowed to witness with spiritual eyes those things that remain hidden to those who do not take the chance and walk in faith through this life…living on the edge as it were. Because much of the pathway of life is hidden it is hard to know the destination at times, but in the collage of persons that God continues to blend into our family, one thing remains obvious: all of us were destined to be touched by adoption…it was God's plan.

Our children

Our treasures from many lands.
You're divinely created by God's loving hands.
As we dedicate these children to our God today,
We stand humbled and awed at God's power and way!
From the Philippines, through birth, from Korea they came
From Africa, and India and Viet Nam just the same.
All God's children, each unique in God's plan
Often of nationalities not easily accepted by man.
Mistakes? I know not—for God has revealed to me,
That our children His servants will one day be.
Through rejection, and confusion, to the world it seems odd—
But we are being refined and molded, commissioned by God!

Appendix

To **B***irth Parents and* **B***iological Families*

Releasing a child to another family can often be the exact plan God had for that child from the very beginning of time. Carefully and prayerfully committing to an adoption plan is a very loving and unselfish act.

Moses was placed in a river (by a godly mother) and later saved an entire people from a life of slavery in a godless nation.

Esther (who's parents had died) was placed in a harem, which no doubt seemed to be at the time a very undesirable turn of events. From her position in the inner court (while being watched and protected by her godly/adoptive uncle) she saved the Jews (God's chosen people) from potential death and persecution.

Joseph was sold into slavery (allowed by God) but he chose to live a godly life (no doubt inspired by the knowledge of God instilled in his life as a young child by a Godly father) being a witness to all who knew of him. This witness gave him favor in the land and ultimately saved his biological family during a famine. All of these stories and more continue to teach us and encourage us through the scriptures today.

In all of these stories the biological families suffered loss, took risks, and made sacrifices within the cultures of their day in order for that person to fulfill their destiny.

Perhaps you come seeking confirmation that the child you are carrying and cannot parent will be safe and loved in another family. We do well to remember that though transplanted into another culture, in reality Joseph, Esther and Moses all enjoyed more material comforts and privileges in their lives than they might have had in their original surroundings—God made it so. At the same time, they were given huge responsibilities.

Find peace in the knowledge that not all of us who conceive will be able to parent the children we choose life for. Once this fact is clearly accepted in your hearts, you will be free to move forward in the spirit and seek what it is that God is purposing you to do with regards to growing your family, or enabling others to add to theirs.

With few exceptions, birth families come into counseling rooms with all sorts of preconceived notions; not only about how the adoption will proceed, but also with a list of supposed requirements they expect the agency and the family they will allow to parent their child to fulfill. Having thoughts and opinions are natural and an important part of the decision making process, as long as there is an openness to the guiding hand of God, who no doubt will reveal a totally different plan than the one so carefully detailed by human notions.

I cannot express enough the importance I place upon the need to seek reputable Christian counseling from the earliest stages of pregnancy. Thankfully there are many options and an abundance of kind people still around to minister to those in difficult circumstances. I pray each birth family reading these pages will find appropriate counsel sprinkled with love, compassion and understanding for all members of the adoption triad.

There are many adoption options as I have outlined in the adoptive parent part of this appendix. Seek and find a comfortable plan for yourself, for adoption is a decision you will be living with for the rest of your life, and there are many very positive and happy endings to this challenging time.

Please remember…life will go on. The tiny baby that you place in another's arms will soon be bonded and loved by others in the best sort of way. You too will need to move on to new relationships and with amended goals and plans for your life. Openness that seems so important presently may not be in the best interest of all involved as life moves forward. At the same time I do believe that in some circumstances on-going relationships in a variety of ways is healthy and vital to life moving on. Only God knows what will be down the road of life, be sensitive to that leading and not to the present needs of those trying to help you, or to your high emotional needs of the day.

Just as spiritual battles come over the family seeking the child God has for them, it will fall upon your life as well. In letters from birth mothers I have found that often as soon as the baby is conceived and the notion of giving life and making an adoption plan for the child considered, confusion and warfare surrounding their lives intensifies. As if pregnancy and its emotional highs and lows are not enough, adding the adoption option will make getting through the months really tough. The devil will go to great lengths to stop the transplanting of a child into a Christian home. But you must put on the full armor of God and stand firm in your decisions for they are good and right in the sight of our Lord—and it is after all, He that we seek to please.

The good news is God's plans are perfect! There will come a time in your walk down the adoption planning path when you realize that all logic will have to be crushed and you will find it absolutely essential to follow your heart, for therein you will find what God has for you and the child destined for adoption…through pain and sacrifice the peace and closure you seek will be eminent.

Finally be strong in the Lord and in the strength of his power
(Ephesians 6:10 NRSV)

To Adoptive Parents

Children come to us as gifts of God, whether biologically or through spiritual adoption. God has a unique intentional plan for each family. The means by which children arrive into a family is irrelevant. God can be trusted to gift us with exactly the children we are to parent. Family planning, like other areas of our lives, should be wholly submitted to God. This includes the number of children and the origin of their conceptions.

Perhaps you come to read these pages motivated to find out more about adoption as a result of your own infertility. Understanding that God opens and closes wombs, we must accept that if God places a desire for more children in our hearts, He indeed must have a plan to give us that which He ordains. Fret not in your barren womb but rejoice, for God has a plan! There is a scripture reference about the children of the desolate one will be more than she who is married (Galatians 4:27). This verse comes to mind frequently when people discuss the present epidemics of infertility and sometimes within the same context, the children awaiting forever homes. God knew from the beginning of time there would be an abundance of children to fill empty arms.

I would like to share some thoughts with those just beginning to consider the adoption of a child. This is especially written for those still grieving over the lost children you now realize you may never conceive and give birth to. Adopted children cannot be substitute children. They should not become members of our families simply because we are unable or choose not to have biological children, though those are certainly valid motivating factors. It is perfectly normal to start down the adoption path seeking a child that would most closely resemble the child that we would give birth to, if that were an option. However, at some point as we work through the issues we must realize that regardless of the reason for pursing adoption, it is a requirement that we place our hopes and dreams in the palm of God's hand, releasing all logic, all control and all our plans to our Heavenly Father…reminding ourselves that all things work together for good.

We must be able to let go of the dream child. Just as there are no perfect adults, there are certainly no perfect children, whether gifted to us by birth or adoption. As Christians, we must arrive at a point where we understand that the children the Lord intended us to have may not be the children of our dreams, but they can and will become our sons and daughters if we seek God and His purpose.

It will become necessary to bequeath to all our children the same things that other parents bequeath the children born to them. These children may not share our genetic make up or our bloodline, but they will share our lifeline. The roots we established upon our marriage will now have a variety of branches and the branches of our family tree will not likely be anything like those we anticipated when we were first married.

We must come to love our children with intense love: a love that keeps them from harm that shares in their hurts, their joys, their dreams and a love that demands obedience which makes a family a safe, secure, happy place to grow up.

Usually the initial motivation to adopt is fairly selfish. We WANT a child with specifics, such as a particular race, gender or age. Maybe we WANT only a healthy child and because of possible predisposition to certain medical challenges that could be passed onto biological children we opt to consider adoption. Please remember there are as many, if not more, unknowns in the genetic compilation of adopted children than we would find in our own imperfect genes.

Perhaps we feel that adoption will allow us more control, allowing us to be selective in choosing a child. I beg the reader to NEVER consider adoption because it is the easy way to add children to a family. Though pregnancy naturally involves some discomfort and certainly a lot of unknowns, adopting a child brings different discomforts and unknowns. There are NO guarantees and adoption is certain to include a bag full of challenges that are not even issues in birthing and parenting biological children.

In spite of the challenges John and I have found adoption to be a most incredible experience, bringing a spiritual awareness and a purpose like nothing else. Each time a child was added to our family we could look back, and in retrospect, see how God had orchestrated events and people in order to bring our walk in line with His will. Those promptings may come for you, too, if you open your hearts to the possibilities presented by present circumstances. Perhaps a waiting child program on television will prick your heart. At one point God brought two different families with very different adoption stories to our small church, just when we needed the nudging from the Holy Spirit to move on toward our mark. Those families were timely resources and spiritual enablers, without likely ever knowing the impact they had on our lives, and ultimately a multitude of people.

I remember shopping in the mall and being especially drawn to particular races of children or suddenly seeing infants or families that represented what God had placed in my heart. It was not just coincidences while in the Philippines the house John rented happened to have another military family living across the street that had recently adopted a little Ameriasian baby girl. Their experiences greatly reduced our mistakes and ultimately lead us directly to Leah, our first adoption.

A glance through the yellow pages of any major metropolitan area and you will quickly realize the adoption arena is vast. While considering what sort of adoption God would have you to pursue, you can simultaneously begin requesting information from local agencies. Most will be glad to send you packets of information and answer questions over the telephone. It is the easiest and quickest way to get a feel for the current climate in adoption.

The Internet enables prospective couples in their search for agencies and also increases the ability of agencies to place children that not so long ago were considered un-adoptable because of workers' inabilities to find appropriate matches for the children entrusted to them. As quickly as you can log onto your Internet server you can also link to agencies from around the world.

Always proceed with GREAT caution as you inquire about different programs and ALWAYS seek and check out references, and verify the validity of the promises made by agencies or facilitators. There are websites to file complaints or to check out agencies, which have had complaints, voiced against them.

Domestic adoption will likely seem the most logical at first. Helping the children in our own nation is necessary and right. Be not deceived, there are multitudes of waiting children in this nation as desperate as those in developing nations. Regardless of ethnic or religious background, country of birth or circumstances for availability, each orphan is anxiously waiting to find love and protection in a forever family.

A family is more likely to be able to bring home a newborn or infant via a domestic adoption because of location and the length of time needed to process international adoptions. Sometimes adopting domestically will allow you to meet the child or children you are considering long before a permanent placement plan is put into motion, enabling a more positive and successful placement in the long run.

Some people advocate saving the children at home, and cannot even consider the option of international adoption. I feel this is a very personal issue, one to be taken up with God. He sees no national boundaries and no distinction among men. I have found His provision to be as effortless in orchestrating and providing for an international adoption as I have in a placement from within our own city. Only God knows where the child He desires you to parent will be born, and only He can direct your paths.

International adoption involves a huge variety of cultures and nations. The options are almost limitless and can be quite overwhelming. Research the various countries, considering things such as physical characteristics and cultures. You will find the qualifications for each country vary greatly and I would suggest researching a good deal before narrowing the field. Then, just when you think you have it all figured out, expect a change! Any veteran of adoption will tell you, the best-laid plans do not always materialize and the path we travel may be totally different than the one we started down in the very beginning.

Requirements vary from country to country and include, but are not limited to, age of parents, number of children already in the home, and the income of the adoptive family. Each country has different travel requirements, and they change from time to time. Expect a lengthy paper trail which is quite time consuming in either domestic or international adoptions, the latter certainly requiring more detail.

At some point in the journey every family is asked if they will consider a special needs child. Have the term defined by the facilitator or social worker: it is a broad term, covering a multitude of medical, physical and age differences.

The special needs could be physical limitations such as cerebral palsy, wartime/deprivation injuries, birth defects or innumerable genetic syndromes. Sometimes siblings are considered "hard to place" because of number of children in the sib group, race or ages. Others also fall within the special needs category: Children born prematurely, alcohol or drug exposed, or those who have no prenatal care, unidentified parents or unavailable medical records. The list goes on and on. Though it was once considered special needs, we are finding that the race of a child is no longer a consideration of any magnitude in this particular category.

As we muddle through the issues, we should be simultaneously seeking God's desires by praying diligently for direction and discernment in order to differentiate between our idea and God's will. Personally I believe that God places the desire in our hearts for a child (using a variety of circumstances such as those I have shared in this book) and then He goes about filling that desire with a specific child or children. I frequently knew in my heart long before the arrival of a child that God intended to bless us with another addition.

For total happiness there has to be a willingness to be God directed. There must come a time when we totally submit to the plan God has. This was especially true for us with the adoption of our more special needs children, such as was the case with Austin, or the addition of babies later in life, as in the placement of Abigail and Aaron. In those instances we have found ourselves hopeless to explain to others why we proceeded to bring home those children under the present circumstances. Those things that are spiritual are nearly impossible to explain in a logical or understandable way to those with blinded or unyielding spirits.

Above all else there must be marital agreement. Adoption, especially of children over a year old, is more like a marriage than a birth. Both parents must come to an understanding of the feelings and needs of each other, and of the newly added child, and talk openly and frequently about their fears, concerns and reasons for moving through the adoption process. There absolutely must be mutual respect and encouragement, and understanding that with God all things are possible (see Matthew 19:26).

Long-term goals will have to be redefined each time there is a change. With each addition comes the dying of some dreams and the birthing of new visions, but there is no gain without pain, so expect to need God on an hour-by-hour basis. Hopefully this is something that we are already attempting to do.

Jesus said: "Again I say to you, if two of you agree on earth about anything they ask, it will be done for them by my Father in heaven" (Matthew 18:19-20).

The only valid reason for adopting a child must ultimately be because we believe that is what God would have us to do. Admittedly we often move forward out of selfish motivation. Hopefully it becomes something we are driven to do; something that is as miraculous as conception and birth itself, and totally God-ordained. Adopting to save a child will not carry you through the hard times of parenting. Adopting to replace a child lost will not carry anyone through the trials of life any easier. Adopting same race children will not guarantee that they will not have identity crisis when we admit that they are not literally flesh of our flesh.

It has been our experience that all persons touched by adoption will in some way have emotional concerns unique to their situation, certainly magnified in the person adopted at an older age or from more traumatic life experiences. There will always be rejection that must be dealt with. Adaptive grieving goes on through out the adopted person's life and varies as much as each individual personality.

Although I often question our circumstances (a personality flaw I have openly shared within the pages of this book), I do have faith that God is in control, working when circumstances would warn against such divine intervention. When we stepped out to bring our children home, there were certainly difficult times. Those testing times have not lessened after the children are secure in our family, or as the years have flown by, but continue to be allowed in order to teach us more about the sovereignty of God and to school us on how to serve Him more effectively.

Press on in your quest and rejoice when God gifts you with just the child or children He has always longed to do!

Be glad for all God is planning for you.
Be patient…and prayerful always.
(Romans 12:12 LB)

To Those who are Adopted

Perhaps at times you feel displaced or as if there are pieces missing in your life. All of us search for identity and purpose in life, as I have shared throughout this book.

Some of our adopted children are very curious about their roots and those unseen faces with which they might share similar genetic characteristics or physical mannerisms. Others seem to seldom consider that they are part of an adoption plan. They have found contentment in their knowledge of the love of Jesus Christ and the plan of an almighty God.

My intent is not to debate the rights and wrongs of, or the reasons or ways that you find yourself grafted into the family you now have.

I want to encourage you to accept your present circumstances and discover God's purpose and plan for you in a positive way.

In the story of Moses in the book of Exodus, we find a young man who grew up and found great purpose in his adoptive environment. He was grounded in the knowledge of God, and once he committed himself to the plan God had for him, he remained faithful and obedient to his Heavenly Father, even though he was separated from his biological family for a season.

Moses was just one example of a child who was hidden for glory: "The woman conceived and bore a son…she hid him three months" (Exodus 2:2). Moses' mother, at great risk to herself and her family, took a step of faith and in so doing initiated a plan that would change the future of an entire culture of people.

Moses was also destined for adoption: "When the child grew up, she brought him to Pharaoh's daughter, and he became her son" (Exodus 2:10).

Releasing a child to grow up away from his or her biological family is usually a very difficult thing to do. But, sometimes it is what must be done in order for all to find the path they are to travel while on this earth. Moses' life was not without tests and trials. He and his family did endure the pain of separation and loss. But…the Israelites were saved from slavery by their simple acts of obedience to God.

You are then, exactly where God knew you would be from the beginning of time. The path you were destined to travel included being released by your biological family into the family or situation you now find yourselves in.

Boldly choose to find what God would have you to do. You will find comfort, peace and blessings abundant in acceptance of this miraculous turn of events. God's perfect will for your life will be found in this environment if you chose to positively move forward.

Destiny
It is not by mistake that you are alive in these times.
His will chose this day, this time in which each of us live.
We must not drift without seeking our divine opportunities.
There will surely be hard and most difficult times, but God is divinely
   controlling all events.
Nothing is left to chance.
We should each then find comfort in knowing the hand of God touches
   all we do, directing, overruling, and sanctifying events.
If our times be good or bad, happy or sad, God knows best how to order
   the daily course…let us diligently seek His face.

My times are in Thy hand.
(Psalm 31:15)

To the Christian Church

It is time for us to move out of our comfort zones and into the realm of serving God as He freely transplants children wherever He feels they will reach their greatest potential. If so called, we need to be willing to nurture and parent even if it is against all logic and cultural preference—if God requests that of us. More importantly, the worldwide church needs to embrace adoption of children as a mission worth supporting in ways identical to the accustomed prayer and organized financial support we historically have offered to those in salaried ministries and on foreign mission fields.

Like Esther, the church must prepare to take risks and accept responsibility for saving the lives of the unborn and the homeless. There is an urgent need for the body of Christian believers to understand that children are truly a mission field as worthy as the most needy of nations. Congregations must enable families to take in the orphans as God leads, just as they would financially support the very same family if that family felt called by God to travel to some distant land and share the gospel with a developing nation.

Few of us would argue that the best situation is for the children first to remain with their birth family. Secondly, it is ideal for them to be placed within their country or culture of birth and with families that most closely resemble what their birth family would likely have looked like. But, the ideology stops there. We live in an imperfect world, where sin and disobedience abound, and where men have free wills. Prejudicial thoughts are sinful, and we all have them in one form or another. The disobedience is in walking away, pretending not to see the desolate children. Free will allows us to say no to our reaching beyond comfort zones and we stay in our worlds all full of materialism and comforts.

Who can honestly forget the orphans created by the Korean War? With little effort we can recall the television programs that brought us the drama of the Viet Nam airlift, or more recently the horror in Romanian orphanages. Television and the Internet have opened our eyes to tragedy and suffering that we would never have known existed a few short years ago.

Now that we know, how can we remain silent and passive?

As many Christian privileges slowly deteriorate worldwide we must intercede on behalf of the children. Identification numbers rather than names, guilty by association with world organizations or religious affiliations have become the norm. Our identities are being swallowed up in one government merger after another. Orphaned children are merely statistics and their continuance within the system ensures state government budgets remain fluid and worldwide it gives governments total control of the destiny of a new generation.

Privileged to live in a nation founded on Godly principals and flourishing because of the truth that God is our enabler we must scoop up the children while the opportunity exists.

We would do well to reconsider our tasks as a body of believers. Kingdom work is about people. Building funds and sound systems are nice perks to our cushy lives, but the souls of the children seem ripe for the harvest, an obvious priority if Christianity is to survive the world crisis.

There are many reasons for the disintegration of the family and the resulting parentless children. Mostly we can blame ourselves for being caught up in rich culture and pleasurable self-satisfying lifestyles that have no room for the 24/7 care of the children. Caring for children is no easy task…but it was Jesus who reminded us that 'such is the kingdom of God'….and 'we must become as a servant to the least of these.'

There are many ways to reroute, amend and restore the destiny of those so sadly affected by our apathy and distractions.

Just imagine what power and enabling lies dormant within America's churches today!

Church members often support with their whole hearts and pocketbooks the decisions of families to travel to some remote place, live on faith, and depend upon God day to day for financial and other material support. Yet, sometimes these same church members scoff at families who bring children not of their own flesh and blood into their homes to nurture and teach of Jesus, perceiving them as irresponsible when they do not have a huge cash flow, large home and abundant college fund set aside before they welcome into their quivers God's children.

Financial, emotional and physical assistance enables adoptive families to help the children who will spread the gospel of Jesus to the next generation. Day to day living expenses often present great challenges and the physical work of caring for children is a huge undertaking. We would do well to under gird families; more so the families who have purposed to help many children.

It is our sincere desire, as seasoned adoptive parents, to assist in outlining a plan with the purpose of enabling churches to grasp this opportunity for ministry and create organized programs along side existing missions works within our churches.

Now you may ask, what can I do? Indeed, there are many ways, let me suggest but a few.

Ultimately Christians must be pro-life, and with that belief must come the conviction to better the lives of those with whom we come in contact, or who are brought to our attention. Crisis pregnancy centers are ever on the front lines, working in the trenches 24 hours a day. Consider the many housekeeping tasks that are necessary in order to keep those offices open. There is always filing, janitorial duties, and counseling to be done. Many need volunteers for answering phones, donating much needed office or medical supplies, even infant, children's and maternity clothing and household items.

There are numerous large adoptive or foster families that would be immensely blessed by the donation of food or other necessary items, gift certificates would be a wonderful help in the ministry of caring for the children. Respite care is another neglected area of ministry.

There will always be a need for sponsorship of children waiting for adoptive families or contributions to funds designated to aid in the placement of special needs children.

I am reminded of the simple yet effective program that encouraged each church to find one family that would adopt one child. Only the Lord knows just how many children found forever families as a result of such a seemingly simple challenge.

Another dream that I have is one where there is no need for a government system to care for the children. It is a place where the love, charity and mission of God's people is so bold that the needs of the children are met by the abundance of God's love, the law of reciprocity and the willingness of a people to meet the challenge.

I believe that we long to see revival in this nation – true soul soaring, spiritual revival. We are hungry for solid foundations for families where commitment to marriage is strong and unconditional and Biblical principals of parenting initiated and allowed without fear of persecution.

I believe that God is asking the church to start with the obvious, a love and dedication to the protection and nurturing of the children, one child at a time.

Whoever welcomes one such child in my name welcomes me,
and whoever welcomes me
welcomes not me but the one who sent me.
(Mark 9:37 NRSV)

Closing

Within the pages of this book, I have shared how God has united us as an adoptive family. Each of us was destined to be touched by adoption. From John's early childhood of being parented first by a single mother, then as the years progressed with stepfamily relationships, to the seeds that God planted early in my heart to nurture little children, to the supposed unplanned conception of our children…our purposes were hidden for a season…but ultimately destined to be eternally altered by the simple act of adoption.

I gaze out at our children playing gleefully in the summer sun. They are tanned in beautiful colors that range from a caramel brown to the boldest walnut black God's skin pallet contains. These are our children, selected by God, and representing the nations of the world. Watching our children at play I am reminded once again of the powerful promises contained within Jeremiah 29:11: "For I know the plans I have for you, says the LORD, plans for welfare and not for evil, to give you a future and a hope."

I am so very glad I can claim that promise for my children as well as myself.

His plans for us are unimaginable: as mighty, as awesome, as unexplainable as the love our Father God has for all His creation. There is a plan for each child conceived-each person now alive. Our purposes are sometimes hidden to the human mind.

God has directed us in a variety of ways-through dreams, visions, people who crossed the paths of our lives and most importantly through the Scriptures. The book of Esther was just one example of God's divine guidance and care over our lives as it proved so instructional and convicting for me during the gifting of Victoria. God's sovereignty and power are seen all through the book of Esther, and indeed throughout all Scripture, and I pray you have seen that to be true in our humble lives as well.

There is such danger in finding excuses to not help the children. It is so easy to think that there are others more qualified: richer, younger, or healthier than we ourselves are. We have faced head-on most excuses and found none acceptable in the eyes of our Heavenly Father. If our Lord knows the beginning and the end, the purposes and the plans, then in reality we have no ground to stand on if we chose to protest, delay or refuse the desires placed in our hearts by God. The following quote has especially spoken to my heart as I have reached the half-century milestone in my life:

"There are two kinds of people, she once decreed emphatically. One kind you can just tell by looking at them at what point they congealed into their final selves. It might be a very NICE self, but you know you can expect no more surprises from it. Whereas, the other kind keep moving forward and making new trusts with life, and the motion of it keeps them young. In my opinion, they are the only people who are still alive. You must be constantly on your guard…against congealing" (Godwin, Gail: The Finishing School).

We may be living comfortably, as Esther was within the inner court. We may be asked to go somewhere we don't want to go, much like Jonah being sent to Nineveh. We may be asked to give up that which provides material comfort to rescue the children. We may need to join Esther in saying "If I perish, I perish" (Esther 4:16). I have not been asked to risk my life as Esther was, but God is surely ever asking if we are willing to make some pricey sacrifices.

"For if thou altogether holdest thy peace at this time, then shall there enlargement and deliverance arise to the Jews from another place; but thou and thy father's house shall be destroyed: and who knoweth whether thou art come to the kingdom for such a time as this?" (Esther 4:14, KJV).

Perhaps, like the Jews, the children John and I thought were ours but we did not get to bring home fell under the circumstances referenced in this Scripture in Esther. Thankfully, God does send others where we fear to tread. My greatest prayer is that if we have indeed missed a child destined for our family that their deliverance did come from another Christian family.

Without Esther, the Jews would likely have perished.

Without the Christians taking the risks that come with the responsibility of more children, I fear many more will perish within the government systems of the world.

Judgment will fall upon the nations that continue to devalue their children. Psalm 127:3 states: "Lo, sons are a heritage from the LORD, the fruit of the womb a reward" and Jesus says in Matthew 19:14: "Let the children come to me, and do not hinder them; for to such belongs the kingdom of heaven."

I do not believe that God approves of all of the circumstances under which children are conceived. Prices are paid-spiritually, emotionally, and physically for those conceived out of the marriage relationship. But, still we must keep our thoughts in perspective.

Somehow, miraculously, at the moment of conception (perhaps before) God creates a soul with a purpose and a plan, and valuable enough that if they would have been the only person ever conceived God would have sent Jesus to save that soul, because He loves each of us so.

I can proclaim with certainty in parenting others I found out who I really was. Children became my umbilical cord to my Heavenly Father. I did not always like what I discovered about myself, but the closer I became to my husband and my children – all gifts from God – the closer I grew to my Savior. It was in the giving away of love that I found it. It was in seeking God's plan that the void was filled. It was in truly believing that I can't out-give God that I realized how inadequate I was and how completely God was meeting all of our needs.

Love is like a pebble dropped into a still pool of clean sparkling water. This is such a simple motion and yet spiritually significant. A cool, smooth stone is released with precision into the center of a garden pool and with synchronism only God could design- the ripples of water grow ever wider until they reach the boundaries of the pool. When carefully dropped into the heart of another person, love ripples, not only through the receiver's heart and soul but ultimately to the edge of time. Its affects are mostly unrealized by the person who took the time to give love away.

It is my prayer that in spite of my own human inadequacies, our children will become like the pebbles in the analogy above. That God will take the limited love John and I were able to give and through our children and the lives touched by our family ripple that love to a multitude of people. As it reaches each boundary, or life, I pray that love is dropped into the life of yet another soul.

I long to do so much more than my human limitations will allow. So, when reality sets in and my human failings take their toll, I pray for the lives that I will never have energy nor time to help. I plead with God to continue to prick the hearts of His people so that more of the children can be saved, for the harvest is plentiful.

> *And now, O Father, glorify Thou Me with Thine own self with the glory which I had with Thee before the world was...Father, I will that they also, whom Thou hast given Me, be with Me where I am; that they may behold My glory, which Thou hast given Me: for Thou lovedst Me before the foundation of the world. (John 17:5,24 KJV)*

I challenge each of you reading these words to ask God what He might have for you to do. Somewhere in this vast universe there is a child with a heart that aches for a home on their promised land.

What dream has God given you that seems impossible? What fleeting thoughts have you denied or even run far from because they seem so unachievable?

Perhaps you are to seek just one of those children hidden safely away, waiting for 'such a time as this' to be rescued. Hopefully for many seasons the window in time will remain open and many will find those children once hidden from them, divinely destined for adoption into Christian families and ultimately into the kingdom of God.

SDG